# The Cuisine of

# Hubert Keller

# The Cuisine of

# Hubert Keller

with JOHN HARRISSON

PHOTOGRAPHY *by* LOIS ELLEN FRANK

TEN SPEED PRESS

BERKELEY, CALIFORNIA

Ten Speed Press
Box 7123
Berkeley, California 94707

Distributed in Australia by E. J. Dwyer Pty. Ltd, in Canada by Publishers Group West, in New Zealand by Tandem Press, in South Africa by Real Books, and in the United Kingdom and Europe by Airlift Books.

Cover and text design by Big Fish Books, San Francisco.
Illustrations by Hubert Keller and Akiko Aoyagi Shurtleff.
Food photography by Lois Ellen Frank, Santa Fe.
Food styling and props by Robert Lambert and Hubert Keller.
Photo on page 6 (top) © 1993 by Ira Schrank, San Francisco.

Library of Congress Cataloging-in-Publication Data on file with publisher.

Printed in Hong Kong

First printing, 1996

1 2 3 4 5 6 7 8 9 10 — 00 99 98 97 96

To my wife and best critic, Chantal, who shared my vision
and without whose support and understanding none of this would
have been possible.

To my parents and to all in this wonderful profession who have inspired me
over the years and taught me to enjoy the quality of life.

# Contents

~~~~~~~~~~~~~~~~~~~~~~~~~~~~~~~~~~~~~~~~~~~~~~~~~~~~~

# CONTENTS

# Contents

# Introduction

OVER THE centuries, food has become an essential part of France's cultural landscape. Not only a primary focus of life, food is an expression of French society and has been lovingly featured in countless novels, poems, and paintings. My own professional experience is a by-product of this historical legacy, in that my apprenticeship and training occurred under the tutelage of various masters, including my father, a **pâtissier.** These mentors all generously shared the knowledge of previous generations.

I grew up in the small town of Ribeauvillé, a picturesque community set among the hills and vineyards in the heart of Alsace, in eastern France about 30 miles south of Strasbourg. Alsace, which lies on the German border, claims a distinctive culinary heritage. This region is particularly renowned for its foie gras, charcuterie (pork and other meat products), fresh fruit, pastries, eaux de vie (especially kirsch), fine white wines, and beers. Growing up over the Pâtisserie Keller, the family business, meant that I was introduced to the professional kitchen at an early age. My older brother and I regularly volunteered to help around the shop. We'd grease the pastry molds, line them with paper, and help with the batters—of course, we'd also do taste tests! As we grew older, we helped by sorting the berries, pitting fruit, rolling out pastry dough, and garnishing tarts. Working with food became second nature to us. It was also fun.

*The Pâtisserie Keller and family house in Ribeauvillé, my hometown in eastern France.*

Because both of my parents were involved in running the **pâtisserie,** my grandmother did much of the cooking at home. She was the one who introduced me to an exciting array of traditional foods, with their wonderful home-cooked flavors and evocative aromas. I was also exposed to formal dining during my early years because my father enjoyed eating out at restaurants. I loved Grandmother's home-cooked meals, but I always looked forward to these excursions.

When I turned sixteen, I decided to follow in my brother's footsteps and

*Top: My parents in front of the Pâtisserie Keller in 1951. Bottom: I am about one year old here with my Dad, Grandma, and brother, Francis.*

apprentice as a pastry chef. (My brother has now assumed my father's position, and runs the family **pâtisserie**.) It so happened that a school classmate of mine was Marc Haeberlin, whose father, Paul, was the renowned chef at L'Auberge de L'Ill, already an acclaimed Michelin three-star restaurant in the nearby town of Illhaeusern. Marc's uncle (Paul's brother), Jean-Pierre, managed the front of the house at L'Auberge. Marc suggested that I speak with his father, who offered me an apprenticeship. I was so aware of the momentous impact this would have on my life that the exact date I began my training is indelibly etched in my memory—July 12. After a few months of working in the pastry kitchen, I felt the desire to learn all aspects of the restaurant kitchen, and after enthusiastically expressing this interest, I was given the opportunity. I have always deeply appreciated my experience at L'Auberge; apprentices often have to endure a rough rite of passage in French kitchens, but we were always treated with respect, as part of the extended family, and given a thorough training. Toward the end of my apprenticeship, I was even sent to Paris to train under Gaston Lenôtre, one of the leading pastry chefs in the country and a true genius. Chef Haeberlin also taught us invaluable lessons about respect, for both ingredients and our profession, as well as about kitchen organization, teamwork, and responsibility. It is a wonderful feeling to know that chef Haeberlin (and Jean-Pierre) has always been proud of the progress I have made as his protégé. I greatly value their friendship, as well as Marc's, who has now taken over most of his father's responsibilities.

I spent a total of four years at L'Auberge before serving my obligatory year of military conscription. While in the military, I trained as a sharpshooter and learned to drive army trucks before being transferred to cook for the general of the Sixth Military District in Lorraine, the largest in France. (Fortunately, I have not had to call on my military skills since.) It was not exactly a taxing post—mostly, I cooked for the general and his wife—but we were kept busy with helping in the garden and picking fresh ingredients, which proved to be another invaluable learning experience. I had never spent any time in a garden before, and the professional military gardeners were happy to teach me and the other cooks about tending plants. Professional chefs do not usually have the time to garden, so direct contact with the soil and plants that provided the raw materials I worked with has remained a special memory.

My only disappointment with the conscription was that I did not get to travel, as I had hoped I would. After completing my required year, and in deference to this wanderlust, I applied for a chef position with Compagnie Paquet, a cruise ship line based in Marseilles. With the cruise ship, I traveled all over the Mediterranean and the coastal regions of northern Europe, the Baltic, and later, the Caribbean. For a while, my cruise ship was based in Fort Lauderdale, where I enjoyed my on-shore leave so much and felt such an affinity for the United States that I became convinced I would someday return to pursue my career.

Meanwhile, back on terra firma, chef Haeberlin recommended that I take a

position he had arranged for me in the South of France, at Domaine Chateauneuf, near Toulon. This was an important step for me because I gained a tremendous amount of confidence by taking on all the responsibilities involved in running a restaurant kitchen and realizing that I could do it successfully. However, I also realized I needed to learn more, so when Jean-Pierre Haeberlin, Paul's brother, called to tell me that the acclaimed Roger Vergé was looking for a saucier chef (the rank below sous chef) at his renowned three-star restaurant, Moulin de Mougins, I did not hesitate to move on again. (This type of rotation to gain experience is expected in professional French kitchens.)

*In the kitchen with Roger Vergé when Sutter 500 opened in 1982.*

Vergé's stunning **"cuisine du soleil,"** based on the lighter style of southern French cooking, was a different concept for me, and I relished the challenge. Most of all, Vergé's creativity broadened my horizons and encouraged me to be even more open to new ideas and innovative ways of approaching ingredients. What I learned at Moulin de Mougins has significantly influenced my cooking ever since. In 1978, I moved on once more, thanks again to the recommendation of Jean-Pierre Haeberlin. This time, I was to work under Jacques Maximin at the Chantecler restaurant at the Hotel Negresco in Nice. At the time, Maximin was blazing a trail with his nouvelle cuisine, and I was fortunate to witness the brilliance of his exciting new style. This was another turning point in my career and personal development as a chef, as I enjoyed the chance to work with a strong staff and the best products available. I felt reinvigorated and motivated, and I would have stayed longer if I had not been offered a position as chef de cuisine at Hotel Le Prieuré in the Loire Valley, another exceptional opportunity. This experience provided me with one of my biggest accomplishments: I gained the restaurant its first Michelin star (the ultimate accolade of culinary excellence) after one year.

Despite all the moving around and varied experiences, I still had the travel bug. With each change of scene I learned so much and I enjoyed the challenges that travel presented. So, in December 1979, when Roger Vergé approached me to open a new restaurant in Brazil, he didn't have to persuade me to accept. And what an opportunity Sao Paulo presented! The city is the cosmopolitan business center of the country and the third largest city in the world. I cooked with new and exotic products and worked with a mostly Portuguese-speaking kitchen staff in a totally different and energizing environment. I took cooking classes to learn about the foods of Brazil, and my horizons broadened exponentially. While I was there, political changes meant that the country's borders were closed, and imports were subject to taxes of 500 percent, so the availability of many familiar products was sharply limited. This too presented an opportunity and a learning experience, as we were forced to make our own flavored oils, vinegars, and mustards, among many other items. Working with Vergé was inspirational; I really admired the experience and ingenuity he shared so generously, especially while I was outside the familiar medium of our own country.

After two years in Brazil, Vergé asked me to open a new restaurant, Sutter 500, in San Francisco. California was at the top of my list of places to live, so I gladly accepted the assignment. I began what was to be a four-year stay that furthered my learning curve. My wife, Chantal, and I fell in love with the Bay Area and were happy to put our roots down. San Francisco is an exciting food town, for many reasons, not the least of which is the twenty-year role it has played in pioneering the U.S. food revolution, which in turn sparked the growth of indigenous regional cuisines and changed the way Americans eat. The plethora of top-quality local growers and suppliers, eager and able to entertain the requests of chefs, and the proximity of one of the greatest wine-growing areas in the world make the Bay Area an inspirational place to live and work.

Eventually, in 1986, Vergé asked me to move again, this time to open a restaurant in Marbella, Spain. But my appetite for travel had subsided, and

Chantal and I couldn't bear the thought of leaving San Francisco. Vergé understood, and instead I accepted a partnership offer extended by Maurice Rouas, the owner of Fleur de Lys, an established French restaurant just a few blocks away on Sutter Street. Maurice had worked at Maxim's in Paris before coming to San Francisco in the 1960s, where he worked at Ernie's and L'Etoile, two of the leading restaurants in the city at the time, before taking on ownership of Fleur de Lys. Maurice felt that I could reshape the menu and take the restaurant to another level. I saw this as the perfect opportunity to establish my own style in an ideal setting before an appreciative and sophisticated audience.

I asked Rick Richardson, my sous chef from Sutter 500, to join me, and he has remained my right-hand man ever since. The other member of our team who has contributed so much to our success is my wife, Chantal. She trained as my pastry chef before taking over the responsibilities of public relations and all aspects of administration, and her boundless support and energy has been tremendously important.

Rick and I created a progressive repertoire based on my interpretations of classic French recipes, dishes I had encountered on my travels, and those I had become familiar with during my career. Despite the various influences, I still observed the defining principles of French cooking. French chefs were the first to assert that the flavors of foods should stand on their own and not be disguised by spice or smothered by other flavorings. New techniques, ingredients (especially herbs and vegetables), and cooking methods were first employed and considered essential in French kitchens. The French were also the first to hold that only the best, freshest, and most perfect seasonal ingredients will do. Like other French chefs, I believe that following these principles directly enhances the food I create.

*Top: Chantal in her office at Fleur de Lys. Bottom: Chantal, Maurice Rouas, and me celebrating my thirty-ninth birthday.* Photo copyright © 1993 by Cameron Anne Hirigoyen

Early on, local newspaperman and personality Herb Caen included favorable notes about Fleur de Lys in several columns. Then **San Francisco Chronicle** food editor Michael Bauer and independent food critic Patricia Unterman reviewed us in glowing terms. National recognition soon followed.

We adapted our menu to the health-oriented style of eating in California and to utilize the rich availability of local ingredients. Very early on, in the mid-1980s, I decided to base the menu on a leaner cuisine, opting for organic produce and free-range meats whenever possible. Our well-informed, health-conscious guests encouraged me to continue this approach. I developed a vegetarian menu,

which was the first of its kind in an upscale restaurant in the United States and I relished the challenge of making meatless food exciting. I also wanted to quash the perception that vegetarian food is bland and dull. Molly O'Neill kindly helped us spread the word in several **New York Times** articles, mentioning or featuring Fleur de Lys and our vegetarian menu.

At the same time, I had refined a selection of lowfat and nonfat recipes, so when Dr. Dean Ornish asked me to contribute to his book **Eat More, Weigh Less,** I was delighted to oblige. This project led to an invitation to the White House, where I was asked to demonstrate my recipes and techniques. It was a wonderful experience of which I am very proud.

In my recipes, I use butter and cream in relatively few dishes. When I do use them, it's only in limited amounts, and certainly in far smaller quantites than the classic recipes call for. Instead, I use many different nonfat flavorings and thickening agents, such as fresh herbs, spices, reduced broths or stocks, puréed roasted garlic, puréed vegetables, and flavored oils and vinegars.

*Top: Showing off my toy in a photo taken for one of Molly O'Neill's stories on Fleur de Lys. Photo copyright © 1993 by Ira Shrank Bottom: Cooking Baeckeoffe at home, Christmas, 1993.*

I also use simple standard techniques, such as using nonstick pans and kitchenware and spray bottles to dispense oil sparingly, to adjust traditional recipes so they are in keeping with contemporary health concerns. When combined, these concepts—using updated techniques to create healthful, flavorful, and often vegetarian food in the French style—define my philosophy and the **raison d'être** or purpose behind this book.

As you read the recipes, you will see that I have included tips and suggestions ("Chef's Notes"), wine recommendations (beginning with Salads), and some sketches of the assembled dishes. These suggestions come from what I have observed while making and serving these recipes at home and in the restaurant. I offer them in hopes you will find them helpful but not limiting in any way. Every cook approaches the same recipe differently, which is one of the reasons cooking is so personal. Above all, I want you to have as much fun as I do when you make my recipes and share them with friends and family.

Bon appetit!

# Fundamentals

*I* FIND IT disconcerting that traditional French cuisine is often perceived and described in narrow and intimidating terms. In its truest definition, the cuisine of France encompasses many styles of food and culinary traditions, from the uncomplicated rustic dishes of Alsace, my homeland, or Provence, a region close to my heart, to the sophisticated and intricate dishes found in many other parts of the country. And so, while all of the recipes in this book are by no means exclusively French in origin, many are French influenced and feature the simpler foods and techniques that the cuisine offers. These recipes are no more difficult than those from other countries and cooking styles that I'm sure you would make without hesitation. I have taken deliberate care to create and test recipes that are based on easy-to-grasp fundamentals and that are specifically designed or modified for the home kitchen. I guarantee you will find them straightforward and enjoyable to make.

From the time I began "apprenticing" in my father's **pâtisserie**, I learned that the theories and practice of traditional French cuisine are based on certain fundamentals. These fundamentals—familiarity with standard ingredients, simple but precise cooking techniques, reliable equipment, and timeless basic recipes—have become so universal that they are now the foundation of fine cooking in many countries, including the United States. In addition to the basics, I also describe some techniques and equipment that are not traditionally defined as French, but that enable me to create the healthful dishes I like to prepare and our guests like to order. If you find this approach as sensible as I do, you may find yourself adjusting your daily cooking practices accordingly. (I would be flattered!) Become familiar with these basics and you will have no difficulty mastering the recipes in this book.

Many of the dishes use terms or call for preparation techniques or basic recipes that are detailed in this chapter. Although you do not have to study this chapter before you start reading the recipes, I highly recommend it. If that feels too restricting, then quickly skim the information so you will know where to find the directions as you need them. Similarly, you may also find the Glossary of Ingredients (see page 216) a helpful source for definitions of unfamiliar foods. As all serious cooks know, gastronomic harmony is ensured only when the scales are mastered before the composition is written. Here's to the rehearsals!

# Notes on Ingredients

In my recipes, I use the following basic ingredients exactly as they are listed, unless the recipe specifies otherwise. For the sake of simplicity, however, I do not include the information given below each time those ingredients appear in a recipe. Please review the list and consult it, as needed, while you cook.

**Butter** is unsalted and chilled.

**Citrus juice** is always freshly squeezed.

**Cream** is light (30% to 36% butterfat).

**Eggs** are large.

**Flour** is all-purpose, unbleached.

**Garlic, shallots,** and **carrots** are peeled.

**Ginger** is fresh and peeled.

**Herbs** are fresh, leaves or needles removed from stems.

**Olive oil** refers to virgin olive oil.

**Onions** are yellow and peeled.

**Parsley** is the standard, ruffled variety.

**Pepper** is always freshly ground and refers to black pepper.

**Salt** is sea salt (see Glossary of Ingredients, page 216).

**Spinach leaves, other greens,** and **leeks** are all washed thoroughly beforehand.

**Sugar** is granulated.

## Basic Equipment

Using the correct equipment yields the best results. While the required equipment (or **batterie de cuisine**) may seem daunting and even unnecessary, nearly all of the items I recommend are found in well-stocked home kitchens. I offer substitutes for the few items that are less common. Here's a list of the basic equipment you will need to make the recipes in this book.

### Baking Pans and Dishes

You will need medium and large roasting and baking pans for the recipes that follow, as well as a baking or cookie sheet, 9 by 5-inch loaf pans, and 4- or 6-ounce ramekins. Occasionally, I call for small molds; these can be purchased at good-quality kitchen stores, but round cookie cutters can often be substituted. An ovenproof casserole is a necessary item in most kitchens; the traditional ones in Alsace are made of earthenware, but cast iron or other nonreactive ovenproof material is equally acceptable. Other baking equipment called for (such as a **kugelhopf** mold) can also be substituted, as described in the following recipes.

### Baking Stone

This optional equipment makes home-baked pizzas and bread better by facilitating an even oven heat. It creates a better heat distribution and will help keep the temperature from falling too far, even if you open the oven door. By absorbing some of the humidity, it also gives the bread a crisp crust.

### Blender

One of the most important tools for vegetarian cooking. Mostly interchangeable with the food processor, but with a tall, narrow food container. Mostly used for puréeing and liquefying, especially for soups, sauces, and smooth drinks. The higher blade speed keeps the natural colors of vegetables (such as spinach or beets) brighter and aerates more than a food processor. It can make purées seem rich and creamy, even when no cream is added.

### Chopping Board

Wood or plastic boards are preferable to marble, which dulls knives and scratches easily. Wash frequently with hot, soapy water when chopping foods, especially when working with meat. Recent findings suggest that wood chopping boards are at least as safe as plastic ones when it comes to retaining bacteria. However, both should be washed vigorously after coming into contact with meat.

### Food Processor

For chopping, puréeing and emulsifying. There are times when a food processor, rather than a blender, is best suited for processing certain ingredients (such as for bread crumbs or stuffings,

as well as dough or mousses, which need mixing at slower speed so that less air is mixed in).
Likewise, blenders work best for other uses, especially when high speed is essential. Preference
is indicated in the recipes that follow.

## Graters

I recommend a box-type grater for cheese, vegetables, and fruits, and a small nutmeg grater.

## Grill

Cast-iron stovetop grills, charcoal- or wood-burning, gas, and electric grills all have a heat
source beneath a rack on which food is placed. Grills are used for cooking meat, poultry, fish,
and vegetables; because grilling requires no (or less) fat, it is a healthful method. In addition,
grills can also impart a desirable roasted, smoky flavor.

## Heavy-Duty Electric Mixer

An indispensable machine with three common attachments: a whip (for cream and eggs); a
paddle (for general mixing); and a dough hook (for kneading bread). Some mixers can also be
fitted with meat grinders, juicers, or power strainers.

## Juicer

There are two types of juicer available: reamers and extractors. Reamers, either manual or
electric, remove juices from citrus fruits. Electric extractors create juice by liquefying raw
fruits, vegetables, and herbs.

## Kitchen Scissors

An underrated kitchen tool; buy good-quality scissors that are strong and sharp. I use mine for
all kinds of purposes, such as cutting lobster tails and kitchen twine, trimming parchment
paper, and snipping fresh herbs (especially chives and basil) for a cleaner cut and to avoid bruising.

## Kitchen Timer

I strongly recommend timers, especially if you don't have one built into your stove.

## Kitchen Twine

For tying and trussing. Available at kitchenware stores.

## Knives and Sharpening Steel

Knives are the most common kitchen tool. Buy high-quality knives that feel comfortable in
your hand (remember that knives, like the hands they fit into, are all different). To cover all the
basic needs, I recommend a serrated slicer (or bread knife), a long (nonserrated) carving knife, a

paring knife, a large chef's knife, an oyster knife, and a utility knife. Buy a good steel and keep all of your knives sharp. Blunt knives can bruise food, affecting its appearance and texture.

## Mandoline
A manually operated stainless steel or plastic slicer with a narrow, rectangular body and adjustable slicing blades. It is invaluable for slicing fruits and vegetables; its blades are razor-sharp. A good plastic mandoline can cost as little as $35; a professional-quality stainless steel mandoline can run as high as $150.

## Measuring Cups and Spoons
Durability and safety are the main factors to consider when selecting these measuring tools. Choose glass or plastic types that are easy to clean; aluminum (which has the disadvantage of being reactive) and plastic are more fragile. I particularly like nesting stainless steel spoons—they last forever.

## Melon Baller (or Parisian Scoop)
Different sized scoops mounted on opposite ends of a stainless steel handle, used for making vegetable or fruit balls.

## Mixing Bowls
A collection of nonreactive bowls in a variety of sizes makes life in the kitchen so much easier. You can never have enough mixing bowls! At the minimum, invest in a stacking set of small, medium, and large bowls.

## Parchment Paper
A heavy greaseproof and waterproof paper ideal for lining baking pans and keeping foods separated or wrapped, among many other uses. Use firm-textured, heavy-quality parchment paper. Available at kitchenware stores.

## Pastry Bags
I recommend a medium and a large bag, with a plain $\frac{1}{2}$-inch tip and a selection of other plain and decorative tips (such as star and fluted).

## Pepper Grinder
I always use a grinder or mill to freshly grind peppercorns whenever a recipe calls for pepper. Freshly ground pepper gives a more pronounced aroma and flavor.

## Potato or Vegetable Peeler
Also ideal for paring fruit thinly or zesting citrus fruit.

## Pots, Pans, and Skillets

Price is not necessarily commensurate with quality or results. I recommend heavy-bottomed, nonreactive, stainless steel pots and pans, and stainless steel and cast-iron skillets, in a variety of sizes. At least one skillet should have 2- to 3-inch-high sides. I especially recommend nonstick pans, which enable cooks to use a lot less oil, shortening, and other fats. The essential pots and pans include a medium and a large sauté pan or skillet; small, medium, and large saucepans; a 12- or 16-quart stockpot; and a double boiler. Avoid aluminum cookware.

## Sieves, Strainers, and Colanders

Sieves and strainers are handheld devices (including the conical chinois) with a stainless steel mesh or screen that retains solids while liquids pass through. I recommend stainless steel equipment, which will never rust. The most useful items are fine- and medium-meshed strainers or sieves and a colander, which is particularly helpful for straining vegetables.

## Single-Edged Razor

Available at art supply stores, this tool can be used to slash the top of bread dough, both for decoration and to help give the loaf a greater surface area, facilitate expansion, and make the bread crustier and lighter.

## Spoons, Spatulas, Ladles, and Brushes

The essentials include a set of different-sized wooden spoons; a large metal spoon for basting and stirring; a large, slotted stainless steel spoon; a long-handled rubber spatula for scraping bowls and pans and folding in ingredients; a set of stainless steel ladles (some have ounce or tablespoon sizes stamped on them, which also makes them valuable measuring tools); a medium-sized pastry brush; and a plastic bulb baster for basting meats and other foods to prevent them from drying out or for drizzling liquids over foods.

## Spray Bottles

Use one to spray water into the oven as bread is baking. This creates humidity, making the bread crustier. Use another for olive oil (and other oils) to spray saucepans, sauté pans, baking sheets, and other cooking pans. This item will significantly reduce the amount of oil you'll use.

## Tongs

Ideal for handling hot foods at a distance or removing food from hot or boiling water or a hot grill, for example. Select stainless steel tongs with a wooden handle.

## Weighing Scales

Very helpful in eliminating the guesswork in measuring quantities of ingredients, and essential for the serious cook. Scales are necessary for baking and pastry making, in which amounts of ingredients must be precise. I recommend kitchen scales that measure up to 2 pounds.

### Whisks (Handheld/Electric)

I prefer using handheld whisks, but electric whisks are fine, especially if you're short of time. The best handheld whisks have supple stainless steel wires. Balloon-shaped whisks work best for egg whites and cream.

### Zester

A small hand tool used for removing the outer skin (but not the white, bitter pith) of citrus fruit in thin strips.

# Techniques, Trucs, and Definitions

**Trucs** literally means "tricks of the trade" in French. The following **trucs** are easily mastered and will become second nature with a little practice.

## Blanch

Briefly immersing vegetables or fruits in boiling water to minimize cooking time, retain texture, set color, or loosen skin. The blanched ingredients are then usually shocked (or refreshed) in ice water (or cold water) to stop the cooking process and to cool them down.

For carrots: Dice or julienne the carrots and add to boiling salted water for about 2 minutes, or just until tender. Shock in an ice-water bath until cool, and drain. Blanching carrots is especially useful if you wish to add them to other ingredients that require a short cooking time.

For garlic: Blanching garlic in two changes of water eliminates its sharpness without reducing the flavor. Peel the cloves of garlic. Bring a quart of water to a boil in a saucepan, add the garlic cloves, and return to a boil. Pour off the water, leaving the garlic in the pan. Refill the pan with 1 quart of water and bring to a boil. Drain and reserve the garlic.

For haricots verts (green beans) and fresh peas: Blanching maximizes the color, flavor, and texture of the beans or peas, keeping them tender and crisp. Add the beans or peas to salted boiling water for 3 to 4 minutes. Shock in an ice-water bath until cool, and drain.

For tomatoes: Blanching enables the tomatoes to be peeled, removing the tough skin. Immerse in boiling water for 20 seconds, and then plunge into cold water. Peel with the tip of a knife.

## Blend

To mix ingredients together until combined and evenly distributed.

## Braise

A cooking technique in which foods are first browned in hot fat, then covered and slowly cooked in a small amount of liquid over low heat, often in the oven.

## Bread Crumbs

The easiest way to make fine grained bread crumbs is to toast or freeze the bread slices first. Then break up or dice the bread and run in a food processor until finely ground.

## Brown

The process of cooking meat or poultry in hot fat until it turns a golden brown color and the outside is firm.

## Chiffonade

Greens or leaves of herbs or vegetables cut into fine strips or ribbons.

## Chop

To cut food into bite-sized pieces. Chopped ingredients are more coarsely cut than minced or diced ingredients, but are cut smaller than cubed ingredients.

## Cleaning Mushrooms

Fresh mushrooms should not be washed before use because they absorb water so readily. However, they should be brushed carefully to remove any dirt or debris. A mushroom brush, an old toothbrush, or even a damp paper towel can be used for this purpose.

## Cleaning Truffles

In the United States, truffles are almost always sold cleaned and brushed (including frozen truffles). If you come by some that are not, clean them with a mushroom brush or soft toothbrush.

## Coulis

A thick sauce or purée. Originally, the term referred to the natural juices of meat or thick soups and broths.

## Cutting Oils and Fats Every Day

One of the best ways is to use nonstick pans and kitchenware. Cast-iron stovetop grills also require less oil than conventional grills. Another effective method is to use some olive oil in a spray bottle for use in making croutons or for lightly oiling pans. Just cover the pan with a fine, even film; there is no need to coat it. If you prefer, whenever a nonstick pan is called for, use a regular pan and spray it lightly with oil.

## Deglaze

To stir liquid (often alcohol based) into a pan at medium heat to dissolve or loosen cooked particles or caramelized drippings remaining in the bottom of a pan (usually after sautéing or roasting).

## Dice

To cut food into small, neat cubes. Diced ingredients are more coarsely cut than minced ingredients, but less coarsely cut than chopped or cubed ingredients. In the recipes that follow, "diced" refers to $1/2$-inch cubes; "finely diced" means $1/4$-inch cubes.

## Filleting a Fresh Salmon

First things first: When you buy a whole salmon, make sure it's fresh. It should have a clean, fresh smell, the gills should be bright red, the eyes should be bright and shiny, the skin smooth and glossy, and the flesh firm. From my experience, to most effectively and easily fillet the salmon, use a long carving knife with medium flexibility. Hold the fish firmly by the head and cut down right behind the gills, until you reach the backbone. Incline the blade of the knife horizontally and continue cutting, sliding along the backbone to the tail of the salmon. Remove the fillet and turn the fish over. Hold the salmon by the head again, repeat the technique, and remove the second fillet.

### Fondue
A French term derived from the word **fondre** ("to melt") that refers to vegetables that are cooked slowly for a prolonged time until they are completely soft and reduced to a pulp. Another meaning of the word (not used in this book) refers to the classic cheese dip.

### Julienne
To cut ingredients (usually vegetables) into sticks, about $\frac{1}{8}$ inch wide, $\frac{1}{8}$ inch thick, and 1 to 2 inches long.

### Mince
To cut food very finely and neatly. Minced ingredients are less coarsely cut than diced, chopped, or cubed ingredients.

### Macerate
Steeping fruit or other ingredients in a liquid (often a spirit or liqueur) to infuse it with flavor.

### Mousseline
A sauce or mixture to which whipped cream or beaten egg whites have been added to give an airy texture. The term also refers to a type of light, airy cake with a delicate texture (and usually a flavored filling and icing).

### Peeling Bell Peppers
See "Roast," below.

### Peeling Tomatoes
See "Blanch," above.

### Pulse
To coarsely chop or mix ingredients in a blender or food processor by turning the machine on and off.

### Purée
Food processed in a blender or food processor by mashing or mixing to a smooth, thick pulp.

### Reduce
Rapidly cooking a liquid to decrease its quantity through evaporation and to thicken it and concentrate its flavors. Reducing to a glaze refers to an even more dramatic reduction, to a syrupy consistency, further enhancing flavor.

### Refresh or Shock
To submerge a cooked ingredient (usually vegetables) in cold or ice water to quickly cool and prevent further cooking. See "Blanch."

## Roast

To cook food (typically meat) with dry heat, usually in an oven. Roasting vegetables (such as bell peppers), however, is often done under a broiler or on a grill so they can be more easily peeled, to remove the tough, bitter skin and to bring out their full, sweet flavors. (Roasting on a grill can also introduce an earthy, sometimes smoky flavor.)

For bell peppers: Preheat the broiler or prepare the grill. Coat each bell pepper with about 1 teaspoon of virgin olive oil. Place under the broiler or on the grill, and turn frequently until the skin is blackened on all sides. When the peppers are charred, let cool slightly, preferably in a sealed paper bag or in a bowl covered with plastic wrap. Peel off the blackened skin with the tip of a sharp knife. Remove the stems, cut the peppers open, and remove the core, seeds, and internal ribs. Chop or dice, and set aside.

For garlic: Roasting garlic sweetens and mellows its flavor. Preheat the oven to 375°. Break up a head of garlic into individual cloves; do not peel. Place in a small baking dish and roast in the oven for 20 minutes. Remove the garlic and let cool. Peel the garlic cloves carefully and use as directed.

## Sauté

A cooking technique using conduction to transfer heat from a hot sauté pan or skillet to food, usually with the aid of a small amount of oil or fat. Ingredients are often cut into small pieces to promote even cooking; sautéing is usually done at high temperatures. In French, **sauter** means "to jump," referring to the technique of pulling the pan toward you in a rapid motion so the ingredients flip or jump up in the air before rearranging themselves in the pan, thus promoting even cooking.

## Scallopine

A thin slice of fish or meat; the term is also used to describe sliced and layered potatoes cooked in a cream sauce. Scalloped ingredients are often dredged in a coating or covered in a batter.

## Sear

To brown food quickly over high heat, usually as a preparation step.

## Seasoning to Taste

The recipes that follow invariably call for "salt and pepper to taste," sometimes at several points throughout the preparation. This is for practical as well as obvious reasons. Although some people are on sodium-free or low-sodium diets, everyone likes more or less salt and pepper according to their palates and tolerances. Moreover, I always keep tasting the food at each step, adjusting the salt, pepper, and other seasonings accordingly. I have instructed you to do the same in the recipes, but if you are unsure what's needed when tasting, be conservative. You can always taste and adjust seasonings when the dish is finished.

### Section

Technique for preparing citrus fruit. Using a small, sharp knife, peel the citrus fruit until the white pith and membranes have been removed. Cut both sides of each section's membrane and let the fruit slip out into a small bowl. Remove all the seeds.

### Shred

To tear or cut into thin but irregular strips.

### Simmer

Cooking a liquid mixture over low heat to keep bubbling at a minimum and to maintain a cooking temperature just below boiling.

### Skinning Hazelnuts

See "Toast," below.

### Slice

To cut ingredients into broad, thin slices (usually herbs or vegetables). When slicing herbs, use a sharp knife or kitchen scissors to maintain the bright colors and to avoid bruising.

### Steam

To cook ingredients directly in the steam created by boiling water or some other liquid, without touching the liquid.

### Sweat

To cook an ingredient in a small amount of oil or fat over low to medium heat, to soften and release moisture, but not to color or caramelize. The technique is used so the flavor of the ingredient is more quickly released when it is then added to other foods.

### Toast

Toasting seeds, dried herbs, and spices intensifies their aromatic qualities and brings out additional flavor tones.

For mustard seeds, cumin seeds, and sesame seeds: Place the seeds in a nonstick pan over medium heat. For mustard seeds, cover three-quarters of the pan to keep them from jumping out. The pan does not need to be covered when toasting cumin and sesame seeds. Shake the pan frequently to toast the seeds evenly. Toast for about 3 to 4 minutes, or until fragrant (the mustard seeds will turn grey and the sesame seeds will be very lightly browned). Remove and let cool.

For almonds, walnuts, pecans, and pine nuts: Place in a nonstick pan over medium-high heat. Stir or flip continuously for about 4 minutes, or until golden brown.

For hazelnuts: Preheat the oven to 375°. Spritz the nuts with water from a spray bottle (this will help you peel the skins later). Place in a single layer on a baking sheet and toast in the oven for 5 to 8 minutes. Remove and let cool. Place in a kitchen towel, twist to secure, and rub the nuts with the towel to loosen the skins.

For ground spices: Place in a dry nonstick pan or skillet and toast over medium heat for 1 or 2 minutes, or until fragrant.

### Water Bath (Bain Marie)

A pan filled with hot or simmering water in which ramekins or baking dishes can be placed to cook, usually in the oven. This method of cooking is particularly effective with custards, mousses, sauces, or delicate foods that should not be cooked over direct heat.

### Wilt

Usually refers to sautéing greens such as spinach, lettuce, or sorrel over heat until the leaves wilt and diminish in volume.

### Whipping

The purpose of this technique (usually applied to cream and eggs or egg whites) is to aerate the ingredient and increase its volume. It may be done with a whisk, rotary beater, or electric mixer. Whipping is often continued until soft peaks form on the surface of the ingredient, indicating thorough aeration. Occasionally, a recipe will call for whipping to stiff peaks, when parts of the surface stand up firmly, at which point the whipping process is maximized—continued whipping will cause the ingredient to "break."

### Zest

The colored, flavorful part of citrus peel that contains the aromatic oils, with none of the bitter white pith.

# Basic Recipes

The broths (the word I use for stocks) in this section form the foundation for many of the recipes in this book. Homemade broths are always best, but if you are short on time, you can substitute a good-quality canned stock, preferably a brand that is sodium-free—you can always season it to taste.

---

# Bouquet Garni

*T*his is a great tool for infusing a little extra flavor to foods. In Europe (and in some specialty stores in the United States), you can buy sachets of dried herbs labeled bouquet garni, but for best results, make your own.

### CHEF'S NOTES

In Europe, it's common to find premade bouquet garni in tea bag-like sachets. These are also available in some gourmet food stores and provide a shortcut if you prefer.

### YIELD: 1

- 4 or 5 sprigs fresh parsley
- 1 sprig fresh thyme
- 1 dried bay leaf
- 3-inch stalk celery
- 1 sprig fresh basil (optional)
- 1 sprig fresh tarragon (optional)
- 1 sprig fresh rosemary (optional)
- 1 sprig fresh cilantro (optional)
- 1 leek leaf (optional)

Bunch the herbs and celery neatly and tie securely with the leek leaf or kitchen twine. Use as directed.

# Brown Chicken Broth

*A* good chicken broth can be served by itself as a soup or used as a base for other soups and sauces. The white wine is optional, but certainly adds a touch of sophistication. As a shortcut, you can use a couple of cans of good-quality chicken stock, add the vegetables and Bouquet Garni called for in this recipe together with a little port, sherry, or wine, and reduce by one-third.

## CHEF'S NOTES

Allow about 2 hours to prepare. You don't have to brown the chicken bones in the oven, especially if you want a paler broth (for example, for a white sauce). An effective way to degrease the broth, if you have the time, is to chill it overnight and when cold, remove the congealed surface fat with a spoon.

YIELD: 3 TO 4 QUARTS

4 to 5 pounds chicken bones (such as wings, necks, and scraps), raw, cooked, or a mixture, cut into 2-inch pieces

2 onions, coarsely chopped

2 stalks celery, coarsely chopped

2 large carrots, coarsely chopped

2 cups dry white wine

1 leek, white part and some of the green, coarsely chopped

2 tomatoes, seeded and diced

2 cloves garlic, crushed

1 Bouquet Garni (page 22)

1 teaspoon salt

8 peppercorns

Preheat the oven to 450°.

Place the chicken bones and scraps in a large roasting pan and roast in the oven for 15 to 20 minutes, turning and basting several times, until golden brown. Mix in the onions, celery, and carrots. Continue roasting for 5 to 10 minutes, turning and basting occasionally to brown evenly.

Remove the pan from the oven and transfer the bones and vegetables to a large stockpot. Pour off the accumulated fat and deglaze the roasting pan with the wine, using a wooden spoon to scrape and dissolve all the food particles on the pan. Add these deglazing juices to the stockpot and add enough water to completely cover the chicken pieces.

Bring to a boil, reduce the heat, and simmer for 10 minutes, skimming any impurities from the surface of the broth. Add the leek, tomatoes, garlic, Bouquet Garni, salt, and peppercorns, and continue to simmer for 1 1/2 hours, skimming the surface as necessary.

Carefully strain the broth through a fine-meshed sieve, discarding the solids. Skim any impurities and adjust the seasonings if necessary. Refrigerate or freeze until needed.

# Beef Broth

*B*eef Broth is the base of so many delicious soups, wonderful stews and sauces with explosive flavors. Although I highly recommend making your own Beef Broth, which is painless and gives dishes a personal touch, you can substitute canned broth if necessary. If you do use the canned form, add water in the ratio of 1 part water to 4 parts broth, a dash of port, a little minced carrot and celery, and simmer for 20 minutes. Then strain and you'll have a respectable broth substitute.

## CHEF'S NOTES

Allow 4 to 5 hours to prepare. Ask your butcher to saw the broth bones for you. You can degrease the broth in the same way that's described for the Brown Chicken Broth (page 23). This broth can be reduced to make an intense demiglace, or cookeddown even further for a really concentrated glace.

### YIELD: 3 TO 4 QUARTS

- 4 to 5 pounds meaty beef bones (such as shank, neck, shoulder, or knuckle) and any beef scraps, cut into 2- or 3-inch pieces
- 2 onions, coarsely chopped
- 2 stalks celery, coarsely chopped
- 2 large carrots, coarsely chopped
- 2 cups water
- 1 large leek, white part and some of the green, coarsely chopped
- 2 tomatoes, seeded and diced
- 2 cloves garlic, crushed
- 1 large Bouquet Garni (page 22)
- 1 teaspoon salt
- 8 peppercorns

Preheat the oven to 450°.

Place the bones and meat scraps in a large roasting pan and roast in the oven for 25 to 30 minutes, turning and basting several times, until golden brown.

Mix in the onions, celery, and carrots. Continue roasting for 5 to 10 minutes, turning and basting occasionally to brown evenly.

Remove the pan from the oven and transfer the bones and vegetables to a large stockpot. Pour off the accumulated fat and deglaze the roasting pan with the water, using a wooden spoon to scrape and dissolve all the food particles on the pan. Add these deglazing juices to the stockpot and add enough water to completely cover the bones.

Bring to a boil, reduce the heat, and simmer for 10 minutes, skimming any impurities from the surface of the broth. Add the leek, tomatoes, garlic, Bouquet Garni, salt, and peppercorns, and continue to simmer for 4 hours, skimming the surface as necessary.

Carefully strain the broth through a fine-meshed sieve, discarding the solids. Skim any impurities and adjust the seasonings if necessary. Refrigerate or freeze until needed.

# Fish Broth

*I*t's definitely worth the time and effort involved to prepare this broth for fish and seafood dishes.

## CHEF'S NOTES
Allow about 1 hour to prepare. This broth can be stored in the refrigerator for up to 3 days in a tightly covered container.

YIELD: 3 TO 4 QUARTS

5 to 6 pounds meaty fish bones (from lean fish such as sole, flounder, cod, sea bass, halibut, or hake)

2 onions, coarsely chopped

2 stalks celery, coarsely chopped

1 leek, white part only, cut in half lengthwise and coarsely chopped

2 cloves garlic, crushed

3 cups dry white wine

1 Bouquet Garni (page 22)

Salt to taste

8 peppercorns

Place all of the ingredients in a large stockpot. Cover with cold water and bring to a boil. Reduce the heat and lightly simmer 20 minutes, skimming any impurities from the surface of the broth. Cover the pan loosely and continue to simmer for 20 to 25 minutes longer.

Carefully strain the broth through a fine-meshed sieve, discarding the solids. Skim any impurities and adjust the seasonings if necessary. Refrigerate or freeze until needed.

# Vegetable Broth

This fragrant, complex broth is absolutely essential when preparing many vegetarian dishes. It can also be substituted for any meat-based broths; it is a lighter flavored and more healthful alternative when preparing soups and sauces. It makes a good sipping broth, too.

### CHEF'S NOTES

Allow about 1 hour to prepare. A good vegetable broth should be clear and light colored. All of the broth recipes freeze well, so double the quantities if you like. You can add just about any fresh vegetables you have on hand, not just the ones I've called for here. For instance, I often use various types of turnips, wild mushrooms, and fresh herbs.

YIELD: 1¼ TO 2 QUARTS

2 leeks, white part and some of the green parts, sliced into ½-inch lengths

½ small celeriac or 2 stalks celery, diced

4 or 5 shallots, coarsely chopped

1 large tomato, blanched, peeled, seeded, and diced

3 cloves garlic, coarsely chopped

3 carrots, diced

10 button mushrooms, diced

3 sprigs fresh parsley

8 to 10 fresh basil leaves

1 sprig fresh thyme

2 sprigs fresh cilantro

2 pinches fresh chervil leaves

2 dried bay leaves

Salt to taste

4 or 5 peppercorns

Place all of the ingredients in a large stockpot. Cover with cold water and bring to a boil. Reduce the heat and lightly simmer for 20 minutes. Remove from the heat, cover the pan and let infuse for 20 minutes.

Carefully strain the broth through a fine-meshed sieve, discarding the solids. Adjust the seasonings if necessary. Refrigerate or freeze until needed.

# Breads

*B*READ IS taken very seriously in France, where you'll hear the refrain "a meal without bread is like a beautiful face without eyes." In France, bread making is an art form as well as a profession. In fact, under French law, a clear distinction is made between the bread makers **(boulangers)** and pastry and cake makers **(pâtissiers)**, and it is a demarcation that is rarely crossed; only **boulangers** may bake and sell bread. The one exception is that the **pâtissiers** make the rich, cakelike **brioche.** In Alsace and Lorraine on Sundays, when the **boulangeries** are closed, **pâtissiers** can make bread as long as it contains some butter.

To many people in the United States, "French bread" refers to the elongated baguette loaf, but back home there are many types of bread. The long thin **ficelle** bread and the wider **pain Parisien** are made in a similar style and shape as the baguette, but have different crust-to-dough ratios, which in turn produce varying textures and shelf life. The free-form **pains paysans** and the traditional large, round **boules,** have low crust-to-dough ratios, and so they keep longer. Breads flavored with herbs and ingredients such as olives and tomatoes were previously rare, but as in the United States, they are becoming increasingly popular.

Experienced professional bakers weigh many factors when making bread, such as the idiosyncrasies of the oven they're using and the humidity that day. It's the same in the home kitchen; with practice you'll come to know when to make small adjustments. If you follow these recipes closely you'll never go too far wrong, so don't be intimidated—bread baking is really very easy and immensely rewarding. Here are a few hints and tips that should help you get the best results:

■ Use a baking stone. Select a thick rectangular stone, which will accommodate any shape of loaf. Baking stones regulate the temperature throughout the oven, even when the oven door is opened, and evenly distribute the heat across the bottom of the bread. If you don't have a baking stone, you can use several pieces of unglazed tile instead.

■ To make crusty yeast breads, use a spray bottle filled with cold water to spritz the walls and floor of the hot oven immediately before baking the bread. This creates the humidity necessary to give the bread a crunchy crust. You may also periodically spray the inside of the oven with water as the bread bakes.

■ Test the health of the yeast. Working with a dough that is "alive" requires special care and attention, which begins with the proofing process. Many of these recipes call for a "sponge." When you make the sponge, check it periodically for activity. If it does not substantially expand in volume and the surface is not covered with many tiny bubbles within the first hour, throw it out and begin again. Sluggish or dead yeast never makes good bread, so don't waste time and flour trying to use it.

■ Bread is best eaten fresh. If you want to store the bread for more than a day or two, wrap it in plastic wrap or foil and keep it refrigerated (this will help prevent the bread from drying out). Yeast breads freeze well, especially when double-wrapped.

I have many dear memories of helping my father make **brioche** in his **pâtisserie**. I hope the recipes in this chapter will provide the inspiration necessary to ensure your meals are always accompanied by wonderful bread, and to make memories while baking with your loved ones.

## ABOUT YEAST

Baker's yeast is a harmless, live single-cell fungus that is used to leaven bread. Yeast converts its food (in the case of breads, sugar, water or milk, and flour) to carbon dioxide, which is what makes bread dough expand and rise. However, the liquid must be the right temperature (105° to 115°) and the air temperature must be warm enough to activate the yeast. If the liquid is too hot, it will kill the yeast; if the liquid or air is too cool, it will impede its leavening action.

Yeast is available both in active dry form (the type I use in the following recipes)—fine, dehydrated granules—and compressed fresh yeast, in moist, cake form. Fresh yeast is highly perishable and thus less practical for the home cook. Dry yeast should be stored in a cool place (such as the refrigerator) and used before the expiration date on the package or label. It can also be frozen and then defrosted before use. If the yeast does not froth or foam during proofing (dissolving it and sugar in water and letting it sit for 10 minutes or so), it is no longer active; discard and start again.

# Crusty Boulettes

*T*HESE CLASSIC French rolls (**boulette** means "little ball") are great for novice home bakers because they are made with a simple, basic dough. If you prefer, the dough can be formed into a baguette-style loaf, although the proper rolling technique is an acquired skill. These rolls are best when eaten immediately (or within three hours of baking) while they are still a little moist. Some French bread, like the long, thin and exquisite **ficelle**, must be eaten the same morning that it's baked, because it dries out quickly and by the afternoon, it's too hard to eat.

## CHEF'S NOTES
Allow 25 to 30 minutes to prepare the dough and about 2 hours for rising and baking. If you like, you can spray the rolls with water, then sprinkle with poppy seeds or sesame seeds just before you bake them.

YIELD: 12 ROLLS

1 tablespoon active dry yeast

1½ cups warm water (105° to 115°)

1 teaspoon sugar

3½ cups unbleached all-purpose flour

2 teaspoons sea salt

Combine the yeast, water, and sugar in the bowl of an electric mixer fitted with a dough hook, and stir until blended. Cover the bowl with plastic wrap and let stand in a warm place for 15 minutes, until the mixture is foamy.

Combine the flour and salt in a mixing bowl, and gradually add to the yeast mixture while mixing on low speed. Mix for 2 to 3 minutes until thoroughly incorporated. Increase the speed to medium and mix together for 10 to 12 minutes, or until the dough is smooth and elastic.

Transfer the dough to a well-oiled bowl and cover with plastic wrap or a damp towel. Let the dough rise in a warm place for about 1 hour, or until doubled in size.

Punch the dough down and turn out onto a lightly floured work surface. Knead the dough by hand for 1 minute. Divide the dough into 2 equal pieces and form each piece into a long rope. Cut each rope into 2 equal pieces, and then divide each of these pieces into 3, making a total of 12 equal-sized pieces of dough. Shape each piece into a ball by rolling between your palm and the work surface.

Place the rolls on a large baking sheet (or 2 sheets measuring 12 by 18 inches) and cover with a damp towel. Let rise in a warm place for 45 minutes to 1 hour, or until doubled in size.

About 30 minutes before the dough is ready to bake, place a baking stone in the oven and preheat to 425°.

Remove the towel from the dough. Using a single-edged razor, slash the top of each roll in a cross pattern with quick and sure strokes. Place the baking sheet on top of the baking stone in the oven, and spray the oven walls and floor generously with cold water. Immediately close the oven door and bake for 15 minutes, or until the crust is golden brown and crisp.

Remove from the rolls from the oven and transfer to a wire rack to cool.

# Provençal Fougasse

*F*OUGASSE, A country-style flatbread, is ideal for those who prefer rustic, crusty-type bread. It makes a simple snack with a glass of wine and is wonderful with dinner. Fougasse is one of the Western world's first recorded breads—the word (like its close cousin, the Italian focaccia) is derived from the Latin word **focus**, which means "fireplace." As this etymology suggests, in the days long before ovens, the ancient Greeks and Romans baked flatbread on the hearth. The Romans introduced this bread to southern France, where it is traditionally made in an oval shape; diagonal slashes, like the veins in a leaf, are made through the dough just before it is baked.

## CHEF'S NOTES

Allow about 30 minutes to prepare the dough and 2 hours 45 minutes to 3 hours 15 minutes for rising and baking. Fougasse is best eaten the same day it's baked, as it does not keep well. If you like, you can flavor the top of the bread pizza-style with sundried tomatoes, pitted olives, or sautéed onions.

YIELD: 1 LOAF

**STARTER**

½ cup warm water (105° to 115°)

2 teaspoons active dry yeast

1 tablespoon sugar

¾ cup unbleached all-purpose flour

**DOUGH**

1¼ cups warm water (105° to 115°)

½ tablespoon active dry yeast

3 slices bacon (optional)

4½ tablespoons virgin olive oil

3½ cups unbleached all-purpose flour

2¾ teaspoons kosher salt

1½ tablespoons minced fresh rosemary needles

To prepare the starter, place the warm water in a small bowl. Sprinkle the yeast and sugar over the water and stir to dissolve. Let stand for 10 minutes in a warm place, until the mixture is foamy. Stir in the flour, cover the bowl with plastic wrap, and let rise at room temperature for 45 minutes to 1 hour, or until doubled in size.

To prepare the dough, combine the water and yeast in the bowl of an electric mixer fitted with a dough hook, and stir together. Let stand for about 10 minutes, or until the mixture is foamy.

Sauté the bacon in a skillet over medium-high heat for 3 to 4 minutes, or until cooked through. Transfer to paper towels to drain. When cool, dice.

Add the starter to the bowl of the electric mixer, add 2 tablespoons of the olive oil, and mix on low speed until thoroughly combined. Gradually add 1 cup of the flour and ³/₄ teaspoon of the salt, and mix until incorporated. Add the remaining 2¹/₂ cups of flour, increase the speed to medium, and mix together for 8 to 10 minutes. Mix in the bacon and ¹/₂ tablespoon of the rosemary; the dough should have a firm consistency.

Transfer the dough to a well-oiled bowl and cover with plastic wrap or a damp towel. Let the dough rise in a warm place for about 1 hour, or until doubled in size.

Punch the dough down and turn out onto a lightly oiled baking sheet. Flatten the dough, using oiled hands, and shape it into an oval, or to fit the pan (it should be no more than 1 inch thick). Cover with plastic wrap or a damp towel and let the dough rise in a warm place for 45 minutes to 1 hour, or until doubled in size.

About 30 minutes before the dough is ready to bake, place a baking stone in the oven and preheat to 425°.

Remove the plastic wrap or towel from the dough and brush the top of the dough with the remaining 2¹/₂ tablespoons of olive oil. Sprinkle with the remaining 2 teaspoons of salt and the remaining 1 tablespoon of rosemary.

Place the baking sheet on top of the baking stone in the oven, and spray the oven walls and floor generously with cold water. Immediately close the oven door and bake for 20 minutes, or until the crust is crisp and golden brown.

Remove the fougasse from the oven and transfer to a wire rack to cool. Serve warm or at room temperature.

# San Francisco Sourdough

*S*AN FRANCISCO is the sourdough capital of the world—even the city's airport sells sourdough bread—so it would be remiss of me not to include this recipe. In France too, rustic loaves are commonly made with **levain**, a sourdough starter, and some starters pass from generation to generation, especially in professional baking families. (The round loaf pictured on the opposite page, centered in front of the basket, is San Francisco Sourdough. Among the other breads pictured are Braided Brioche, Black Olive Bread, and Crusty Boulettes.)

## CHEF'S NOTES

Allow 3 to 5 days to begin the starter, about 30 minutes to prepare the dough, and $3\frac{1}{2}$ to 5 hours for rising and baking. Replenish the remaining starter by adding 1 cup of warm water (105° to 115°) and $2\frac{1}{2}$ cups of bread flour. Cover and let stand at room temperature for 24 hours. Then refrigerate for up to a week or freeze; the starter will die unless you keep using and replenishing it. Before reusing, allow the starter to slowly thaw at room temperature until it bubbles again.

### YIELD: 2 LOAVES

### SOURDOUGH STARTER
- $1\frac{1}{4}$ cups room-temperature water (about 70°)
- 1 teaspoon active dry yeast
- 1 tablespoon sugar
- 3 cups bread flour

### DOUGH
- 1 cup warm water (105° to 115°)
- ½ tablespoon active dry yeast
- 1 tablespoon sugar
- 9 ounces sourdough starter
- 4 cups plus 3 tablespoons bread flour
- ½ tablespoon salt
- 2 tablespoons cornmeal, for sprinkling

To prepare the starter, place the water in a high-sided nonreactive bowl. Sprinkle the yeast and sugar over the water and stir to dissolve. Mix until blended, and let stand in a warm place for 10 minutes, or until the mixture is foamy. Stir in the 3 cups of flour and blend for 1 to 2 minutes until the starter is soft and sticky. Cover with plastic wrap. Let stand at room temperature for at least 3 or 4 days, and up to 5 days. The starter should bubble and smell sour. Stir the starter once a day during this time, mixing in any crust that forms on top. When the starter is ready, remove 9 ounces to use for the dough.

To prepare the dough, place the water, yeast, and sugar in the bowl of an electric mixer fitted with a dough hook. Mix to blend, and let stand for 10 minutes in a warm place, or until the mixture is foamy. Stir in the starter and mix at low speed until thoroughly combined. Gradually add the 4 cups of flour and the salt, increase the speed to medium, and mix together for 8 to 10 minutes; the dough should have a fairly sticky but elastic consistency. Turn out the dough onto a lightly floured work surface and knead by hand for 1 minute. Form into a ball, place in a well-oiled bowl, and cover with plastic wrap or a damp towel. Let rise in a warm place for 2 to 3 hours, or until doubled in size.

Punch the dough down and turn out again onto a lightly floured work surface. Knead the dough by hand for 1 minute, and divide into 2 equal pieces. Shape each piece into a round loaf. Sprinkle a baking sheet with the cornmeal. Transfer the loaves to the sheet. Cover with a damp towel to prevent a crust from forming, and let the dough rise in a warm place for 1 to $1\frac{1}{2}$ hours, or until almost doubled in size. Periodically spray the towel with water to keep it damp.

About 30 minutes before the dough is ready to bake, place a baking stone in the oven and preheat to 425°.

Just before you are ready to bake the loaves, remove the towel and spray the loaves with water. Dust with the remainin 3 tablespoons of flour. Using a single-edged razor, make 2 parallel ½-inch-deep slashes on the top of the dough with quick and sure strokes. Then make 2 more parallel slashes at a 45-degree angle, to form a diagonal criss-cross pattern. Place the baking sheet on the baking stone, and spray the oven walls and floor generously with cold water. Immediately close the oven door and bake for 25 to 30 minutes, or until the crust is golden brown and the loaves sound hollow when tapped. Remove the loaves from the oven and transfer to a wire rack to cool.

# Black Olive Bread

*O*LIVE BREAD is sold in the South of France, but is not nearly as common or popular there as it is in California. I particularly enjoy crusty, round **boule**-style bread like this one, which we often serve at Fleur de Lys. This versatile, flavored bread goes very well with sheep or goat cheese, cold or barbecued meats, and most fish. After a day or two, it's best toasted.

## CHEF'S NOTES

Allow 35 to 40 minutes to prepare the dough, and 3 to 3½ hours for rising and baking. Sprinkling the surface of the risen loaf with flour and then slashing the top of it before baking creates a rustic appearance as the slashes open up and the surface browns at a different rate than the rest of the crust. The dough can also be made into dinner rolls, if you prefer. Prepare the dough as directed for the loaf, but bake 15 to 20 minutes at 425°

**YIELD: 1 LARGE LOAF OR 8 TO 10 ROLLS**

**STARTER**

½ cup warm water (105° to 115°)

½ tablespoon active dry yeast

1 teaspoon sugar

⅔ cup bread flour

**DOUGH**

⅔ cup rye flour

¼ cup whole wheat flour

2½ cups bread flour

1½ teaspoons sea salt

1 cup warm water (105° to 115°)

2 teaspoons active dry yeast

4 tablespoons virgin olive oil

¾ cup large pitted Greek kalamata or other black olives

1 tablespoon whole wheat flour

To prepare the starter, place the warm water in a bowl. Sprinkle the yeast and sugar over the water and stir to dissolve. Let stand for 10 minutes in a warm place, or until the mixture is foamy. Stir in the bread flour, cover the bowl with plastic wrap, and let rise in a warm place for 45 minutes to 1 hour, or until doubled in size.

To prepare the dough, combine the rye flour, whole wheat flour, bread flour, and salt in a mixing bowl and set aside. In the bowl of an electric mixer fitted with a dough hook, combine the water and yeast, and stir together. Let stand for about 10 minutes, or until the mixture is foamy.

Add the starter to the bowl of the electric mixer, add the olive oil, and mix on low speed until thoroughly combined. Gradually add the dry ingredients, increase the speed to medium, and mix together for 8 to 10 minutes. Mix in the olives. The dough should have a firm consistency.

Transfer the dough to a well-oiled medium bowl and cover with plastic wrap or a damp towel. Let the dough rise in a warm place for 45 minutes to 1 hour, or until doubled in size.

Punch the dough down and turn out onto a lightly floured work surface. Knead the dough by hand for 1 minute. Form into a ball and place smooth side down (seam side up) in a large shallow bowl lined with a dry, clean kitchen towel. Cover the dough with another kitchen towel and let the dough rise in a warm place for about 1 hour, or until doubled in size.

About 30 minutes before the dough is ready to bake, place a baking stone in the oven and preheat to 425°.

Remove the top towel from the dough and place a lightly oiled baking sheet over the bowl. Invert the bowl, placing the dough onto the baking sheet. Remove the bottom towel, gently brush the dough with water, and sprinkle lightly with the 1 tablespoon of whole wheat flour.

Using a single-edged razor, make 2 parallel ½-inch-deep slashes on the top of the dough with quick and sure strokes. Then make 2 more parallel slashes at a 45-degree angle, to form a criss-cross pattern.

Place the baking sheet on top of the baking stone in the oven, and spray the oven walls and floor generously with cold water. Immediately close the oven door and bake for 35 to 40 minutes, or until the crust is golden brown and the loaf sounds hollow when tapped.

Remove the loaf from the oven and transfer to a wire rack to cool.

# Nori Bread

NORI, A Japanese ingredient, is edible seaweed, pressed and dried into paper-thin sheets often used for wrapping sushi. This is a nutritious and healthful low-calorie bread, with a crisp, golden crust and flavors that make it the perfect match for fish or seafood. It was inspired by a recipe I once read in a French cookbook and has been one of my favorites for some time now. It makes a great conversation piece.

## CHEF'S NOTES

Allow 35 to 40 minutes to prepare the dough, and 3 to $3^1/_2$ hours for rising and baking. You can bake the dough in loaf pans, shape the dough in a free form on a baking sheet, or divide it into rolls (makes 14 to 16).

YIELD: 2 LOAVES

### STARTER

½ cup warm water (105° to 115°)

½ tablespoon active dry yeast

1 cup bread flour

### DOUGH

3 cups cold water

¾ ounce nori

½ tablespoon active dry yeast

4 cups bread flour

2 teaspoons sea salt

To prepare the starter, place the warm water in a bowl. Sprinkle the yeast over the water and stir to dissolve. Let stand for 10 minutes in a warm place, or until the mixture is foamy. Stir in the flour, cover the bowl with plastic wrap, and let rise in a warm place for 45 minutes to 1 hour, or until doubled in size.

Meanwhile, to prepare the dough, place the cold water in a bowl and soak the nori sheets for about 10 to 15 minutes. Remove the nori from the water and drain thoroughly on paper towels. Strain the soaking liquid into a saucepan and bring to a boil over medium heat. Add the soaked nori and continue simmering for 15 minutes. Remove from the heat and set aside to cool. Reserve about $1^1/_2$ cups of the infused water to moisten the dough later. Remove any excess moisture from the nori by blotting it with paper towels. Mince the nori.

Combine the yeast and the $1^1/_2$ cups of infused nori liquid in the bowl of an electric mixer fitted with a dough hook. Let stand for about 10 minutes, or until the mixture is foamy.

Add the starter to the bowl of the electric mixer and mix on low speed until thoroughly combined. Gradually add the bread flour and salt, increase the speed to medium, and mix together for 8 to 10 minutes. Reduce the speed to low and mix in the minced nori. The dough should have a firm consistency.

Transfer the dough to a well-oiled bowl and cover with plastic wrap or a damp towel. Let the dough rise in a warm place for 45 minutes to 1 hour, or until doubled in size.

Punch the dough down and divide it into 2 equal pieces. Flatten one piece and shape it into a rectangle. Fold in half lengthwise (so that one long edge meets the other) and press the seam together. Roll the dough, pressing the seam firmly with each turn. Stretch the ends as necessary to maintain a rectangular shape. Place the finished roll of dough in a lightly oiled 8 by 4-inch loaf pan and repeat the process for the other piece of dough.

Cover the two loaves with plastic wrap or a damp towel and let the dough rise in a warm place for 45 minutes to 1 hour, or until doubled in size.

About 30 minutes before the dough is ready to bake, place a baking stone in the oven and preheat to 425°.

Remove the plastic wrap or towel from the dough and place the loaf pans on top of the baking stone in the oven. Spray the oven walls and floor generously with cold water. Immediately close the oven door and bake for 25 to 30 minutes, or until the crust is crisp and golden brown.

Remove the loaves from the oven and turn out onto a wire rack to cool.

# Rye Bread with Raisins

*I*N MANY French restaurants, rye bread is served with the cheese course—a classic combination—and we do the same at Fleur de Lys. My personal favorite is rye bread studded with sweet raisins. (It also makes great breakfast toast.) Because rye flour naturally contains less gluten than other flour, this bread is denser than most. It also has a longer shelf life than other breads, because the crisp crust retains the bread's moisture very effectively.

### CHEF'S NOTES

Allow 30 to 35 minutes to prepare the dough and 3 to 3$^1/_2$ hours for rising and baking. To truly appreciate rye bread at its best, I let it rest for at least 2 hours after baking. High-gluten flour is a hard wheat flour with high protein. It is often added to low-gluten soft flours, such as rye, to help produce well-risen bread. If you prefer, you can substitute half of the raisins in this recipe with the same amount of chopped walnuts or pecans.

### YIELD: 2 LOAVES

**STARTER**

1¼ cups warm water (105° to 115°)

1 tablespoon active dry yeast

1 cup rye flour

1 cup bread flour

**DOUGH**

2 cups rye flour

2½ cups bread flour

2 tablespoons high-gluten flour (optional)

1½ teaspoons sea salt

1¼ cups warm water (105° to 115°)

1 scant tablespoon active dry yeast

1 cup raisins, rinsed, blanched, and drained

2 tablespoons cornmeal, for sprinkling

To prepare the starter, place the warm water in a mixing bowl. Sprinkle the yeast over the water and stir to dissolve. Let stand for 10 minutes in a warm place, or until the mixture is foamy. Mix the flours together in a separate mixing bowl and stir into the yeast mixture until incorporated. Cover the bowl with plastic wrap and let rise in a warm place for 45 minutes to 1 hour, or until doubled in size.

To prepare the dough, combine the dry ingredients (rye flour, bread flour, gluten flour, and salt) in a mixing bowl and set aside. Combine the water and yeast in the bowl of an electric mixer fitted with a dough hook, and stir together. Let stand for about 10 minutes, or until the mixture is foamy.

Add the starter to the bowl of the electric mixer and mix on low speed until thoroughly combined. Gradually add the dry ingredients and mix until incorporated. Increase the speed to medium and mix together for 8 to 10 minutes. Mix in the raisins; the dough should be stiff.

Transfer the dough to a well-oiled bowl and cover with plastic wrap or a damp towel. Let the dough rise in a warm place for 45 minutes to 1 hour, or until doubled in size.

Punch the dough down and divide into 2 equal pieces. Shape into round loaves. Sprinkle a baking sheet with the cornmeal. Place the loaves on the baking sheet. Cover with plastic wrap or a damp towel and let the dough rise in a warm place for 45 minutes to 1 hour, or until doubled in size.

About 30 minutes before the dough is ready to bake, place a baking stone in the oven and preheat to 425°.

Remove the plastic wrap or towel from the dough. Using a single-edged razor, make 2 parallel ½-inch-deep slashes on the top of the loaves with quick and sure strokes. Then make 2 more parallel slashes at a 45-degree angle, to form a criss-cross pattern.

Place the baking sheet on top of the baking stone in the oven, and spray the oven walls and floor generously with cold water. Immediately close the oven door and bake for 25 to 30 minutes, or until the crust is golden brown. Watch the bread carefully toward the end and cover with an aluminum foil tent, if necessary, as the bread turns dark brown very quickly.

Remove from the oven and transfer the loaves to a wire rack to cool.

# Braided Brioche Loaf

*T*HIS RECIPE has been in my family for three generations. The rich dough, made with eggs, milk, and butter, is wonderfully versatile. It can be made into croissants, Danish pastries filled with flavored pastry creams, or bread of all shapes and sizes. This bread is perfect for breakfast or as a snack. If you want to use it for toast, just bake the dough in two 8 by 4-inch loaf pans. The traditional French **moules à brioche** is baked in a special mold and distinguished by its topknot. During the Christmas season, pastry shops sell brioche shaped into people or animals (**pain décoratif**) for children. My father's trademark shape was **le petit bonhomme** ("the little man"), with currants for eyes and buttons. The children of our town often took them to school in their lunch boxes or enjoyed giant "**bonhommes**" at home with their families.

## CHEF'S NOTES

Allow about 35 minutes to prepare the dough and 2 hours 45 minutes to 3 hours 15 minutes for rising and baking. For a savory brioche to serve with dinner, cut the sugar by half; for a sweeter version, you can brush the loaf with a simple frosting immediately after removing it from the oven. If you like, sprinkle the loaf with sliced almonds or chopped pecans after brushing it with the egg wash for the second time.

YIELD: 1 LOAF

### STARTER
½ cup warm milk (about 105° to 115°)

2 tablespoons active dry yeast

½ cup unbleached all-purpose flour

### DOUGH
5 cups unbleached all-purpose flour

¾ cup sugar

Pinch of sea salt

5 eggs

6 tablespoons milk, at room temperature

1 cup butter, diced, at room temperature

### EGG WASH
2 egg yolks

1 teaspoon water

To prepare the starter, place the warm milk in a bowl and add the yeast and flour. Stir together, cover with plastic wrap, and let stand for 10 to 15 minutes in a warm place, or until the mixture is foamy.

To prepare the dough, combine the flour, sugar, and salt in the bowl of an electric mixer fitted with a dough hook. Stir in the eggs and milk, and mix on low speed for 5 to 8 minutes. Gradually add the butter and continue mixing for 5 to 8 minutes longer. Add the starter and mix for 10 minutes, or until the dough is smooth and elastic and forms a ball. Add more flour if necessary.

Transfer the dough to a well-oiled bowl and cover with plastic wrap or a damp towel. Let the dough rise in a warm place for 1¹/₂ to 2 hours, or until doubled in size.

Punch the dough down, divide it into 3 equal pieces, and turn out onto a lightly floured work surface. Gently roll each piece of dough into ropes of equal length and thickness (about 1 inch in diameter and 15 inches long). Place the ropes next to each other and begin braiding in the middle of the strands (this helps ensure the ends will be even). When the first half of the loaf has been braided, rotate the loaf and braid the other side, again working from the middle to the end. Pinch the ends together and tuck them under the loaf. Lightly butter a baking sheet. Place the loaf on the sheet.

For the egg wash, beat the egg yolks and water together in a bowl, and gently brush the loaf with it. Let the dough rise in a warm place, uncovered, for about 45 minutes, or until doubled in size.

About 30 minutes before the dough is ready to bake, place a baking stone in the oven and preheat to 350°.

Just before baking, gently brush the loaf a second time with the egg wash. Place the baking sheet on top of the baking stone in the oven, immediately close the oven door, and bake for 35 to 40 minutes, or until golden brown.

Remove the loaf from the oven and transfer to a wire rack to cool.

# Henri's Authentic Kugelhopf

*M*Y HOMETOWN, Ribeauvillé, is the **kugelhopf** capital of the world. This distinctive sweet bread is a traditional specialty of Alsace, and every June, Ribeauvillé holds a medieval fair to celebrate. Today, the local pastry shops set up wood-fired ovens on street corners and bake authentic **kugelhopfs** in specially shaped earthenware molds. People come from all over Alsace and beyond to enjoy the festivities—and, of course, the **kugelhopf**. This family recipe has been handed down over the generations, and it's the one my father, Henri, and my brother bake at the family **pâtisserie**. When we were growing up, my brother and I would help my father by cleaning and buttering the intricate molds and placing the almonds inside.

## CHEF'S NOTES

Allow about 35 minutes to prepare the dough and 3 hours 45 minutes to 4 hours 45 minutes for rising and baking. **Kugelhopf** is usually eaten with a glass of wine in the afternoon or served with breakfast. In Alsace, more and more people have taken to serving it with evening cocktails. **Kugelhopf** molds can be difficult to find, but bundt pans will work just fine.

YIELD: 1 LOAF

**STARTER**

½ cup warm milk (about 105° to 115°)

2 tablespoons active dry yeast

½ cup unbleached all-purpose flour

**DOUGH**

5 cups unbleached all-purpose flour

½ cup granulated sugar

Pinch of sea salt

3 large eggs

1 cup milk, at room temperature

¾ cup butter, diced, at room temperature

2 tablespoons kirsch

¼ cup raisins

20 almonds, with skin

2 tablespoons confectioners' sugar

To prepare the starter, place the warm milk in a bowl and add the yeast and flour. Stir together, cover with plastic wrap, and let stand for 10 to 15 minutes in a warm place, until the mixture is foamy. To prepare the dough, combine the flour, sugar, and salt in the bowl of an electric mixer fitted with a dough hook. Stir in the eggs and milk and mix on low speed for 5 to 8 minutes. Gradually add the ³⁄₄ cup of butter and the kirsch, and continue mixing for 5 to 8 minutes longer. Add the starter and mix for 10 minutes, or until the dough is smooth and elastic and forms a ball. Add more flour if necessary. Mix in the raisins.

Transfer the dough to a well-oiled bowl and cover with plastic wrap or a damp towel. Let the dough rise in a warm place for 1¹⁄₂ to 2 hours, or until doubled in size.

Meanwhile, brush an 11- or 12-inch kugelhopf mold with the remaining tablespoon of butter, taking care to butter each flute to prevent any unmolding problems. Place 1 almond in each flute (the number of flutes in kugelhopf pans varies, so you may have extra almonds).

Punch the dough down, form into a ball, and make a hole in the middle with your thumb. Fit the dough around the mold tube and settle it into the mold (the mold should be about two-thirds full). Cover with plastic wrap or a damp towel and let the dough rise in a warm place for 1¹⁄₂ to 2 hours, or until the dough rises to the rim of the mold.

About 30 minutes before the dough is ready to bake, place a baking stone in the oven and preheat to 400°.

Remove the plastic wrap or towel from the mold and place the mold on top of the baking stone in the oven. Immediately close the oven door, and bake for 45 minutes, or until golden brown and the kugelhopf sounds hollow when tapped. If the surface browns quickly (check halfway through the baking time), cover with an aluminum foil tent. Remove from the oven. Place the rack over the mouth of the pan and invert to unmold. Place the kugelhopf on a wire rack to cool. Using a sifter, dust the kugelhopf with the confectioners' sugar. To serve, cut with a serrated knife.

# Alsatian Dried-Fruit Christmas Bread

TRADITIONALLY, THIS bread (called **schnetzwecka**, or "slice loaf," in the Alsatian dialect) was served on Christmas Eve before midnight mass. These days, Alsatians commonly enjoy it for breakfast on Christmas Day or New Year's Day. Make it during the holiday season—or any time—as an accompaniment for morning or afternoon coffee or as an after-dinner treat. It's a very dense, sweet bread that should be cut into very thin slices—you'll only want to eat a little at a time because it's so intensely flavored.

## CHEF'S NOTES

Allow 2 days to soak the dried fruit, about 30 minutes to prepare the dough, and 2 hours 15 minutes to 2 hours 45 minutes for rising and baking. Because this bread uses Brioche dough, I suggest baking a batch of both breads on the same day. The loaf will keep up to 2 weeks, stored in an airtight container in the refrigerator. For more about kirsch, see page 225.

YIELD: 2 LOAVES

DRIED FRUIT MIXTURE
½ cup golden raisins

½ cup dried currants

1 cup diced dried pears

1 cup diced dried apricots

1 cup diced dried figs

1 cup diced dates

½ cup dried cherries

1 cup coarsely chopped walnuts

2 cups kirsch

½ teaspoon ground cinnamon

⅓ recipe Brioche dough (page 41)

EGG WASH
1 egg yolk

½ teaspoon water

8 to 10 walnuts or skinless almonds

Combine all the ingredients for the dried fruit mixture in a nonreactive bowl and mix thoroughly. Cover with plastic wrap and refrigerate for 2 days, stirring from time to time.

Prepare the brioche dough. About 30 minutes before the dough is ready to bake, place a baking stone in the oven and preheat to 375°.

Punch the dough down, drain the fruit mixture, and stir it vigorously into the dough. Transfer the dough to a lightly floured work surface, and divide it into 2 equal pieces. Shape each piece into a loaf about 8 inches long and 2 1/2 inches wide. Lightly butter a baking sheet. Place the loaves on the baking sheet.

For the egg wash, beat the egg yolk and water together in a bowl and gently brush the loaves with it. Gently press the walnuts or almonds into the top of the loaf in a line in the middle or in swirls (alternate nuts at a 45° angle).

Place the baking sheet on top of the baking stone in the oven, immediately close the oven door, and bake for 45 to 55 minutes, or until golden brown.

Remove the loaves from the oven and transfer to a wire rack to cool. To serve, slice with a serrated knife.

# Kugelhopf with Bacon, Onion, and Walnuts

This is another of my family's recipes. It's a version of the modern, savory **kugelhopf** that has been created by Alsatian pastry chefs within the last twenty years or so. Savory **kugelhopfs** have become very popular because they go so well with many different meals. This one's also excellent toasted, with Munster cheese (from Alsace) or other creamy cheese.

## CHEF'S NOTES

Allow about 45 minutes to prepare the dough and 3 hours 45 minutes to 4 hours 45 minutes for rising and baking. This bread can be kept in an airtight container or plastic bag in the refrigerator for up to 4 days. However, I recommend slicing and toasting it after the second day.

### Yield: 1 loaf

**STARTER**

½ cup warm milk (about 105° to 115°)

2 tablespoons active dry yeast

⅛ cup unbleached all-purpose flour

**DOUGH**

2 slices bacon, diced

1 large onion, finely diced

Pinch plus 1½ tablespoons sea salt

5 cups unbleached all-purpose flour

½ cup sugar

3 eggs

1 cup milk, at room temperature

¾ cup butter, diced, at room temperature

2 tablespoons kirsch (optional)

1 cup cooked and finely diced ham

¼ cup walnuts, coarsely chopped

¼ teaspoon whole fresh thyme leaves

2 tablespoons finely minced fresh parsley

20 almonds, with skin

To prepare the starter, place the warm milk in a bowl and add the yeast and flour. Stir together, cover with plastic wrap, and let stand for 10 to 15 minutes in a warm place, or until the mixture is foamy.

To prepare the dough, fry the bacon in a skillet over medium heat for 3 to 4 minutes, or until cooked through. Remove the bacon from the skillet, drain on paper towels, and set aside. In the rendered bacon fat, sauté the onion over medium heat for 8 to 10 minutes, or until tender. Season with the pinch of salt, remove from the skillet, and drain on paper towels. Combine the flour, sugar, and the 1½ tablespoons of salt in the bowl of an electric mixer fitted with a dough hook. Stir in the eggs and milk and mix on low speed for 5 to 8 minutes. Gradually add the butter and the kirsch, and continue mixing for 5 to 8 minutes longer. Add the starter and mix for 10 minutes, or until the dough is smooth and elastic and forms a ball. Add more flour if necessary. Mix in the bacon, onion, ham, walnuts, thyme, and parsley. Transfer the dough to a well-oiled bowl and cover with plastic wrap or a damp towel. Let the dough rise in a warm place for 1½ to 2 hours, or until doubled in size.

Butter an 11- or 12-inch kugelhopf mold, taking care to butter each flute to prevent any unmolding problems. Place 1 almond in each flute. Punch the dough down, form into a ball, and make a hole in the middle with your thumb. Fit the dough around the mold tube and settle it into the prepared mold (it should be about two-thirds full). Cover with plastic wrap or a damp towel and let the dough rise in a warm place for 1½ to 2 hours, or until the dough rises to the rim of the mold. About 30 minutes before the dough is ready to bake, place a baking stone in the oven and preheat to 400°.

Remove the plastic wrap or towel from the mold and place the mold on top of the baking stone in the oven. Immediately close the oven door, and bake for 45 minutes, or until golden brown and the kugelhopf sounds hollow when tapped. If the surface browns quickly (check halfway through the baking time), cover with an aluminum foil tent.

Remove from the oven, unmold, and place the kugelhopf on a wire rack to cool. To serve, cut with a serrated knife.

# Fig and Honey Bread

Figs and honey are a popular combination in Alsace, where dried figs and dates are widely available in winter and are traditional Christmas snacks. Both figs, which were originally brought to Alsace by the Romans, and dates are used extensively in baking. Like kugelhopf or the Alsatian Dried-Fruit Christmas Bread, this light, sweet bread goes best with coffee, or eau de vie (brandy). I think you'll enjoy the exotic flavors of the rum, vanilla, and cinnamon. You can use a combination of figs and apricots instead of just figs, if you prefer.

### CHEF'S NOTES

Allow about 30 minutes to prepare the dough and 45 to 50 minutes for baking. For best results, let the bread rest for a day before serving to allow the flavors and moisture to marry and become fully absorbed. This recipe doubles successfully and the bread freezes well.

### Yield: 1 loaf

1½ cups unbleached all-purpose flour

2 teaspoons baking powder

½ teaspoon ground cinnamon

1 vanilla bean

1 cup diced dried figs

¾ cup water

¼ cup dark rum

¼ cup butter, softened

¾ cup honey

1 egg, beaten

1 cup walnuts or hazelnuts, toasted and chopped

Place a baking stone in the oven and preheat to 350°. Grease the bottom of an 8-inch loaf pan with butter, and line with 3 rectangular pieces of waxed or parchment paper. Grease the paper with butter and set aside.

Sift the dry ingredients (flour, baking powder, and cinnamon) together into a bowl and set aside.

Split the vanilla bean in half lengthwise and scrape the seeds into a saucepan. Add the vanilla pod, figs, water, and rum, stir together, and cook over low heat for about 10 minutes, or until the figs have absorbed all the liquid and are soft. Remove and discard the vanilla pod.

Transfer the figs to a mixing bowl and let cool until lukewarm. Fold the butter and the honey into the figs, and then fold in the egg and nuts. Gently mix in the dry ingredients until incorporated.

Pour the batter into the prepared loaf pan, place on top of the baking stone in the oven, and bake for 45 to 50 minutes, or until a toothpick inserted in the center comes out clean.

Remove the loaf from the oven and turn out onto a wire rack to cool. Wrap tightly and keep at room temperature for 24 hours before serving. To serve, slice with a serrated knife.

# Soups

LTHOUGH SOUPS are often satisfying, healthful, and excellent for entertaining, they are a frequently overlooked course. Soups are an important element of the menu at Fleur de Lys—we always have a hot soup and a cold soup, whatever the season—and our guests express their approval with emptied bowls.

At L'Auberge de l'Ill in Illhaeusern, where I trained as an apprentice in Alsace, Monsieur Daniel, Paul Haeberlin's "right arm," would prepare the **soupe du jour** following Escoffier's traditional recipes to the letter. The Haeberlin family and staff would also eat this soup at lunch and dinner. It was a wonderful environment in which to learn how to create and appreciate perfect soups.

Robust soups are an integral part of Alsatian cuisine, in home cooking as well as in the best restaurants. They are often the prelude for lunch and dinner, which was invariably the case at our house. Typically, homemade Alsatian soups are prepared using choice leftovers and whatever fresh ingredients are on hand. They often contain smoked meat, which is a traditional food of the region.

Although the soups I serve at the restaurant and include in this chapter are not in the rustic, hearty Alsatian style that I grew up with, my philosophy and approach to soups are grounded in my early experiences. I like to make updated versions of classic soups, reinterpreted in keeping with contemporary health concerns and trends. More specifically, I enjoy taking traditional combinations of ingredients and giving them a sparkle or twist by reducing the fat content, adding an ingredient or two to lift the flavors of the soup, or personalizing them with garnishes.

The straightforward soups in this chapter are mostly vegetarian or lowfat. The others feature the delicate flavors of seafood. Whatever their classification, these recipes challenge the traditional French approach to soup making by demonstrating that you don't have to add meats or generous amounts of butter and cream to create flavorful soups. In both the vegetarian and lowfat soups, I use fine-quality olive oil and puréed fresh vegetables to achieve the richness commonly provided by meats, butter, and cream. After you try a few, I'm sure you'll agree the taste is not compromised but heightened. These soups may not pass muster with Monsieur Daniel back at L'Auberge, but I think the forward-thinking Haeberlin family would understand.

# Green Lentil and Sorrel Soup

*T*HIS IS a flavorful, lowfat, low-cholesterol vegetarian dish that updates the hearty, traditional combination of lentils and sorrel in French soups. Sorrel has a pleasantly acidic flavor and is a herb that's used a lot in Alsace. The use of herbs like sorrel has changed dramatically over the last twenty years or so, in France as well as the United States. When I was learning to cook, the herbs we most frequently used were chervil, parsley, chives, and sorrel. We rarely used some of today's most common herbs, such as basil or cilantro, which now find their way into many Alsatian kitchens.

### CHEF'S NOTES

Allow about 1 hour to prepare. Sorrel grows more acidic as it matures, so try to find young leaves. Peak season for sorrel is spring.

SERVES: 4

⅔ cup dried green or French lentils, picked through and rinsed

5 cups Vegetable Broth (page 26) or water

Salt and pepper to taste

1 Bouquet Garni (page 22)

1 small onion, finely diced

2 cloves garlic, minced

1 small carrot, finely diced

4 ounces fresh sorrel leaves (about 3 cups), chopped

1 tablespoon honey

2 tablespoons finely sliced fresh chives

Bring a large saucepan of water to a boil and blanch the lentils for about 1 minute to remove any bitterness. Drain, return the lentils to a clean saucepan, and cover with the broth. Bring to a boil over high heat, season with salt and pepper, and add the Bouquet Garni. Reduce the heat to a simmer, cover the pan, and cook for 15 to 20 minutes.

Add the onion, garlic, and carrot, and cook for about 20 to 25 minutes longer, or until the lentils are tender.

Meanwhile, warm a nonstick sauté pan and heat the chopped sorrel for about 2 to 3 minutes, or until the leaves have wilted. Remove from the heat and set aside.

When the lentils have cooked, remove the Bouquet Garni and discard. Stir in the wilted sorrel, honey, and chives. Adjust the consistency by adding more broth or water if it is too thick. Adjust the seasonings if necessary. Ladle the hot soup into warm bowls and serve immediately.

# Black Bean and Spinach Soup

THIS VEGETARIAN soup contains flavor combinations that I first experimented with at La Cuisine du Soleil, the restaurant I opened in Brazil for Roger Vergé. Black beans were new to me, but because they are a staple in Brazil, they quickly became familiar. In fact, black beans are an integral component of the national dish **feijoada**, a cassoulet-style meat-and-bean stew served with rice and garnished with greens and orange segments. This recipe borrows flavors from that beloved dish.

## CHEF'S NOTES

Allow about 1¹/₂ hours to prepare. You can make this recipe more like the traditional **feijoada** by adding a few slices of cooked Italian sausage and 2 tablespoons of cooked white long-grain rice, or you can enjoy the rustic, hearty soup exactly as it is.

SERVES: 4

⅔ cup dried black beans, picked through and rinsed

3 tablespoons chopped onion

2 tablespoons chopped celery

1 teaspoon minced garlic

1 teaspoon grated ginger

1 tablespoon orange zest

Pepper to taste

6 cups Vegetable Broth (page 26) or water

5 ounces fresh spinach leaves

Salt and pepper to taste

¼ cup nonfat plain yogurt, for garnish

8 orange segments, sectioned, for garnish

1 tablespoon chopped fresh cilantro, for garnish

Place the beans, onion, celery, garlic, ginger, orange zest, and pepper in a large heavy-bottomed saucepan. Add the broth and bring to a boil, stirring occasionally. Reduce the heat to a simmer, cover the pan, and cook for about 1 hour, or until the beans are tender. (The cooking time varies depending on the age and type of black beans.)

Meanwhile, warm a nonstick sauté pan and heat the spinach over medium-high heat for about 2 or 3 minutes, or until wilted but still bright green. Season with salt and pepper, and remove from the heat. Let cool slightly, mince, and set aside.

When the beans are tender, place one-third of them in a blender and purée until smooth. Return the puréed beans to the soup and stir in the minced spinach. Adjust the seasonings if necessary and return to a simmer.

Ladle the soup into rimmed shallow soup plates. Garnish by spooning 1 tablespoon of the yogurt onto the center of the soup, add 2 orange segments and sprinkle with the cilantro. Serve immediately.

# Curried Split Pea Soup

*S*PLIT PEAS, like lentils and beans, are inexpensive and store well, and they are essential to have on hand for those times you don't have time or energy to go out and shop for a meal. The traditional French split pea soup, **Potage Saint Germain,** is made with ham and bacon, but this smooth-textured, sweet and spicy version is meatless. The simple addition of a little curry powder adds sparkle and an exotic touch, lifting all the other flavors of the soup

### CHEF'S NOTES

Allow about 1 hour 15 minutes to prepare. If you want, this soup can be made into a more substantial meal by adding $1^1/2$ tablespoons diced smoked ham or sliced lobster per person (6 tablespoons total). You can prepare this soup in advance and reheat it just before serving.

SERVES: 4

1 tablespoon virgin olive oil

¾ cup diced onion

⅓ cup diced celery

⅓ cup diced carrot

½ tablespoon curry powder

1 cup dried split peas, picked through and rinsed

1½ quarts Vegetable Broth (page 26) or water

1 small handful fresh spinach leaves, coarsely chopped

Salt and pepper to taste

½ cup cubed white sandwich bread

Heat the olive oil in a large heavy-bottomed saucepan. Add the onion, celery, and carrot, and sauté over medium heat for 5 minutes, stirring frequently. Stir in the curry powder and mix well to coat all the vegetables. Add the split peas and broth and bring to a boil, stirring occasionally. Cover with a lid, reduce the heat, and simmer for about 40 minutes, or until the peas are tender.

Add the spinach, salt, and pepper, and continue simmering for 5 minutes longer. Remove from the heat and let cool slightly. Transfer to a blender or food processor, in batches if necessary, and purée until smooth.

Preheat the oven to 375°.

Return the soup to a clean saucepan, heat through, and adjust the consistency by adding more broth or water if it is too thick. Adjust the seasonings if necessary and keep warm.

Place the bread cubes in a single layer on a baking sheet and toast in the oven for 8 to 10 minutes, or until golden brown. Watch the croutons carefully and stir occasionally so they don't burn.

Ladle the hot soup into warm serving bowls, garnish with the croutons, and serve immediately.

# Spicy Tomato and Ginger Soup

THIS IS an ideal vegetarian soup for the summer, when tomatoes are at their very best. I recently created it when working on new ways to feature summer tomatoes, which we do every year while they're in season. The soup proved very popular and earned a place on our summer menus. Try to find young, pliable ginger as it will give the soup a particularly spicy and zingy accent. You can transform the character of the soup by varying the garnish—cooked shrimp, lobster, crabmeat, or sea scallops all work particularly well and can be added at the last minute.

## CHEF'S NOTES

Allow about 1 hour to prepare. This is a versatile soup that can be served hot, at room temperature, or chilled. I like to serve it with toasted garlic bread.

SERVES: 4

2 tablespoons virgin olive oil

1 onion, thickly sliced

1 small leek, white part only, cut in half lengthwise and thickly sliced (about ½ cup)

1 stalk celery, thickly sliced

1 carrot, thickly sliced

2 large cloves garlic, minced

3 cups Vegetable Broth (page 26) or water

2 tablespoons finely grated ginger

Salt and pepper to taste

12 fresh basil leaves

2 pounds ripe tomatoes, blanched, peeled, seeded, and coarsely chopped

½ tablespoon honey

3 tablespoons cream or half-and-half

Heat the olive oil in a heavy-bottomed saucepan and sweat the onion, leek, celery, carrot, and garlic over medium heat for about 10 to 12 minutes, or until almost soft but not brown. Add the broth, ginger, salt, and pepper, and bring to a boil. Reduce the heat and simmer for 15 minutes.

Mince 6 of the basil leaves and add to the pan with the chopped tomatoes and honey. Return to a simmer and cook for 10 minutes. Remove from the heat and let cool slightly. Transfer to a blender or food processor and purée (in batches if necessary) until smooth.

Return the soup to a clean saucepan and bring to a simmer. Stir in the cream and adjust the seasonings. Finely mince the remaining basil leaves. Ladle the soup into shallow soup bowls, sprinkle with the finely minced basil, and serve immediately.

# Caramelized Onion and Fava Bean Soup

THIS VERSION of the traditional French onion soup is a healthful low-calorie dish that combines flavor and robust character with good looks. The secret for success with this recipe is not to rush the onions, but to cook them gently over low heat, so their full caramelized flavor emerges. Adding the vinegar gives the soup a tantalizing sweet and sour quality and balance (called **gastrique** in France) that is unusual for an onion soup.

### CHEF'S NOTES

Allow about 1 hour to prepare. This soup can be prepared 2 or 3 hours ahead of time, as long as you add the diced tomato and fava beans at the last minute and reheat the soup over medium heat until it is just hot. This way, the beans stay bright green and firm and the tomato will show its full fresh flavor. Likewise, toast the bread just before serving.

SERVES: 4

- 1½ tablespoons virgin olive oil or butter
- 1½ pounds onions, thinly sliced
- 5 cups Vegetable Broth (page 26) or water
- Salt and pepper to taste
- 1 pound unshelled fava beans (about 1 cup shelled)
- 1½ tablespoons sugar
- 1 tablespoon water
- 1½ tablespoons red wine vinegar
- 6 tablespoons port
- 1 tomato, blanched, peeled, seeded, and diced
- 4 thick crusty slices of French country-style bread, toasted
- 4 ounces Comté or Emmentaler cheese, grated (optional)

Heat the olive oil in a large heavy-bottomed saucepan. Add the sliced onions and sauté over low heat for about 30 minutes, stirring constantly, or until they are soft and golden brown.

Add the vegetable broth, season with salt and pepper, and bring to a boil. Cover the pan and simmer for 30 minutes.

While the soup is simmering, bring a saucepan of salted water to a boil and blanch the fava beans for 2 minutes. Remove with a wire mesh strainer and refresh under cold running water. Drain, peel off the thick skin of the beans, and set aside.

Combine the sugar and water together in a small saucepan and cook over medium heat until the mixture becomes golden caramel in color. Remove from the heat and stir in the vinegar and port. Return to the heat and bring the mixture to a boil, stirring continuously until the caramel is completely dissolved. Strain into the broth.

Gently stir in the peeled beans and tomato, and adjust the seasonings if necessary. Divide the bread and cheese among side plates. Ladle the hot soup into warm bowls and serve immediately.

# Garlic and Saffron Soup

THIS RECIPE is based on the authentic Provençal **soupe d'ail doux** (sweet garlic soup), made with garlic, onion, and bread. It's a popular, basic peasant soup that's very quick and easy to make. I've enhanced its wonderful flavor here (and added color) with a little saffron. Garlic is healthful—it's believed to be a natural antibiotic and an excellent digestive aid, and to purify the blood and may prevent heart disease and cancer. Regardless, many people are wary of its pungency, but blanching removes its sharpness without diminishing its flavor or health benefits, so you can enjoy this soup and still ward off vampires!

## CHEF'S NOTES

Allow about 40 minutes to prepare. You can give this soup an unusual touch by placing a warm poached egg on a slice of toasted baguette bread in each soup bowl, which is a common presentation in peasant-style soups (especially garlic-based ones) from the South of France. Then, ladle the hot soup all around and sprinkle the finely sliced chives over the egg.

SERVES: 4

- 1 tablespoon virgin olive oil
- 2 small leeks, white part only, cut in half lengthwise and thickly sliced (about 1 cup)
- 3 or 4 whole heads garlic, peeled and blanched
- 1 quart Vegetable Broth (page 26) or water
- Salt and pepper to taste
- ¼ cup peeled and finely diced white potato
- Large pinch of saffron threads
- 1 cup cream or half-and-half
- 3 tablespoons blanched, peeled, seeded, and diced tomato (optional)
- 2 tablespoons finely sliced fresh chives, for garnish

Heat the olive oil in a heavy-bottomed saucepan and sweat the leeks over medium heat for about 6 minutes, or until soft, stirring often. Add the blanched garlic cloves, broth, salt, and pepper, and bring to a boil. Add the potato and saffron threads, reduce the heat, and simmer for about 7 or 8 minutes, or until the potato is soft. Stir in the cream and return to a boil. Immediately remove the soup from the heat and let cool slightly.

Transfer to a blender or food processor, in batches if necessary, and purée until smooth. Return the soup to a clean saucepan, heat through, and adjust the seasonings if necessary. Stir in the diced tomato, if desired.

Ladle the hot soup into warm soup bowls, sprinkle with the chives, and serve immediately.

# Chilled Beet and Ginger Soup

*I* DEVELOPED THIS simple, healthful soup for Dr. Dean Ornish's book, **Eat More, Weigh Less.** Root vegetables are underutilized by most people, which is a shame because they can be very flavorful. Beets are particularly overlooked, perhaps because they color other foods (and anything else they come into contact with, including clothing) an indelible red. The yogurt binds the dish and gives it a creaminess without the high fat content of cream, while the vinegar and ginger hit the high notes.

### CHEF'S NOTES

Allow about 15 minutes to prepare and at least 1 hour to chill. This soup must be served chilled—the balance of flavors as well as the color are lost when heated. I like to serve this soup with sliced, toasted French bread on the side.

SERVES: 4

1 clove garlic

8 beets, peeled and cubed

1-inch length ginger

½ cup nonfat plain yogurt

Juice of 1 lemon

1 tablespoon Spanish sherry vinegar or balsamic vinegar

Salt and pepper to taste

1 teaspoon fresh chervil leaves, for garnish

Run the garlic, beets, and ginger through a juicer and combine the juices in a mixing bowl. Stir in the yogurt, lemon juice, vinegar, salt, and pepper. Refrigerate for at least 1 hour.

Just before serving, adjust the seasonings if necessary. Ladle the chilled soup into rimmed shallow soup plates and sprinkle with the chervil.

# Carrot and Fresh Pea Soup
# with Cinnamon Croutons

*J*UST ABOUT everybody enjoys the classic combination of peas and carrots, and they never tasted better together than in this recipe. I first tasted the pairing of carrot and cinnamon in a savory flan we made at L' Auberge de L'Ill. I liked that flan so much, the flavors stayed with me and resurfaced in this soup. The texture of the unexpectedly sweet-spiced croutons perfectly offsets the creamy soup. You can prepare this soup 2 or 3 hours in advance, and when you're ready to serve it, stir in a little cream at the last minute. This adds a comforting touch, although it's by no means a necessity.

### CHEF'S NOTES

Allow about 1 hour to prepare. If you use frozen peas, buy a good-quality brand and defrost them at the last minute. To make a delicious pasta topping, add some blanched carrots, peas, and chiffonade of basil to any leftover soup.

SERVES: 4

1 tablespoon virgin olive oil

½ cup finely diced onion

2 cups finely diced carrots

1 small leek, white part only, cut in half lengthwise and thickly sliced (about ½ cup)

1 quart Vegetable Broth (page 26) or water

Pinch of sugar

Salt and pepper to taste

½ cup peeled and finely diced white potato

1 cup shelled young fresh peas (about 1 pound pods), or frozen petits pois

CINNAMON CROUTONS

1 tablespoon virgin olive oil

1½ cups diced bread (¼-inch cubes), from brioche or French baguette

¼ teaspoon ground cinnamon

¼ cup cream or half-and-half

1 tablespoon chopped chives, for garnish (optional)

Heat the olive oil in a heavy-bottomed saucepan and sweat the onion, carrots, and leek over medium-high heat for 6 to 8 minutes. Add the broth, sugar, salt, and pepper, and bring to a boil.

Add the potato, cover the pan, and reduce the heat to a simmer. Cook for 15 minutes, or until the vegetables are tender. Add the peas and continue simmering for 10 minutes longer. Remove from the heat and let cool slightly.

Meanwhile, prepare the croutons. Heat the olive oil in a heavy skillet over medium heat. Add the bread cubes and sauté for about 3 minutes, or until they turn a golden brown all over. Sprinkle the cubes with the cinnamon and set aside to cool.

Transfer the soup to a blender or food processor and purée (in batches if necessary) until smooth. Return the soup to a clean saucepan, heat through, and adjust the consistency by adding more vegetable broth or water if it is too thick. Stir in the cream and adjust the seasonings if necessary.

Ladle the hot soup into shallow soup bowls and float the croutons on top, or set them on the side. Sprinkle with the chives and serve.

# Chilled Cucumber and Dill Soup

*T*HIS BRIGHTLY colored and very refreshing soup pairs cooling cucumber with aromatic dill and pungent mustard. It's definitely an eye-catcher for any buffet, and its flavors will dazzle the palate. At Fleur de Lys, we sometimes give the soup an elegant twist by placing a scoop of vodka sorbet on a cucumber rose in the center of the bowl, topped with Beluga caviar.

## CHEF'S NOTES

Allow about 15 minutes to prepare, and at least 1 hour to chill. You can also use this soup as a low-calorie salad dressing for mixed greens, a cold pasta, or rice salad.

SERVES: 4

- 6 young English or hothouse cucumbers, about 10 to 12 inches long, peeled, seeded, and diced
- 2 teaspoons chopped dill
- ½ tablespoon Dijon-style mustard
- 1 teaspoon Spanish sherry vinegar or champagne vinegar
- ¼ cup nonfat plain yogurt
- Salt and pepper to taste
- 10 radishes, finely minced
- 4 small sprigs fresh dill, for garnish
- 1 teaspoon black mustard seeds, toasted, for garnish

Place the cucumbers, dill, mustard, vinegar, yogurt, salt, and pepper in a blender and purée until smooth. Adjust the seasonings if necessary and transfer to a mixing bowl. Refrigerate for at least 1 hour.

Just before serving, stir half of the minced radishes into the soup. Ladle the soup into rimmed shallow soup plates and sprinkle with the remaining minced radishes. Garnish with the dill and toasted mustard seeds, and serve immediately.

# Chilled Tomato and Red Bell Pepper Soup with Caviar

*M*UCH OF the preparation for this Mediterranean-style summer soup can be done in advance, which makes it ideal for entertaining. It also makes an impressive lunch dish. If you wish, serve the soup warm. If you thicken the soup by reducing it, you'll have a tasty sauce for grilled poultry, fish, scallops, or pasta.

### CHEF'S NOTES
Allow about 45 minutes to prepare and at least 1 hour to chill. The caviar garnish is optional, but it's one of nature's greatest delicacies, so add it if you can.

### SERVES: 4

1 tablespoon virgin olive oil

1 onion, chopped

2 cloves garlic, minced

2 tomatoes, blanched, peeled, seeded, and diced

4 red bell peppers, roasted, peeled, seeded, and chopped

Pinch of minced fresh thyme

8 fresh basil leaves, coarsely chopped

1 teaspoon sugar

Salt and pepper to taste

6 cups Brown Chicken Broth (page 23)

¼ cup peeled and finely diced white potato

1 tablespoon Spanish sherry vinegar or champagne vinegar

¼ cup light cream

20 fresh watercress leaves, or 4 pinches minced fresh chervil, for garnish

4 teaspoons osetra caviar or American sturgeon caviar (optional), for garnish

Heat the olive oil in a saucepan and sauté the onion over medium heat for about 3 minutes, or until translucent. Add the garlic, tomatoes, bell peppers, thyme, basil, sugar, salt, and pepper and cook for 5 minutes longer. Add the broth and potato, and bring to a boil. Reduce the heat to a simmer and cook for 20 minutes.

Transfer to a blender or food processor and purée (in batches if necessary) until smooth. Strain into a mixing bowl, and let cool. Refrigerate for at least 1 hour.

Just before serving, stir in the vinegar and cream, and adjust the seasonings if necessary. Ladle the soup into rimmed shallow soup plates and garnish by sprinkling with the watercress. Place 1 teaspoon of caviar in the center of each serving. Serve immediately.

# Cream of Spinach with Crabmeat

*D*ON'T LET the title of this recipe deceive you—there is no cream in this soup! It does, though, have a smooth, creamy consistency. It's my variation of a recipe that Roger Vergé created for the opening of La Cuisine du Soleil in Sao Paulo, where I was the opening chef. Vergé in turn had derived his inspiration from the Jamaican callaloo, a soup made with large-leafed spinachlike greens (callaloo), pork, and rice. The crab lifts the flavor of the soup, but you can use sautéed scallops, shrimp, or lobster, or you can leave out the seafood completely for a vegetarian version.

## CHEF'S NOTES

Allow about 45 minutes to prepare. I highly recommend mincing the spinach before simmering in the soup as you will find it much quicker and easier to purée. I also prefer puréeing this soup in a blender rather than a food processor, because it gives much smoother results and the color remains truly more appealing.

SERVES: 4

- 1 tablespoon virgin olive oil
- 2 cups chopped onion
- 1 clove garlic, chopped
- 1 quart Vegetable Broth (page 26) or water
- Pinch of sugar
- Salt and pepper to taste
- 2 tablespoons shredded, dried unsweetened coconut (optional)
- ¼ cup peeled and finely diced white potato

- 1 to 1¼ pounds fresh spinach leaves, rolled up in bundles and minced
- 8 ounces fresh jumbo lump crabmeat or Maine crabmeat
- 4 teaspoons sour cream, for garnish
- Sweet paprika, for garnish

Heat the olive oil in a heavy-bottomed saucepan over medium heat. Sweat the onion and garlic, stirring often, for 6 to 8 minutes or until soft. Add the vegetable broth, sugar, salt, pepper, coconut, and potato, and bring to a boil. Reduce the heat and gently simmer for 10 to 12 minutes. Stir in the spinach and continue simmering for another 3 minutes.

Transfer the soup to a blender and purée (in batches if necessary) until very smooth. Adjust the seasonings if necessary.

Divide the crabmeat evenly among 4 warm soup bowls. Ladle the hot soup over the crab. Spoon 1 teaspoon of the sour cream in the center of each bowl and sprinkle with the paprika. Serve immediately.

# Mussel, Leek, and Potato Soup

*I*N THE Mediterranean region of southern France, **moules à la marinière** is a popular steamed mussel dish made with wine, garlic, shallots, thyme, and parsley. This is my version in soup form.

## CHEF'S NOTES

Allow about 45 minutes to prepare. You can easily transform this recipe into a pasta sauce by reducing it until it thickens.

**S e r v e s :  4**

### Mussel Broth

1 tablespoon virgin olive oil

¼ cup minced shallots

1 teaspoon minced garlic

1½ cups dry white wine

Pinch of salt

2 tablespoons chopped fresh parsley

4 pints mussels, scrubbed and debearded

### Soup Base

1 tablespoon virgin olive oil

1 small leek, julienned

¼ cup peeled and diced white potato

2 tablespoons minced shallots

Salt and pepper to taste

1 tablespoon cream

1 tomato, blanched, peeled, seeded, and diced

3 tablespoons finely sliced fresh chives

To prepare the broth, heat the olive oil in a large saucepan over medium-high heat. Add the shallots and garlic and soften for 1 minute without browning. Add the wine, salt, parsley, and mussels, and cover the pan. Turn up the heat to high, and cook for about 5 minutes, or until the mussels have just opened. Remove the mussels immediately with a slotted spoon and set aside to cool. Discard any that remain unopened. Take care not to overcook the mussels or they will be tough.

Strain the broth through a fine sieve into a glass measuring cup and add enough water to make 3 cups. When the mussels are cool, remove the meat from the shells and set aside; discard the shells and strained solids.

To prepare the soup base, heat the olive oil in a large saucepan, and sauté the leek, potato, and shallots over medium heat for 3 to 4 minutes. Add the 3 cups of reserved mussel liquid and season with salt and pepper. Bring to a low boil and lower the heat to a gentle simmer. Cook for 5 or 6 minutes.

Add the reserved mussels, cream, tomato, and chives. Bring to a gentle boil and adjust the seasonings if necessary. Ladle into warm soup bowls and serve immediately.

# Lobster and Coconut Milk Soup with Ginger and Lemongrass

*A* COUPLE OF years ago, the queen of Thailand booked Fleur de Lys's entire dining room for one evening during an unofficial visit to the United States. She requested our usual menu, plus a dish of my choosing that contained traditional Thai flavors. This is the soup recipe I created, and it was a hit that evening. It has been so popular with our customers ever since that it has become one of my signature dishes; it was even featured in **Food & Wine** magazine. The soup has a pretty contrast of colors and delightful taste that comes from the richness of the lobster and the coconut broth blended with all the fresh herbs and vegetables.

## CHEF'S NOTES

Allow about 1 hour to prepare. Canned coconut milk is quite acceptable and a lot less work than making fresh from coconut meat. I prefer brands from Thailand or Malaysia, which are usually sold in 14-ounce cans at Asian specialty markets. Shake the cans well before opening.

SERVES: 4 TO 6

**Coconut Broth**

4 stalks lemongrass

5 cups canned unsweetened coconut milk

1 stalk celery, diced

¼ cup minced ginger

6 tablespoons freshly squeezed lemon juice

1 tablespoon minced garlic

¼ cup minced fresh cilantro

1 cup dry white wine

Salt and pepper to taste

1 live lobster (about 1½ pounds)

1 tablespoon virgin olive oil

1 onion, thinly sliced

1 carrot, thinly sliced

1 small leek, julienned

Salt and pepper to taste

16 fresh basil leaves, coarsely chopped

2 tablespoons finely sliced fresh chives

3 ounces haricots verts, blanched and sliced into 1-inch lengths

1 large tomato, blanched, peeled, seeded, and diced

To prepare the broth, crush the lemongrass with the back of a knife or cleaver, or use a mallet. Place in a large stockpot and add the coconut milk, celery, ginger, lemon juice, garlic, cilantro, white wine, salt, and pepper. Stir together and bring to a boil.

Add the lobster, head first, and poach for 10 to 12 minutes; remove and let cool. Strain the broth through a fine sieve, and set aside.

Break the lobster in two where the tail meets the body. Using scissors, cut the underside of the tail and remove the meat in one piece. Break off the claws, carefully crack the shells, and remove the meat. Dice the lobster meat into small bite-sized pieces, and set aside.

Heat the olive oil in a saucepan and sauté the onion, carrot and leek over medium-high heat for 2 minutes. Season with salt and pepper and add the strained coconut broth. Bring to a boil, reduce the heat to barely a simmer, and cook for about 3 to 5 minutes longer, stirring occasionally.

Stir in the basil, chives, haricots verts, tomato, and lobster meat, and return to a boil over high heat. Adjust the seasonings if necessary. Transfer to a tureen (or ladle directly into bowls if you prefer), and serve immediately.

# Asparagus Soup with Oysters

HE CLASSIC, delicate flavors of this unpretentious soup are a popular combination, and asparagus lovers find it irresistible. It is no less delicious for being simple and easy to make. The soup can be made ahead, but it's important to reserve the oysters until you're ready to serve. Once you pour the soup over the oysters, their flavor will immediately infuse the dish, creating a deliciously sharp-edged combination of tastes.

## CHEF'S NOTES

Allow about 45 minutes to prepare. Don't reheat leftover oysters in the soup, or their texture and flavor will be compromised. To reheat, strain and heat the soup, then add the oysters and cook just until heated through.

SERVES: 4

- 1 tablespoon virgin olive oil
- 2 small leeks, white part only, cut in half lengthwise and thickly sliced (about 1 cup)
- 1 quart Vegetable Broth (page 26) or water
- ¼ cup peeled and finely diced white potato
- Pinch of salt

- 1 pound asparagus, each spear cut into 4 or 5 lengths
- 12 freshly shucked oysters, with their liquor reserved
- Salt and pepper to taste
- 1½ tablespoons cream or half-and-half
- 4 sprigs fresh chervil, for garnish

Heat the olive oil in a heavy-bottomed saucepan. Add the leeks and sauté over medium heat for 5 to 8 minutes, stirring occasionally, or until soft but not brown. Add the broth, potato, and salt, and bring to a boil. Reduce the heat to a simmer and cook for 10 minutes. Add the asparagus slices and simmer for another 8 to 10 minutes, or until the asparagus is tender.

Meanwhile, coarsely chop the oysters and place in a mixing bowl with the reserved oyster liquor. Set aside.

Transfer the soup to a blender and purée until very smooth. Season with salt and pepper and strain through a fine mesh strainer into a clean saucepan. Return to a boil, stir in the cream, and adjust the seasonings, if necessary.

Divide the chopped oysters and their juices among 4 warm soup bowls, and ladle the soup over the oysters. Garnish with the chervil.

# Truffled Vichyssoise

*L*EEK AND potato soup is a longstanding, popular French tradition, and there are many variations on this theme. The addition of watercress, for example, turns it into the delicious **potage au cresson**; blended with cream and chilled, you have the perfect soup for summer—and my idea of sophisticated comfort food. Although this classic soup is named after the French spa and resort town of Vichy, it was devised by Louis Diat, the chef of the Ritz Carlton Hotel in New York in 1910. My version contains considerably less cream that the traditional recipe. The heady aroma and rich taste of the truffle dresses it up and gives it a delightfully elegant touch.

### CHEF'S NOTES
Allow 30 minutes to prepare and 6 to 8 hours to chill. I prefer to use black truffle oil for this recipe, but white truffle oil works equally well. When shopping for truffle oil, don't be surprised to find that both types are the same color.

### SERVES: 4

1 tablespoon virgin olive oil

2 small leeks, white part only, cut in half lengthwise and thickly sliced (about 1 cup)

1 small black truffle (about 1 ounce), julienned

1 clove garlic, finely minced

1 quart Vegetable Broth (page 26) or water

Salt and pepper to taste

1 potato, peeled and finely diced (about ¼ cup)

1 cup cream or half-and-half

1 tablespoon black truffle oil (optional)

Heat the olive oil in a heavy-bottomed saucepan. Add the leeks and sweat for about 5 minutes. Add the truffle and garlic, stirring often, and continue to sweat for 3 minutes longer, or until the leeks are soft. Add the broth, salt, and pepper, and bring to a boil. Add the potato, reduce the heat, and simmer for about 7 to 8 minutes, or until the potato is soft. Immediately remove the soup from the heat and let cool slightly.

Transfer the soup to a blender in batches, and puree until very smooth. Transfer the soup to a clean saucepan, add the cream, and adjust the seasonings if necessary. Bring the soup to a boil over high heat, remove from the heat and let cool to room temperature. Cover and refrigerate the soup until well chilled, about 6 to 8 hours.

When ready to serve, stir the truffle oil into the soup and ladle the soup into the bowls. Serve immediately.

# Watercress, Bay Scallop, and Potato Soup

WATERCRESS IS used extensively in Alsace, where it is a common crop. We ate it in salads all the time at home and I remember appreciating its peppery flavor even as a child. This soup is my adaptation of Paul Haeberlin's famous **Soupe de Grenouille** (frogs' legs soup) which he makes with a watercress base. Scallops have a delicate flavor, similar to frogs' legs, but they're a lot less intimidating for most people. This creamy soup is excellent year-round.

### CHEF'S NOTES

Allow about 45 minutes to prepare. Take care not to overcook the watercress. Adding the watercress as late as possible preserves its wonderfully intense color. You can substitute spinach for the watercress if you like.

### SERVES: 4

1 tablespoon plus 1 teaspoon virgin olive oil

1 onion, minced

2 small leeks, white part only, cut in half lengthwise and thinly sliced (about 1 cup)

1 quart Vegetable Broth (page 26) or water

¼ cup peeled and finely diced potato

Salt and pepper to taste

2 bunches fresh watercress (tender leaves and stems only, reserving a few leaves for garnish), coarsely chopped (about 3½ to 4 cups)

1½ tablespoons cream or half-and-half

5 ounces bay scallops, washed and patted dry

Croutons (page 76), for garnish (optional)

Heat 1 tablespoon of the olive oil in a heavy-bottomed saucepan. Add the onion and leeks and sweat over medium heat, stirring often, for about 5 to 8 minutes, or until soft but not brown. Add the broth, potato, salt, and pepper, and bring to a boil. Reduce the heat and gently simmer for 10 to 12 minutes, or until the potato is tender.

Stir in the chopped watercress and continue simmering for another 5 to 6 minutes. Stir in the cream and continue simmering for 1 minute longer.

Transfer the soup to a blender and blend (in batches if necessary) until smooth. Adjust the seasonings if necessary. Return the soup to a clean saucepan and heat through.

Season the scallops with salt and pepper. Place a sauté pan over medium heat, and add the remaining 1 teaspoon of olive oil. Add the scallops and panfry for 2 to 3 minutes, or until browned and cooked through. Divide the scallops among 4 warm soup bowls. Ladle the hot soup over the scallops and garnish with the reserved watercress leaves and croutons.

# Salads

*I* SOMETIMES compare the development and progression of my salads to learning how to play a musical instrument. I started with the basics—practicing the scales—during my apprenticeship in Alsace, and then began to play real music while working in the South of France. As I learned the possibilities and grew to appreciate the range of variation, I began to create and compose on my own. In Alsace, I was taught to make salads using a single type of green or lettuce, occasionally adding some radicchio or treviso for variety. In the South of France, I was introduced to the possibilities of mixed salads, including the region's typical mesclun mix of greens. (A standard mesclun consists of young greens and lettuces such as oak leaf, mustard greens, Bibb, radicchio or treviso, frisée, spinach, and arugula. This variety gives a combination of flavor, color, texture, and spiciness. Young greens are ideal because they are uniformly tender and bite-sized, so all their leaves can be used. This mesclun-style mixture remains my preference for most salads.) While working in the South of France, I also developed a fondness for the popular niçoise style of salad, full of mixed greens and delicious ingredients such as potatoes, haricots verts, garlic, onion, olives, capers, anchovies, tuna or other seafood, hard-boiled eggs, and tomatoes. These rustic salads appealed to me more than the formal style of salads served elsewhere.

Over the years, I have developed other preferences also adapted from French culinary practices. For instance, I particularly enjoy warm salads, especially those that combine warm and cold elements, effectively releasing the ingredients' fragrances. (Warm salads and vinaigrettes are a feature of contemporary French cuisine; they work on the same principle as hot apple pie served with ice cream.) As in the French tradition, it's important for my salads to be vibrant, well arranged, and exciting to look at. With the right vinaigrette, a beautiful salad will sing. Think of this chapter as a symphony of my favorite single-green, mesclun, rustic, and warm salads.

I hope you will not view these salads as immutable compositions, but as models for experimenting with your favorite ingredients. Try matching the versatile vinaigrettes in this chapter with salads other than the ones they're presented with, or create your own. Vinaigrettes can contribute exciting flavors and colors that transform a salad and give it a whole new identity, from traditional French to Asian to Indian. Substitute freely, following an approximate pattern of flavor, color, textures, and heat—don't limit yourself if the exact ingredient is unavailable. I also encourage you to experiment with the way you serve salads. In France, for example, salads are never combined with the cheese course, but at Fleur de Lys, I offer a mixed green salad with fruit and cheese, which works well and has proved very popular. When it doesn't feel right to serve a salad with the cheese course or as a starter, you might make one large salad and serve it with the main course. However you decide to construct and serve your salads, be sure to celebrate their fresh flavors and satisfying textures as often as possible.

# Crisp Potato Pancakes with Goat Cheese on Mixed Lettuce

*I* ALWAYS ENJOY cooking this recipe for large parties or cooking classes. In fact, the first time I made this was at a local AIDS research benefit organized by food critic, writer, and restaurateur Patricia Unterman. This was the warm cheese course I prepared for 600 guests. I also serve this salad at Fleur de Lys where our loyal patrons swear the pancakes are the crispiest and most delicious they've ever tasted.

## CHEF'S NOTES

Allow about 20 minutes to prepare. When preparing the potatoes, do not soak or rinse them in water to wash away the starch. In these pancakes, you need the starch to help bind the potatoes together. You can use molds to shape the pancakes, for a less rustic look.

Recommended Wines: A light fruity red wine, such as a Beaujolais, or a white wine with high acidity, such as a Sauvignon Blanc.

SERVES: 4

VINAIGRETTE

1 tablespoon Spanish sherry vinegar, or balsamic vinegar

½ teaspoon Dijon-style mustard

Salt and pepper to taste

3 tablespoons virgin olive oil

1 small clove garlic, minced

1 tablespoon minced shallot

2 tablespoons finely sliced fresh chives

2 baking potatoes (about 1 pound), peeled and thinly julienned (preferably using a mandoline)

Salt and pepper to taste

1½ tablespoons virgin olive oil

4 ounces fresh goat cheese

1 tablespoon finely sliced fresh chives

4 cups loosely packed mixed baby lettuce (about 4 ounces), such as oak leaf, mustard greens, Bibb, radicchio, frisée, spinach, and arugula

To prepare the vinaigrette, whisk together the vinegar, mustard, salt, and pepper in a mixing bowl. Whisk in the olive oil, garlic, and shallot until emulsified. Stir in the chives and set aside. (The vinaigrette can be made ahead of time, but use within 1 hour or so, or the garlic will become too strong.)

Using your hands, firmly squeeze any moisture out of the potatoes. Place in a mixing bowl and toss lightly with a sprinkling of salt and pepper.

Heat 1 tablespoon of the olive oil in a large skillet over medium-high heat, and place a thin (¹/₄-inch) layer of the potatoes in the skillet, forming a round pancake about 2 ¹/₂ inches across. Spread one-quarter of the goat cheese on top of the potato layer, not quite to the edges, and sprinkle with one-quarter of the chives. Cover with another layer of potatoes, making sure that the goat cheese is completely covered. Working quickly, repeat for the remaining 3 pancakes.

Cook for 3 to 4 minutes, or until the potatoes have turned golden on one side. With a spatula, carefully turn the pancakes over, adding the remaining ¹/₂ tablespoon of the olive oil to the pan. Cook for about 3 minutes longer, until the second side turns golden.

Meanwhile, gently toss the greens with the vinaigrette, and adjust the seasonings if necessary. Arrange a mound of the tossed greens in the center of each serving plate. Remove the potato pancakes from the skillet, drain on paper towels, and place one on top of each salad. Serve immediately.

# Spicy Melon and Grapefruit Salad

THIS IS certainly a healthful salad, and the combination of mint, grapefruit, and melon is bright and refreshing—it'll get those taste buds and appetites geared up for the rest of the meal. Black pepper goes well with many different kinds of fruit and in this recipe, its heat is balanced by the sweetness of the fruit and wine.

### CHEF'S NOTES

Allow about 15 minutes to prepare and at least 1 hour to chill. This salad is an eye-catcher served buffet-style, and it also looks particularly striking when served in black china bowls.

Recommended Wines: A Sauternes wine, a California late harvest Sauvignon Blanc, or a Semillon.

SERVES: 4

1 fully ripe cantaloupe melon, cut in half and seeded

½ fully ripe honeydew melon, cut in half and seeded

1 grapefruit, peeled and sectioned

12 fresh mint leaves

¼ teaspoon freshly cracked pepper, or to taste

½ cup dessert wine, such as Sauternes, California late harvest Sauvignon Blanc, or Semillon

Using a melon baller, scoop out the flesh of each melon and place in a mixing bowl. Add the grapefruit sections. Cut 4 of the mint leaves into chiffonade, using sharp scissors so the leaves are not bruised, and add to the mixing bowl together with the pepper and wine. Gently toss all the ingredients together. Cover the bowl with plastic wrap and refrigerate for at least 1 hour (and up to 24 hours).

To serve, divide the salad equally among 4 salad bowls. Spoon the liquid in the mixing bowl over the fruit and garnish with the remaining mint leaves.

# Spiced Fava Bean Salad with Fennel and Lentils

The elegant fava bean has a delicate flavor and appealing texture. One of the traditional ways it's used in France is in a cake **(la gallette des rois)** that's made to celebrate January 6 (the twelfth day of Christmas). A dried fava bean is placed inside the almond filling of the cake, which is sold with a golden cardboard crown. Whoever gets the slice of the cake with the bean inside wins the crown. My father used to make lots of these cakes in his **pâtisserie**, and at home we'd cheat by trying to detect a slightly raised crust, which would give away the location of the bean! This simple and sophisticated salad, low in fat and high in fiber and vitamins, is another way to enjoy the delectable fava bean. Use the freshest ingredients you can find.

## CHEF'S NOTES

Allow about 1 hour to prepare. If you prefer, use a milder chile (for example, half a poblano or green Anaheim). If you really don't like the heat of chiles, use about one-quarter of a green bell pepper instead.

Recommended Wines: A moderately rich, balanced Sauvignon Blanc from France or California.

SERVES: 4

1 cup dried green or French lentils, picked through and rinsed

1½ quarts water

1 small onion

¼ teaspoon salt

Pinch of pepper, or to taste

¼ cup shelled fresh fava beans

1 fennel bulb, trimmed, cored, and thinly sliced

1 stalk celery, finely diced

1 tomato, blanched, peeled, seeded, and diced

1 or 2 hot green chiles (such as jalapeños or serranos), seeded and diced

2 tablespoons minced fresh cilantro

2 tablespoons minced fresh parsley

1½ tablespoons freshly squeezed lemon juice

1½ tablespoons virgin olive oil

1½ tablespoons soy sauce

4 cups loosely packed mixed baby lettuce (about 4 ounces), such as oak leaf, mustard greens, Bibb, radicchio, frisée, spinach, and arugula

12 fresh endive leaves

Bring a large saucepan of water to a boil and blanch the lentils for about 1 minute to remove any bitterness. Drain and return the lentils to a clean saucepan, and cover with the 1½ quarts of water. Bring to a boil over high heat, add the onion, and season with salt and pepper. Reduce the heat to a simmer, cover the pan, and cook for about 20 minutes, or until just tender. Discard the onion, drain the lentils, and let them cool in a mixing bowl.

Bring a saucepan of salted water to a boil and blanch the shelled fava beans for 2 minutes. Remove with a wire mesh strainer and refresh under cold running water. Drain, peel off the thick skin of the beans, and add to the lentils.

Add the fennel, celery, tomato, chiles, cilantro, parsley, lemon juice, olive oil, soy sauce, salt, and pepper, and toss together very gently. Adjust the seasonings if necessary. To serve, decoratively arrange the baby lettuce and endive leaves on each plate. Top with the fava bean salad and serve immediately, or keep chilled until ready to serve.

# Celeriac, Truffle, and Walnut Salad

**W**HY NOT combine two wonders that lurk just beneath the soil: truffles and celeriac! This recipe is a good example of the contrasts—between exotic and common ingredients, crunchy and soft textures, and different colors and flavors—that I enjoy matching when I develop dishes. Celeriac, or celery root, is underutilized, which is a mistake because it has an earthy celery-parsley flavor and is highly versatile—it can be cooked or used raw.

### CHEF'S NOTES

Allow about 30 minutes to prepare. To prevent the celeriac from discoloring, work quickly. If necessary, cut and season the celeriac in batches to prevent it from yellowing. The salad will be more tender and flavorful if you let it steep in the refrigerator for several hours. When refrigerated, it keeps for at least a day or two. I like to serve this salad with plenty of grilled or toasted crusty country-style bread.

Recommended Wines: A perfumed, spicy white wine from the Rhône Valley, such as a Chateauneuf-du-Pape.

### SERVES: 4

DRESSING

2 tablespoons mayonnaise

3 tablespoons cream

1½ tablespoons Dijon-style mustard

Salt and pepper to taste

SALAD

1 celeriac (about 1 pound)

2 tablespoons freshly squeezed lemon juice

Salt and pepper to taste

1 Granny Smith apple, peeled, halved, and cored

2 or 3 tablespoons coarsely chopped and toasted walnuts or pecans

1 small black truffle (about 1 ounce), finely minced

2 tablespoons finely minced fresh chives

Celery leaves, for garnish (optional)

Whisk together all the dressing ingredients in a mixing bowl and set aside.

Peel the celeriac, cut into chunks, and shred with a mandoline or in a food processor. Immediately place the shreds in a large mixing bowl and toss with the lemon juice, salt, and pepper. Shred the apple in the same manner and toss with the celeriac and lemon juice. Add the dressing, walnuts, minced truffle, and half of the chives. Toss together until evenly coated. Adjust the seasonings if necessary.

Arrange the salad on a large serving platter. Garnish with some celery leaves and sprinkle with the remaining chives.

# Blue Prawn Pasta Salad with Basil, Artichokes, and Olives

ERE'S ONE of the most delightful summer pasta salads. It has a Mediterranean flair and is best made with good-quality niçoise or halved kalamata olives. Prepare this salad when large fresh basil leaves are abundant and fresh tomatoes are red, ripe, and full flavored. Orzo is a versatile pasta (although the word means "barley" in Italian). It's about the same size as rice, for which it can be substituted in all kinds of recipes.

### CHEF'S NOTES

Allow about 1 hour to prepare. Orzo may be labeled as "riso" pasta and can be used to make risottos. You can use long-grain rice or small pasta shells in this recipe instead, if you prefer.

Recommended Wines: A lean Chablis or California Chardonnay.

SERVES: 4

4 artichokes

1 lemon, cut in half

1 cup orzo

5½ tablespoons virgin olive oil

1 ear corn, husked and silk removed

12 blue prawns or jumbo Gulf shrimp (about 1 pound), heads removed, shelled, and deveined

Salt and pepper to taste

1 tomato, blanched, peeled, seeded, and diced

¼ cup pitted niçoise olives

8 fresh basil leaves, minced

1½ tablespoons Spanish sherry vinegar or freshly squeezed lemon juice

Zest of 1 lemon, minced

12 Boston lettuce leaves (inner leaves from the heart)

8 whole fresh basil leaves, for garnish

1 tomato, cut into wedges (optional), for garnish

Bring a large saucepan of water to a boil. To prepare the artichokes, cut off the stems and thorny tips of the leaves. Trim the bottom so that none of the hard green skin remains. As you work, rub the cut portions of the artichokes with the lemon to prevent discoloration. Place the trimmed artichokes in the boiling water and cook for about 20 to 30 minutes, until tender when pierced with a knife. Remove from the boiling water, drain, and let cool. When the artichokes have cooled, scoop out the chokes with a teaspoon, and slice the hearts. Place in a mixing bowl.

Meanwhile, to cook the orzo, place 2 quarts of salted water in a saucepan and bring to a rolling boil. Add the orzo and ½ tablespoon of the olive oil, and boil over medium heat, uncovered, for about 10 to 12 minutes, or until the pasta is done. Drain in a fine-holed colander and refresh under cold running water. Drain again and add to the mixing bowl.

Bring another saucepan of salted water to a boil and cook the corn for 3 to 4 minutes. Drain and set aside to cool. Cut the kernels from the cob with a knife and transfer to the mixing bowl.

Season the prawns with salt and pepper. Heat 1 tablespoon of the olive oil in a large skillet and cook the prawns over high heat for 2 minutes on each side. Remove from the pan, set aside to cool, and add to the mixing bowl, along with the tomato, olives, and minced basil.

Whisk together the remaining 4 tablespoons of olive oil with the vinegar, lemon zest, salt, and pepper in a separate mixing bowl, and pour over the pasta salad. Gently toss together and adjust the seasonings if necessary.

To serve, line a platter with the lettuce leaves. Spoon the salad in the center, in a dome shape (alternatively, put the salad in a bowl and invert quickly). Garnish with the whole basil leaves, and arrange the tomato wedges around the edge of the salad.

# Chantal's Wild Rice and Mussel Salad with Basil and Pine Nuts

*I* LOVE USING wild rice whenever I can. My wife Chantal does too, and this is her recipe. She prepared it for a "potluck" buffet-style party hosted by a friend who lives on the other side of the Berkeley Hills in the East Bay. Our good friends Marimar Torres, the owner of the Torres winery in Spain, and Jacques Pépin were also among the guests, and everyone loved Chantal's salad.

## CHEF'S NOTES

Allow about 1 hour to prepare and 1 hour to chill. The pine nuts add an appealing crunchiness and a Mediterranean twist.

Recommended Wines: A full-flavored California Chardonnay.

SERVES: 4

---

3 tablespoons virgin olive oil

6 tablespoons finely diced onion

¼ cup wild rice, rinsed and drained

2 cups Vegetable Broth (page 26) or water

Salt and pepper to taste

½ cup long-grain white rice

1 teaspoon minced garlic

½ cup finely diced carrots

1½ cups dry white wine

2 pounds mussels, scrubbed and debearded

2½ teaspoons Spanish sherry vinegar or red wine vinegar

¼ cup shelled young fresh peas (about 4 ounces pods), blanched for 1 minute, or frozen petits pois (unblanched)

2 tablespoons pine nuts, toasted

1 fennel bulb, trimmed, cored, and finely minced

1 tomato, blanched, peeled, seeded, and diced

8 fresh basil leaves, finely julienned

1 head radicchio, leaves separated

Leaves of 1 bunch arugula

---

Heat 1 teaspoon of the olive oil in a saucepan, add 1 tablespoon of the onion, and sauté over medium heat until translucent and golden. Add the wild rice and stir for 1 minute. Add 1 cup of the broth or enough to cover the rice by ¼ inch, and season lightly with salt and pepper. Cover and simmer for 35 to 40 minutes, or until al dente, adding broth as needed. When the rice is cooked, the liquid should be just evaporated; if it is not, uncover and stir gently until it is. Transfer the rice to a bowl and let cool.

Heat 2 teaspoons of the olive oil in a clean saucepan, add 2 tablespoons of the onion, and sauté over medium heat, until translucent and golden. Add the white rice and stir for 1 minute. Add the remaining 1 cup of broth or enough to cover the rice by ¼ inch, and season lightly with salt and pepper. Cover and simmer for 15 minutes, or until tender, adding broth as needed. When the rice is cooked, the liquid should be just evaporated; if it is not, uncover and stir gently until it is. Let cool for 5 minutes, then fluff with a fork.

Heat the remaining 2 tablespoons of olive oil in a clean saucepan, add the remaining 3 tablespoons of onion, and sauté the garlic and carrots over medium heat for 2 minutes, or until soft. Add the wine and mussels, cover, and raise the heat to high. Cook for 5 minutes, or just until the mussels open. Remove immediately and set aside to cool. Discard any unopened mussels. Strain the broth through a fine sieve into a clean saucepan and reserve the cooked vegetables. Over high heat reduce the broth to ½ cup.

Remove the mussels from the shells, reserving a few in the half shell, and place in a large mixing bowl. Add the reserved vegetables, both cooked rices, the reduced cooking liquid, vinegar, peas, pine nuts, fennel, tomato, and basil. Season with salt and pepper and toss gently. Refrigerate for 1 hour. Transfer the salad to a serving platter. Arrange the radicchio and arugula leaves, alternating, and the mussels in the half shell all around the salad.

# Warm Bay Scallop and Haricot Vert Salad with a Light Curried Vinaigrette

*T*HIS IS one of my favorite salads because the mix of flavors and textures come together really well. The curry powder, horseradish, and mustard in this recipe provide several nuances and layers of heat. Horseradish always reminds me of Alsace, where it's often used as a condiment for **pot-au-feu**, the meat and vegetable stew traditionally served on Sundays. This tradition dates from the 1600s and the reign of Henry IV, who decreed that all his subjects should have **la poule au pot** (chicken stew) on Sundays—an early version of "a chicken in every pot"!

## CHEF'S NOTES

Allow about 35 minutes to prepare. Bay scallops, mostly found on the East Coast, have a sweeter, richer flavor and crisper texture than sea scallops and average about 100 to the pound. If they're unavailable, use quartered sea scallops. The fresher the better, of course, especially because fresh scallops release less liquid when cooked, which makes for better searing. The vinaigrette can be prepared up to 1 hour ahead of time, but don't let it stand longer because the garlic will become too strong.

Recommended Wines: A dry, mature Riesling, preferably from Alsace.

SERVES: 4

### LIGHT CURRIED VINAIGRETTE

1 tablespoon Spanish sherry vinegar or champagne vinegar

½ teaspoon Dijon-style mustard

Salt and pepper to taste

3 tablespoons virgin olive oil

1 small clove garlic, minced

1 tablespoon minced shallot

1 tomato, blanched, peeled, seeded, and diced

2 tablespoons finely sliced fresh chives

1 tablespoon sliced almonds, lightly toasted

### CROUTONS

8 slices French baguette bread, about ½ inch thick

½ tablespoon virgin olive oil

1 teaspoon drained prepared horseradish

3 tablespoons whipped cream

Salt to taste

### SALAD

1 head Belgian endive

1 small head radicchio

1 small head green leafy lettuce, such as Bibb, romaine, or frisée

12 ounces haricots verts, trimmed and blanched

1 tablespoon virgin olive oil

12 ounces fresh bay scallops

Salt and pepper to taste

1 teaspoon curry powder

To prepare the vinaigrette, whisk together the vinegar, mustard, salt, and pepper in a mixing bowl. Then whisk in the olive oil, garlic, and shallot until emulsified. Add the tomato, chives, and almonds, and set aside.

To prepare the croutons, preheat the oven to 375°. Lightly brush both sides of the bread slices with the olive oil and place on a baking sheet. Toast in the oven for about 10 minutes, or until crisp and golden. Meanwhile, combine the horseradish, whipped cream, and salt in a mixing bowl and keep refrigerated until needed.

Separate and wash the leaves of the endive, radicchio, and lettuce. Pat dry and set aside. When you are ready to put the salad together, reheat the haricots verts by briefly plunging into boiling water. Remove immediately and drain. Heat the olive oil in a skillet and season the scallops with the salt, pepper, and curry powder. Briefly sauté the scallops over high heat for about 45 seconds to 1 minute, tossing occasionally.

Place the scallops and warm haricots verts in the mixing bowl with the vinaigrette, gently toss together, and adjust the seasonings if necessary. Arrange the beans in the center of each serving plate with the radicchio and lettuce around them and the endive leaves sticking out from the mound like spokes. Spread the horseradish and cream mixture on the croutons, and serve 2 croutons on the side of each plate.

# Red and Green Cabbage Salad Dressed with Cumin Seeds and Sherry Vinegar

*A*LSACE IS famous for its traditional **choucroute**, the cooked cabbage dish that's the French equivalent of sauerkraut, only better! In times gone by, it was a mainstay of the region, as cabbage was one of the few winter greens available in the days before refrigeration. This simple, hearty recipe returns to these roots. In Alsace, both red and green cabbage are traditionally used, although only the green is made into **choucroute** and salads because the red cabbage "bleeds" too readily. I avoid this problem here by mixing the cabbages at the last minute to keep their colors distinct. Be sure to let the red cabbage sit for at least 20 minutes or so after it's combined with the vinegar, because the pickling process makes it strikingly bright and translucent.

### CHEF'S NOTES

Allow about 1 hour to prepare. This salad is beautiful when served with grilled chicken, squab, quail, pork chops, or even salmon. For an unusual and eye-catching presentation, consider hollowing out an attractive large squash or pumpkin or a large red or green cabbage and serving the salad inside.

Recommended Wines: A young French or Californian Sauvignon Blanc.

### SERVES: 4 TO 6

- 3 slices bacon, ¼ inch thick (optional)
- 1 small red cabbage, about 12 ounces, outer leaves removed
- 1 green cabbage (about 1 pound), outer leaves removed
- 6 tablespoons Spanish sherry vinegar or red wine vinegar
- ½ teaspoon cumin seeds
- Salt and pepper to taste
- 1 small carrot, diced
- 1 Golden Delicious apple, peeled, cored, and finely diced
- 3 tablespoons finely minced fresh parsley
- 3 tablespoons walnuts, coarsely chopped and lightly toasted
- 3 teaspoons sugar
- 2 tablespoons virgin olive oil

Heat a nonstick sauté pan and fry the bacon over medium heat until crisp and golden. Remove and drain on paper towels. When cool, dice the bacon.

Meanwhile, bring 5 to 6 quarts of salted water to a rolling boil in a large saucepan. Split the cabbages in half lengthwise, remove the stalk and core, and shred as for coleslaw, keeping the shreds of each cabbage separate. First blanch the red cabbage in the boiling water for 1 minute. Remove with a slotted spoon and immediately transfer to an ice bath. Drain thoroughly and set aside in a bowl. Repeat for the green cabbage and set aside in a separate bowl.

Bring the vinegar to a boil in a small saucepan. Pour half of the hot vinegar over the red cabbage and half over the green cabbage. Toss each cabbage well. Sprinkle the cumin seeds evenly over each bowl of cabbage, season with salt and pepper, and set aside for 20 minutes to allow the cabbage to pickle.

Bring 2 cups of salted water to a boil in a small saucepan and cook the carrot for about 5 minutes, or until tender. Remove and immediately transfer to an ice bath. Drain, and add to the green cabbage together with the reserved bacon, diced apple, parsley, walnuts, sugar, and olive oil.

Combine all the ingredients in a large mixing bowl and toss together thoroughly. Adjust the seasonings if necessary and serve immediately.

# Artichoke Heart, Salmon, and Sea Scallop Salad with Citrus Vinaigrette

T HIS SALAD has been a popular item on the menu at Fleur de Lys for some time. Because it enjoys such popularity, I like to teach how to prepare it in my cooking classes. The vinaigrette, which was developed by Rick Richardson, my chef de cuisine, also works well with rock shrimp mousseline and other delicately flavored shellfish dishes.

### CHEF'S NOTES
Allow about 1 hour to prepare. The salmon and scallops make a nice visual contrast, yet they have the advantage of similar cooking times.

Recommended Wines: A rich and zesty white wine with spicy tones, such as a Pinot Gris from Alsace or a Sauvignon Blanc from France or California, or a crisp sparkling wine.

### SERVES: 4

**CITRUS VINAIGRETTE**

1 orange, peeled and sectioned

1 lime, peeled and sectioned

1 cup freshly squeezed orange juice

2 teaspoons freshly squeezed lime juice

2 teaspoons freshly squeezed lemon juice

¼ teaspoon Dijon-style mustard

Salt and pepper to taste

3 tablespoons virgin olive oil

**MUSTARD VINAIGRETTE**

2 teaspoons red wine vinegar

¼ teaspoon Dijon-style mustard

Salt and pepper to taste

2 tablespoons virgin olive oil

4 artichokes

1 lemon, cut in half

Salt and pepper to taste

1 skinless fillet of salmon (10 to 12 ounces)

8 large sea scallops (about 12 ounces)

1 tablespoon virgin olive oil

4 cups loosely packed mixed baby lettuce (about 4 ounces), such as oak leaf, mustard greens, Bibb, radicchio, frisee, spinach, and arugula

1 teaspoon red peppercorns

To prepare the Citrus Vinaigrette, cut the citrus sections into 4 or 5 pieces and set aside. Heat the orange juice in a saucepan and reduce to 2 tablespoons over high heat, about 5 minutes. Transfer to a mixing bowl and add the lime and lemon juices. Whisk in the mustard, salt, and pepper, then whisk in the olive oil until emulsified. Place in a saucepan and set aside. To prepare the Mustard Vinaigrette, whisk together the vinegar, mustard, salt, and pepper in a mixing bowl. Whisk in the olive oil until emulsified. Adjust the seasonings if necessary.

Prepare the artichokes (see page 74), rubbing the cut portions with the lemon. When cool, remove the artichoke bottoms. Finely slice at an angle and fan out each bottom. Lightly brush a large baking pan with olive oil. Place the artichoke fans in the pan, and season with salt and pepper. Cut the salmon fillet crosswise into 8 slices ½ inch thick, season with salt and pepper, and place in the pan with the artichokes. Slice each scallop into 2 medallions, season with salt and pepper, and place in the pan. Brush each ingredient with the olive oil.

Place the baby lettuces in a mixing bowl and toss lightly with the Mustard Vinaigrette. Arrange the dressed lettuce in the center of each serving plate. Warm the Citrus Vinaigrette over medium heat, adding the orange and lime sections and the pink peppercorns. Adjust the seasonings if necessary and keep warm.

Heat the broiler. Place the baking pan under the broiler for about 3 minutes (do not turn the ingredients). Place a broiled artichoke bottom on each salad. Cover each artichoke bottom with a slice of salmon, and arrange 2 scallop slices on top. Add a second salmon slice and top with 2 more scallop slices. Spoon the Citrus Vinaigrette over the fish, and serve immediately.

# Lobster and Lentil Salad with a Cucumber Vinaigrette

*T*HIS DISH will surprise your guests. The lobster and lentils are hidden inside the salad "cakes," which are lined with carrot and topped with tomato. The combination of the rich lobster, humble yet healthful lentils, and everyday vegetables makes an elegant and exotic salad that can be served as a delicious light meal.

## CHEF'S NOTES

Allow about 1 1/2 hours to prepare. You can substitute shrimp for the lobster or leave out the seafood entirely for a tasty vegetarian version (just increase the Lentil Salad ingredients by half). I recommend slicing the carrot with a mandoline.

Recommended Wines: A medium-bodied Alsatian Riesling.

SERVES: 4

1 Bouquet Garni (page 22)

Salt and pepper to taste

1 live Maine lobster, about 1 1/4 to 1 1/2 pounds

1 tablespoon virgin olive oil

1/2 tablespoon freshly squeezed lemon juice

### LENTIL SALAD

1 cup dried green or French lentils, picked through and rinsed

1 1/2 quarts water

1 small onion

Salt and pepper to taste

1 large, long carrot

3 ripe tomatoes, blanched, peeled, seeded, and finely diced

1 stalk celery, finely diced

1/2 small red onion, finely diced

1/4 teaspoon minced ginger

1 1/2 tablespoons freshly squeezed lemon juice

1 1/2 tablespoons soy sauce

1 tablespoon virgin olive oil

1 English or hothouse cucumber, thinly sliced

### CUCUMBER VINAIGRETTE

1 English or hothouse cucumber, peeled, seeded, and diced

1 teaspoon Spanish sherry vinegar or balsamic vinegar

1/2 teaspoon Dijon-style mustard

Salt and pepper to taste

### GARNISH

6 teardrop and cherry tomatoes, cut in half and hollowed out

12 red peppercorns

4 teaspoons osetra caviar

12 chives

Add the Bouquet Garni, salt, and pepper to a large stockpot of boiling water. Add the lobster, head first and poach 10 to 12 minutes; remove and let cool. Break the lobster in two where the tail meets the body. Using scissors, cut the underside of the tail and remove the meat in one piece. Break off the claws, crack the shells, and remove the meat. Dice the meat, reserving four 1-inch round pieces, and transfer to a small bowl. Dress with the olive oil and lemon juice, and season with salt and pepper. Keep refrigerated.

To prepare the salad, bring a large saucepan of water to a boil and blanch the lentils for 1 minute. Drain and return the lentils to a clean saucepan, and cover with the water. Bring to a boil over high heat, add the onion, and season. Reduce the heat to a simmer, cover, and cook for 30 minutes, or until just tender. Discard the onion, drain the lentils, and let cool in a bowl.

While the lentils are cooking, cut the carrot lengthwise into 8 strips 1/8 inch thick; trim the strips to 3/4 inch wide and 5 to 6 inches long. Bring a saucepan of water to a boil and blanch the carrot strips for 1 minute. Immediatelt transfer to a bowl of ice water. Drain and set aside.

Season the diced tomatoes with salt and pepper, and place in a fine sieve over a bowl to drain; set aside.

Add the celery, red onion, ginger, lemon juice, soy sauce, olive oil, salt, and pepper to the lentils. Toss together and adjust the seasonings, if necessary. Place the cucumber slices, overlapping, in a circle in the center of each serving plate.

To prepare the vinaigrette, place the cucumber, vinegar, and mustard in a blender and pulse 5 times, or until smooth. Season with salt and pepper; and set aside.

Place a $3^{1}/_{4}$ by $^{3}/_{4}$-inch mold over the cucumber slices on each plate. Line the molds with 2 carrot strips, placed end to end (trim the carrot strips to fit). Divide the lobster among the molds. Top with the lentil mixture, packing it down firmly. Cover the lentils with a layer of the drained tomatoes, smoothing them down until they are level with the top of the mold. Wipe away any liquid that has leaked from under the molds. Pipe the vinaigrette into the tomato halves; garnish each with a red peppercorn. Carefully unmold each "cake." Garnish each with 1 lobster claw, 1 piece of reserved lobster meat, and 1 teaspoon caviar. Insert 3 chives into each cake. Place the tomato halves to the side of each salad, and serve.

# Crayfish Salad with Toasted Hazelnuts and Mango

THIS IS another recipe I developed as opening chef at La Cuisine du Soleil in Sao Paulo. It combines the classic French green bean salad with produce that was locally available in Brazil—including mangoes and jumbo prawns called **camaraon pistola**, so called because they were shaped like the handle of a pistol. As an alternative, lobster or shrimp can be used instead of crayfish, which are a popular delicacy in France but little used in the United States outside the South.

## CHEF'S NOTES

Allow about 1 hour to prepare. The same salad can also be presented on a bed of baby lettuce seasoned with a little of the vinaigrette, if you prefer.

Recommended Wines: A young, fruity California Chardonnay.

SERVES: 4

- 1 stalk celery, diced
- 1 small onion, diced
- 1 small carrot, diced
- 1 sprig fresh parsley
- 1 dried bay leaf
- 1 sprig fresh thyme
- Salt and pepper to taste
- 24 live crayfish or extra-large shrimp, or the meat from 1 lobster
- 1 pound haricots verts, trimmed and blanched
- 16 hazelnuts, toasted and chopped
- 1 tomato, blanched, peeled, seeded, and diced
- 1 mango, peeled, pitted, and diced

VINAIGRETTE

- 1 tablespoon tarragon vinegar
- ½ tablespoon Dijon-style mustard
- Salt and pepper to taste
- 2 tablespoons virgin olive oil
- 1 small clove garlic, minced
- 1 teaspoon minced fresh tarragon

- 1 head endive (16 leaves), for garnish (optional)

Add the celery, onion, carrot, parsley, bay leaf, thyme, salt, and pepper to a large stockpot of boiling water. Reduce the heat and simmer for about 5 minutes.

Turn up the heat and bring the water back to a rolling boil. Add the crayfish and poach for 4 to 5 minutes. Remove the crayfish and let cool. Strain and reserve 2 tablespoons of the cooking liquid for the vinaigrette.

When the crayfish have cooled, separate the tails away from the body and gently pull the meat from the tails in one piece; transfer to a mixing bowl. Reserve 12 of the crayfish heads to garnish the salads.

Thoroughly drain the haricots verts and add to the crayfish tail meat, together with the hazelnuts, tomato, and mango. Season with salt and pepper.

To prepare the vinaigrette, whisk together the vinegar, mustard, salt, and pepper in a mixing bowl. Then whisk in the olive oil, garlic, tarragon, and the reserved 2 tablespoons of cooking liquid until emulsified. (The vinaigrette can be prepared ahead of time, but don't let it stand for longer than 1 hour because the garlic will become too strong.)

Pour the vinaigrette over the crayfish mixture and toss together gently. Arrange the salad in the center of each serving plate. Around each salad, place 3 crayfish heads and 3 endive leaves alternately, like the spokes of a wheel. Serve immediately.

# Grilled Tuna with Asparagus and a Marinated Vegetable Vinaigrette

THE MARINATED vegetable vinaigrette is another recipe I developed in Brazil, and it's based on **molho apimentada**, a South American accompaniment for grilled or barbecued meats. The **molho** is a rustic vinaigrette that contains lots of diced onion. My version is a colorful, savory mix of vegetables and herbs that goes wonderfully well with all kinds of fish, chicken, and grilled meats. The more finely and uniformly you dice the vegetables for the vinaigrette, the faster and more effectively they'll cure, so for best results, prepare them by hand rather than in a food processor. You can experiment by using green or yellow zucchini, cucumber, radish, daikon, or turnips instead of, or in addition to, the vegetables called for—the more variety, the better.

## CHEF'S NOTES

Allow about 45 minutes to prepare. It takes a couple of days for the flavors of the marinated vinaigrette to really develop and intensify, so it's best prepared ahead (the colors and textures hold up fine). Cover the mixture tightly and keep it refrigerated. Let it warm up at room temperature for 30 minutes or so before assembling the salads.

Recommended Wines: A full-bodied Pinot Gris from Alsace or a Sauvignon Blanc from France or California.

SERVES: 4

### MARINATED VEGETABLE VINAIGRETTE

- 2 tablespoons hazelnut oil or virgin olive oil
- 2 teaspoons Spanish sherry vinegar or red wine vinegar
- 2 tablespoons finely diced red onion
- 2 tablespoons finely diced celery
- 2 tablespoons finely diced carrot
- 2 tablespoons seeded and finely diced red bell pepper
- 1 tablespoon finely sliced fresh chives
- 1 tablespoon minced fresh cilantro
- Salt and pepper to taste

### FRENCH DRESSING

- 1 tablespoon Spanish sherry vinegar or red wine vinegar
- 1/2 teaspoon Dijon-style mustard
- Salt and pepper to taste

- 3 tablespoons virgin olive oil
- 2 teaspoons minced shallot
- 1 clove garlic, minced

- 4 thick tuna steaks (about 5 ounces each)
- 20 asparagus tips, about 3½ inches long
- 3 cups loosely packed mixed baby lettuce (about 3 ounces), such as oak leaf, mustard greens, Bibb, radicchio, frisée, spinach, and arugula
- 4 pinches minced fresh chervil
- 1 head endive
- 1 ripe tomato, blanched, peeled, seeded, and cubed
- 8 thin slices toasted French baguette bread
- Salt and pepper to taste
- 4 edible flowers, for garnish (see page 222)

To prepare the vegetable vinaigrette, whisk the hazelnut oil and vinegar together in a mixing bowl. Add all the remaining vinaigrette ingredients and gently mix together. Set aside at room temperature until ready to serve.

To prepare the French Dressing, whisk together the vinegar, mustard, salt, and pepper in a mixing bowl. Whisk in the olive oil, shallot, and garlic until emulsified. Set aside. (The dressing can be prepared ahead of time, but don't let it stand for longer than 1 hour because the garlic will become too strong.)

Prepare the grill. Place the tuna steaks on a plate and brush lightly with 1 tablespoon of the French

Dressing, coating evenly on both sides. Marinate in the refrigerator for about 10 to 15 minutes. Meanwhile, bring a saucepan of salted water to a boil and blanch the asparagus for 4 to 5 minutes, or until just tender. Immediately transfer to an ice bath. When cool, drain and transfer to a mixing bowl, dress with 1 tablespoon of the dressing, and set aside.

Grill the tuna over a hot flame for about 1½ minutes per side for rare, and no longer than 2 to 3 minutes per side for medium-rare (overcooking the tuna will dry it out).

In a mixing bowl, gently toss the lettuce with the remaining French Dressing. Make of bed of lettuce on each serving plate. Arrange the dressed asparagus tips over the lettuce in a fan shape, opening toward the upper edge of the plate. Place the tuna on top of the lettuce and over the stem ends of the asparagus. Garnish with the chervil. Fan the endive leaves next to the tuna. On the other side of the tuna, spoon some of the vegetable vinaigrette. Place the tomato next to the vinaigrette, and the toasted bread next to the tomato. Lightly season with salt and pepper, garnish with the edible flowers, and serve immediately.

# Goujonnettes of Sole Served Warm over Vegetables with a Chardonnay and Olive Oil Vinaigrette

**G**oujonette IS the French word for small, angle-cut strips of fish. The word comes from **goujon**, a small freshwater fish that lives in schools. In this straightforward, lowfat, full-flavored dish with concentrated colors, flavors, and essences, the **goujonettes** are strips of imported Dover sole. It's inspired by the classic **truite au bleu**—fresh-killed trout that's cooked immediately so the skin turns blue. One of my first tasks as an apprentice at L'Auberge de L'Ill was to prepare the trout.

## CHEF'S NOTES

Allow about 45 minutes to prepare. Although I prefer to use the delicate imported Dover sole for this recipe, you can substitute a firm and flavorful fish, such as flounder, striped sea bass, salmon, or John Dory.

Recommended Wines: A rich and earthy Californian Chardonnay.

SERVES: 4

### CHARDONNAY AND OLIVE OIL VINAIGRETTE

2 tablespoons tarragon vinegar

1 tablespoon Chardonnay

Salt and pepper to taste

3 tablespoons virgin olive oil

1 teaspoon finely minced fresh tarragon

1 tablespoon finely minced fresh parsley

2 tablespoons finely sliced fresh chives

1 tomato, blanched, peeled, seeded, and diced

### VEGETABLES

½ cup thinly sliced baby carrots

½ cup thinly sliced red onion

½ cup thinly sliced leek

½ cup thinly sliced young turnip

1 to 1¼ pounds fillet of imported Dover sole, cut into even slices, about 2 inches long by ½ inch wide

4 cups loosely packed mixed baby lettuce (about 4 ounces), such as oak leaf, mustard greens, Bibb, radicchio, frisée, spinach, and arugula

1 tablespoon edible flower petals (page 222)

Salt and pepper to taste

1 tablespoon chopped chives

To prepare the vinaigrette, whisk together the vinegar, wine, salt, and pepper in a large mixing bowl. Whisk in the olive oil, tarragon, parsley, and chives until emulsified. Stir in the tomato. Reserve 1 tablespoon of the vinaigrette.

Bring 2 cups of salted water to a boil in a saucepan. Add the vegetables, cover, and boil over medium heat for 4 to 5 minutes, or until tender. Remove the vegetables, drain well, and reserve the cooking liquid in the pan. Place the cooked vegetables in the mixing bowl with the vinaigrette and toss together. Cover, and keep warm.

Season the strips of sole (goujonettes) with salt and pepper. Bring the pan of cooking liquid back to a simmer and poach the goujonettes in it for 2 to 3 minutes. Carefully remove the fish from the water with a slotted spoon and transfer to the mixing bowl with the warm vegetables and vinaigrette. Toss together very gently, being careful not to break the goujonettes. Adjust the seasonings if necessary.

Cover a serving platter with the baby lettuce. Sprinkle the lettuce with the edible flower petals. Arrange the goujonettes and vegetables on top of the lettuce and drizzle the remaining 1 tablespoon of vinaigrette over the whole salad. Sprinkle with chives and serve immediately.

# Roasted Venison Loin over Field Greens with Black Chanterelle Vinaigrette

VENISON MAY be a recent newcomer to the North American market, but it is already very popular because of its healthful qualities. It's lean, tender, and low in cholesterol, yet very flavorful. Because of this, you can serve less per portion than other red meats, which compensates for its relative expensiveness. I recommend cooking venison to medium-rare; it dries out if cooked further, because of its low fat content. Wild chanterelle mushrooms have a limited season and shelf life, so I recommend buying them in dried form and rehydrating them. The soaking liquid can then be used to flavor sauces or broths or reduced and added to vinaigrettes. Black chanterelles are stronger and earthier than the golden ones, and lend dishes a distinctly different flavor. This recipe has wonderful earthy and nutty flavors.

### CHEF'S NOTES

Allow 24 hours for marinating and about 1 hour to prepare. As an elegant decorative option, serve 1 peeled and halved hard-boiled quail egg per plate.

Recommended Wines: An earthy California Chardonnay.

SERVES: 4 TO 6

1 pound boneless loin of venison, trimmed

MARINADE
½ cup diced onion

¼ cup diced carrot

2 cloves garlic

1 dried bay leaf

½ tablespoon juniper berries, crushed

1/2 teaspoon freshly cracked black pepper

2 cups robust red wine, such as Cabernet Sauvignon

BLACK CHANTERELLE VINAIGRETTE

½ ounce dried black chanterelle mushrooms

2 cups warm water

3½ tablespoons peanut oil

3 tablespoons Spanish sherry vinegar or red wine vinegar

2 tablespoons walnut oil

Salt and pepper to taste

1 tablespoon peanut oil

2 cups loosely packed curly chicory (about 2 ounces)

2 cups loosely packed mâche (about 2 ounces)

1 cup loosely packed arugula (about 1 ounce)

1 cup loosely packed radicchio (about 1 ounce)

1 large tomato, blanched, peeled, seeded, and diced

1 tablespoon minced fresh chervil leaves

Place the venison loin in a nonreactive baking dish. Add all of the marinade ingredients, cover, and marinate the venison in the refrigerator for 24 hours.

To prepare the vinaigrette, place the chanterelle mushrooms in a small mixing bowl, cover with the warm water, and soak for at least 30 minutes. Remove the mushrooms from the soaking liquid and set aside in a bowl. Strain the soaking liquid to remove any grit or sand, and transfer to a saucepan. Over high heat reduce the liquid to 2 tablespoons and set aside.

Meanwhile, wash the rehydrated mushrooms in cold water, drain, and pat dry with paper towels. Heat ½ tablespoon of the peanut oil in a nonstick sauté pan and sauté the chanterelles over medium heat for 2 minutes. Season with salt and pepper and remove from the heat. Chop the mushrooms and add them to the saucepan together with the reduced cooking liquid and the remaining 3 tablespoons of the peanut oil, the vinegar, and walnut oil. Whisk together, season with salt and pepper, and set aside.

Preheat the oven to 375°.

Remove the venison from the marinade and pat dry with paper towels. Strain the vegetables from the liquid (discarding the liquid), and set aside. Heat the 1 tablespoon of peanut oil in a small ovenproof roasting pan or sauté pan over medium heat. Season the marinated venison with salt and pepper, add to the pan, and sear for 2 to 3 minutes per side.

Remove the venison from the pan, add the strained marinated vegetables, and sauté for 2 minutes, stirring frequently. Place the seared venison on top of the vegetables, and transfer the pan to the oven. Roast for about 9 or 10 minutes, or until medium-rare. Remove the venison from the pan and keep warm, covered with foil. Discard the vegetables (or use for stock). The vegetables flavor the venison and prevent it from touching the pan and scorching.

Combine the chicory, mâche, arugula, and radicchio in a mixing bowl, and toss with $1^1/_2$ tablespoons of the Black Chanterelle Vinaigrette. Divide the dressed greens between 4 serving plates.

Slice the venison loin into thin slices (about $^1/_8$ inch thick), and place on top of the greens in a fan, opening out toward the top edge of the plates. Garnish the bottom edge of each plate with a spoonful of diced tomato. Heat the remaining vinaigrette over low heat and when warm, drizzle over the venison slices. Spoon the chanterelle mushrooms over the venison, dividing them equally. Garnish with the chervil and serve immediately.

# Appetizers

*M*ANY OF the recipes in this chapter, like the menu at Fleur de Lys, were influenced by my early professional experiences in the South of France. The difference in culinary style that I encountered in that region had an enormous impact on me. The Mediterranean ingredients and cooking techniques were a revelation and provided lasting inspiration for my cooking. Likewise, the exciting style of cooking and the vibrant ingredients—especially the different types of seafood—that I encountered in Brazil made an equally strong impression. Many of my favorite flavor combinations and compositions, discovered during these formative years, remain in my appetizer repertoire today.

Appetizers preface the meal and set the tone for everything that follows. For that reason, I like to feature colorful ingredients with lots of flavors, so the palate and all the senses are properly tuned. The recipes in this chapter—some of which are straight off our menu—are dramatic opening acts perfect for entertaining because they look (and taste) much more complicated than they are. Many of them can be doubled or tripled and served as lunch or main course portions.

Almost all of the recipes in this chapter are vegetarian or feature seafood instead of meat. This is not deliberate, although it is representative of the first courses I like to create and serve at Fleur de Lys. This style of appetizers, and its success in the restaurant, is in large part due to the encouragement of our appreciative, health-conscious guests. After all, we **are** in California! I enjoy going the extra distance to respond to the health needs and requests of our guests, and while it is often a challenge, the endeavor is invariably rewarding. Sometimes, it can be downright fun.

# Alsatian Onion Tart

W HEN MY parents ran the family **pâtisserie** in Alsace, they not only baked cakes and sweet pastries, but also savories such as **pâte en croûte**, quiche Lorraine, **friands** (puff pastries), and this onion tart. This is a traditional, authentic family recipe that my father gave me, and I haven't changed a thing. A similar version from the South of France, called **pisaladière**, uses anchovies and olives. At Fleur de Lys, I serve tiny slices of this tart as canapès; it's also a great party hors d'oeuvre cut into diamonds or squares. It's a versatile dish—you can serve it hot or at room temperature, and you can dress it up by servng it with a little Watercress Sauce (page 102), topped with caviar or diced fois gras.

## CHEF'S NOTES

Allow about $1^{1}/_{2}$ hours to prepare. This tart also makes a satisfying main course for lunch, served with frisée lettuce and Baguette croutons (cut into cubes) from page 76. If you prefer a vegetarian version, simply leave out the bacon. Brushing the pastry with a little beaten egg white helps prevent it from getting soggy during baking.

Recommended Wines: A full-bodied Alsatian Pinot Gris or a dry Alsatian Riesling.

SERVES: 4 TO 6

PASTRY DOUGH
$1^{1}/_{4}$ cups flour

$^{1}/_{4}$ teaspoon salt

$^{1}/_{2}$ cup chilled butter, diced

4 tablespoons ice water

FILLING
$5^{1}/_{2}$ tablespoons butter

4 onions, thinly sliced (about 7 cups)

1 clove garlic, minced

1 tablespoon minced fresh thyme

Salt and pepper to taste

$^{1}/_{2}$ cup water

3 slices bacon, cut into $1^{1}/_{2}$ inch strips

$^{1}/_{2}$ cup flour

$1^{1}/_{2}$ cups milk

3 eggs

Pinch of nutmeg

To prepare the pastry dough, place the flour, salt, and butter in a food processor and mix for about 10 seconds, or until the mixture resembles coarse meal. Add the ice water and pulse 3 or 4 times; the dough should form numerous small lumps at this stage but not a ball. (If a ball forms, the dough has been overmixed.)

Immediately transfer the dough to a work surface and press the dough together with your hands to form a thick, flattened disk. (This helps even chilling and makes it easier to roll out).

Wrap the dough in plastic wrap and chill for at least $1^{1}/_{2}$ to 2 hours. The dough can be prepared up to 24 hours ahead.

Preheat the oven to 375°.

Unwrap the chilled pastry dough on a work surface and roll out in a circle about $^{1}/_{16}$ inch thick. Place in a 9-inch pie pan, bringing the dough up the sides and trimming it off. Prick the bottom of the pastry dough at $^{1}/_{2}$-inch intervals with a fork.

Lightly butter the shiny side of a 12-inch square of aluminum foil and line the pastry shell with it, shiny side down. Cover the foil with about $1^{1}/_{2}$ cups of dry beans or pastry weights. Bake the pastry shell in the oven for 20 to 25 minutes.

While the pastry shell is baking, prepare the filling. Heat $1^{1}/_{2}$ tablespoons of the butter in a heavy-bottomed saucepan and add the onions, garlic, thyme, salt, pepper, and water. Cover the pan and cook over low heat for 25 to 35 minutes, stirring often, until the onions are soft and light amber colored. Remove from the heat and let cool.

Remove the pastry shell from the oven, discard the beans (or remove the weights) and remove the foil. Bake for a few minutes longer, or until the pastry shell turns a light golden color. Remove from the oven and place on a wire rack to cool.

Fry the bacon in a small skillet for about 3 to 4 minutes over medium-high heat, or until cooked but not crispy. Remove from the heat, drain on paper towels, and set aside. In a saucepan, combine the remaining 4 tablespoons of the butter and the flour, and cook over low heat for 2 to 3 minutes, gently stirring. Slowly whisk in the milk, and stir continuously until the mixture thickens. Remove from the heat and fold in the eggs one at a time. Season with salt, pepper, and nutmeg. Fold in the reserved bacon and the onion mixture. Spoon the filling into the pastry shell and spread it evenly.

Bake in the oven for 30 to 35 minutes, or until the filling is just set. Slice and serve hot or at room temperature.

# Eggplant and Zucchini Pie with Roasted Bell Pepper Sauce

ORIGINALLY, I created this recipe as a side dish for lamb chops, but it makes a wonderful appetizer. The bright sauce contrasts wonderfully with the green zucchini and tomato on the pie. It's a great way to begin a vegetarian meal. Although it's a little labor intensive, the pie shell, filling, and sauce can all be made several hours ahead of time, which makes it ideal for entertaining.

## CHEF'S NOTES

Allow at least 2 hours to make the pastry shell and about 1 hour to complete the preparation. If you prefer, you can serve two miniature pies (prepare in $3^{1}/_{2}$-inch tart pans) per plate rather than one large pie.

Recommended Wine: A fresh, fruity Rosé, such as Côtes de Provence.

SERVES: 6 TO 8

1 recipe Pastry Dough (page 92), flattened into a disc and chilled

FILLING

3 eggplant, ends cut off and cut in half lengthwise

5 tablespoons butter

½ cup flour

2 cups milk

4 ounces goat cheese

4 eggs

Nutmeg to taste

Salt and pepper to taste

1 teaspoon finely minced garlic

12 small plum tomatoes, thinly sliced

4 small zucchini (about 1 pound), thinly sliced

½ cup fresh bread crumbs

1 teaspoon fresh thyme leaves

1 tablespoon virgin olive oil

ROASTED RED BELL PEPPER SAUCE

¼ tablespoon virgin olive oil

1 onion, minced

2 cloves garlic, finely minced

3 plum tomatoes, blanched, peeled, seeded, and diced

1 large red bell pepper, roasted, peeled, seeded, and diced

½ teaspoon fresh thyme leaves

1 teaspoon sugar or honey

Salt and pepper to taste

6 fresh basil leaves, minced

Preheat the oven to 375°.

Unwrap the chilled pastry dough and roll out in a circle about $^{1}/_{16}$ inch thick. Place in a 9-inch pie pan (preferably with a removable bottom) bringing the dough up the sides and trimming off. Prick the bottom of the pastry dough at $^{1}/_{2}$-inch intervals with a fork.

Lightly butter the shiny side of a 12-inch square of aluminum foil and line the pastry shell with it, shiny side down. Cover the foil with about $1^{1}/_{2}$ cups dry beans or pastry weights. Bake the pastry shell in the oven for 20 to 25 minutes.

Remove from the oven, discard the beans (or remove the weights), and remove the foil. Bake for a few minutes longer, until the pastry shell turns a light golden color. Remove from the oven and place on a wire rack to cool.

Lower the oven temperature to 350°. To prepare the filling, lightly brush a baking pan with olive oil. Place the eggplant halves skin side up on the pan and roast in the oven for 40 to 45 minutes, or until completely tender. Remove from the oven and set aside to cool. When cool, carefully scoop out the flesh and transfer to a strainer, discarding the skin. Let drain for 20 minutes, then coarsely chop.

Melt the butter in a saucepan over low heat. Stir in the flour and cook for 2 to 3 minutes, or until blended.

ring, alternate the tomato and zucchini slices over the filling, overlapping. Repeat with an inside ring, but work counter-clockwise.

Sprinkle the pie with the bread crumbs and thyme, and drizzle with the olive oil. Season with salt and pepper. Set the pie on a baking sheet, place in the center of the oven, and bake for 30 minutes.

To prepare the sauce, combine the olive oil and onion in a saucepan and sauté over medium heat for 3 minutes, or until translucent. Stir in the garlic, tomatoes, bell pepper, thyme, sugar, salt, and pepper, and cook for 15 minutes, or until it thickens. Adjust the seasonings if necessary and stir in the basil. Keep warm. Remove the pie from the oven and unmold onto a warm serving dish or cut into slices. Serve with the sauce on the side.

# Stuffed Eggshells with Provençale Ratatouille

*I* LOVE TO prepare this dramatic appetizer for large parties—eggshells make great natural containers. I created a spectacular display of 800 eggshells at the Aspen Food and Wine Classic, and they proved to be a real conversation piece. I've experimented with many different fillings, such as salmon, chicken, shrimp, and tuna, but this is my favorite. The combinations of fillings and garnishes are unlimited, so be creative.

## CHEF'S NOTES

Allow about 30 minutes to prepare. Alternative fillings include Poor Man's Caviar (page 98); Cauliflower Purée (page 102), topped with caviar, chives, and an edible flower petal; or Blue Prawn Pasta Salad (page 74) with a minced prawn garnish. I like to crown the shells with black and white sesame seeds, which is easy to do. Dip the rims of the eggshells in lightly beaten egg white, sprinkle with sesame seeds, and let set before filling.

Recommended Wine: A light and crisp Rosé from southern France.

SERVES: 4

### EGGS
8 extra-large eggs

Salt and pepper to taste

¾ teaspoon extra virgin olive oil

4 fresh basil leaves, thinly sliced

### PROVENÇALE RATATOUILLE
3 tablespoons extra virgin olive oil

½ cup diced onion

¼ cup seeded and diced red bell pepper

1 large tomato, blanched, peeled, seeded, and diced

1 teaspoon finely minced garlic

½ teaspoon fresh thyme leaves

Salt and pepper to taste

½ cup unpeeled, diced baby zucchini

½ cup unpeeled, diced baby eggplant

4 basil leaves, thinly sliced

1 tablespoon mayonnaise

8 small sprigs rosemary, for garnish

To prepare the eggs, cleanly slice off the top of one end of each egg with a sharp knife and discard the tops. Empty the eggs into a mixing bowl, gently rinse the eggshells, and invert them on a dry cloth. Whisk the eggs with the salt and pepper just until the yolks and whites are blended.

Heat the ³/4 teaspoon of olive oil in a small skillet. Add the eggs and cook over low heat, stirring constantly with a small whisk until the eggs are thick and creamy; take care not to overcook them. Remove the skillet from the heat, stir in the basil, and adjust the seasonings if necessary. Transfer to a mixing bowl, cover with plastic wrap, and let cool.

To prepare the ratatouille, heat 1 ¹/2 tablespoons of the olive oil in a heavy saucepan and cook the onion over low heat for about 3 to 4 minutes, or until soft and translucent. Add the bell pepper and cook for another 3 minutes. Stir in the tomato, garlic, thyme, and a pinch of salt and pepper, and continue cooking for another 8 minutes, being careful not to overcook. Remove from the heat and set aside. Heat another ¹/2 tablespoon of the olive oil in a sauté pan and sauté the zucchini over medium heat for about 3 to 4 minutes, or until lightly colored. Season with salt and pepper, add to the tomato mixture, and set aside.

Using the same pan, heat the remaining 1 tablespoon of olive oil and sauté the eggplant over medium heat for 5 minutes, or until soft. Season with salt and pepper, and transfer to a colander to drain. Add the eggplant to the zucchini and tomato mixture, and sprinkle with the basil. Cook the mixture over medium heat for 3 to 4 minutes, stirring gently. Adjust the seasonings if necessary and set aside to cool.

Just before serving, stir the mayonnaise into the scrambled eggs to give a creamy texture. Fill each shell about three-quarters full with the scrambled eggs. Top with a spoonful of ratatouille, and garnish with a sprig of rosemary.

# Poor Man's Caviar

THIS DISH, based on puréed eggplant, is very popular in Provence. It's commonly served as a dip in bars and cafes there, and its healthfulness may explain why everyone in the South of France seems to live so long. It keeps well in the refrigerator for up to three days and makes a wonderful accompaniment for cold cuts or **charcuterie**, rustic bread, picnic foods, or meat terrines.

### CHEF'S NOTES

Allow about 1 hour to prepare. For an attractive presentation, serve the dip in a hollowed-out savoy cabbage, sprinkled with chopped chives and garnished with quartered red radishes. Coarsely minced black olives (1 ½ tablespoons) or finely chopped anchovies (1 teaspoon) can be mixed in for a little variation.

Recommended Wines: A moderately rich, balanced Sauvignon Blanc or Semillon.

3 eggplant, ends cut off and cut in half lengthwise

3 tablespoons virgin olive oil

1 small onion, minced

1 large red bell pepper, seeded and finely diced

3 cloves garlic, minced

8 fresh basil leaves, minced

2 tablespoons finely sliced fresh chives

Juice of 1 lemon

2 tomatoes, blanched, peeled, seeded, and finely diced

Salt and pepper to taste

Preheat the oven to 350°.

Lightly brush a baking pan with olive oil. Place the eggplant slices (skin side up) on the pan and roast in the oven for 40 to 45 minutes, or until they are completely tender. Remove from the oven and set aside to cool. When cool, carefully scoop out the flesh and transfer to a strainer, discarding the skin. Let drain for 20 minutes, then coarsely chop. Set aside.

Heat 1 tablespoon of the olive oil in a large nonstick sauté pan and sweat the onion, bell pepper, and garlic for 4 to 5 minutes, until soft but not colored. Remove from the heat and let cool. Transfer to a mixing bowl, add the eggplant, basil, chives, lemon juice, tomatoes, the remaining 2 tablespoons of olive oil, the salt, and pepper, and mix together well. Keep refrigerated until ready to serve.

Serve chilled in a chilled bowl or at room temperature with toasted French country bread.

# Scrambled Eggs with Truffles

WHEN I feel like spoiling myself for breakfast, I make this dish. It's like dancing with angels…only better! It's a simple yet incredible dish that takes me straight back to my days as an apprentice at L'Auberge de L'Ill in Alsace, where we were meticulously taught the classic recipe **les oeufs brouilles du curé.** It took a while to master the art of cooking the eggs just right, and only then were we taught to make the truffle sauce and prepare truffle medallions. Looking back on it, it was very brave of Paul Haeberlin to let us apprentices loose on something as precious as truffles, but he was teaching us an invaluable lesson in self-esteem and respect for the profession. Alas, not every French chef shows such faith in his or her apprentices or takes such an enlightened approach.

### CHEF'S NOTES

Allow about 15 to 20 minutes to prepare. If at all possible, avoid using canned truffles, which just aren't the same. This is a perfect precursor to a multicourse brunch or it can be served as an appetizer for lunch or dinner.

Recommended Wine: A great white Burgundy, such as a Corton-Charlemagne.

**TRUFFLE SAUCE**

2 fresh or frozen black truffles (about 1½ ounces each)

1 tablespoon butter

Salt and pepper to taste

2 tablespoons port

2 tablespoons cream

**EGGS**

10 extra-large eggs

1 tablespoon finely sliced fresh chives

Salt and pepper to taste

1 tablespoon butter

12 fresh whole chives, for garnish

4 slices freshly toasted rustic bread

Cut 4 thin slices of truffle, cover, and set aside for garnish. Mince the remaining truffles.

Melt ¹/₂ tablespoon of the butter in a small skillet over medium heat. Add one-quarter of the minced truffles, and stirring continuously, cook for 1 minute. Add the salt, pepper, and port, and bring to a boil. Reduce the mixture by half, stirring occasionally. Stir in the cream and simmer for 1 minute. Stir in the remaining ¹/₂ tablespoon of butter, adjust the seasonings if necessary, and keep warm. If the sauce seems a little thick, add up to ¹/₂ tablespoon of water.

Break the eggs into a mixing bowl and whisk in the chives, salt, and pepper, beating just until the yolks and whites are blended.

Melt ¹/₂ tablespoon of the butter in a small skillet over low heat. Stir in the remaining minced truffles and cook for 2 minutes, stirring occasionally. Add the eggs and stir continuously with a small whisk, until the eggs are thick and creamy. Remove the skillet from the heat, fold in the remaining ¹/₂ tablespoon of butter, and adjust the seasonings if necessary.

Divide the scrambled eggs among warm serving plates. Drizzle the sauce around the eggs and garnish each serving with 3 chives, placed in the eggs upright, and a slice of truffle. Serve immediately with the bread.

# Tomatoes Stuffed with White Mushrooms and Sage Leaves

THESE STUFFED tomatoes, based on the traditional stuffed vegetable dish from the South of France, **farcis Provençeaux**, make a delicious appetizer. They can also be served as an accompaniment for meat or poultry dishes, or even as a main course, depending on the size of the tomatoes. They can be served hot or at room temperature (my preference in the summer), and they may be prepared in advance, which makes them ideal for entertaining.

## CHEF'S NOTES

Allow about 30 minutes to prepare. You can make this dish entirely vegetarian by substituting Vegetable Broth (page 26) for the Beef Broth and replacing the ham with a few more white mushrooms or $\frac{1}{2}$ tablespoon of chopped large black olives, such as kalamatas.

Recommended Wines: A light and fruity California Merlot or a young red Bordeaux, preferably a St. Émilion.

- 4 firm ripe tomatoes 2½ to 3 inches in diameter, cored
- Salt and pepper to taste
- 1½ tablespoons virgin olive oil
- 1½ tablespoons minced onion
- 8 white or brown mushroom caps, finely diced
- 2½ tablespoons finely diced ham
- 6 to 8 fresh sage leaves, minced
- 1 tablespoon port or Madeira wine (optional)
- 2 tablespoons Beef Broth (page 24)

Preheat oven to 400°.

Cut a ½-inch-thick slice off the top of each tomato and set aside. (Later the tops will act as lids.) Carefully hollow out the tomatoes with a spoon or melon baller, and discard the seeds and pulp. Season the inside of the tomatoes lightly with salt and pepper, and turn upside down on a plate to drain for about 5 minutes.

Meanwhile, heat ½ tablespoon of the olive oil in a small saucepan and sauté the onion over low heat until translucent, stirring frequently with a wooden spoon. Increase the heat to medium-high, add the mushrooms, and sauté while stirring and tossing until the pieces of mushroom begin to separate from each other, about 3 to 4 minutes.

Stir in the ham, sage, port, and broth. Season with salt and pepper, and cook for 5 minutes, stirring continuously. Make sure the mixture does not scorch or burn on the bottom of the pan. Remove from the heat.

Brush the outsides of the tomatoes with the remaining 1 tablespoon of olive oil. Stuff the mushroom mixture inside the tomatoes and cover the stuffing with the tomato "lids." Arrange the tomatoes in a baking dish just large enough to hold them.

Top each of the tomatoes with a drizzle of olive oil and bake in the oven for 20 minutes; the stuffing should be heated through and the tomatoes should still hold their shape. Remove from the oven and serve, or let cool to room temperature.

# Tuna Tartar and Jicama Ravioli

*T*HIS RECIPE is a good example of what can be done by using just two main ingredients and focusing on the way they're presented. Seasoning the jicama with salt tenderizes it and makes it less brittle without affecting its crunchiness. The jicama ravioli can be filled with beef tartar, finely diced vegetables, or even wild rice. Or if you prefer, substitute salmon for the tuna. Serve the ravioli plain, on toasted croutons, or around a green salad.

## CHEF'S NOTES

Allow at least 1 hour to chill the jicama and about 35 minutes to prepare.When making tartar, I recommend chopping the meat by hand with a very sharp large knife rather than using a food processor or meat grinder, which mashes, compacts, and heats it.

Recommended Wine: A well-structured California Zinfandel.

SERVES: 4

1 jicama (about 1 pound)

Salt to taste

1 pound sushi-quality tuna fillets

2 teaspoons Dijon-style mustard

1 teaspoon virgin olive oil

1 tablespoon soy sauce

1 teaspoon minced shallot

1 teaspoon minced fresh cilantro

2 teaspoons freshly squeezed lemon juice

Salt and pepper to taste

Peel the jicama and finely slice crosswise into irregular circles, using a mandoline. Place the jicama slices in a single layer, without overlapping, on a large baking sheet. Season lightly with salt and cover with another layer of jicama. Season again with salt, and continue layering and salting until you have used all of the jicama (you will need 40 slices). Refrigerate, covered with plastic wrap, for at least 1 hour and up to 24 hours.

Meanwhile, trim the dark oily portions from the tuna and discard. Slice the tuna into thin strips and then cut the strips into very fine dice. Refrigerate immediately.

Combine the mustard, olive oil, soy sauce, shallot, cilantro, lemon juice, salt, and pepper in a mixing bowl. Add the diced tuna and gently mix together. Keep refrigerated.

Lay 20 slices of the jicama on a work surface. Place 1 teaspoon of the tartar in the middle of each slice. Place a second slice of jicama over the filling and gently press the edges together with your fingers to seal each ravioli.

Using a 3-inch fluted cookie cutter, cut a neat circle out of each ravioli slice, discarding the extra jicama. Serve 5 ravioli per person.

# Cauliflower Purée Topped with Caviar and Blue Potato Chips

NEW YEAR'S Eve is a special occasion at Fleur de Lys—it's an exciting, festive night when all our regular customers join us, just like family. Each year I create an eight-course set menu that features all new dishes, and this exotic recipe is one of my recent favorites. Blue potatoes are an ancient variety originally from the South American Andes, and they are becoming increasingly popular and more readily available. The crunchy texture of the potato chips contrasts with the silky purée, and their striking, bright blue color lends a dramatic look to this delicious dish.

## CHEF'S NOTES

Allow about 1 hour to prepare. The flavor and texture of the blue potatoes are similar to russet potatoes; you can substitute any small, round, red-skinned potato or even blanched asparagus tips if you prefer.

Recommended Wines: A full-bodied California sparkling wine or a great Champagne.

SERVES 4

### POTATOES

1 quart water

⅔ cup white wine vinegar

1½ tablespoons salt

2 blue potatoes (about 6 ounces), unpeeled

### CAULIFLOWER PURÉE

1 large cauliflower, outer leaves removed, separated into florets

3 tablespoons cream

Salt to taste

White pepper to taste

### WATERCRESS SAUCE

1 small bunch watercress, stemmed

1 teaspoon virgin olive oil

1 tablespoon minced shallot

2 tablespoons dry white wine

1 tablespoon cream

Salt and pepper to taste

### GARNISH

3 tablespoons golden, salmon, or sturgeon caviar

1 tablespoon minced fresh chives

1 hard-boiled egg yolk, chopped

Preheat the oven to 350°.

To prepare the potatoes, place the water, vinegar, and salt in a saucepan and bring to a boil. Remove from the heat. Using a mandoline, cut the potatoes into paper-thin slices (to yield 32 to 40 chips) and drop them, one by one, into the hot water. Cover the pan and let sit for about 30 minutes.

Line a baking sheet with parchment paper and lightly brush the paper with olive oil. Drain the potatoes in a strainer. Place the potato slices side by side on the paper with just enough space between them so that they do not touch (otherwise they will stick together). Lightly brush a second sheet of parchment paper with olive oil and place on top of the potato slices, oil side down.

Transfer to the oven and bake for 15 to 18 minutes, or until the potatoes turn a beautiful dark blue color and are almost translucent. Remove from the oven and set aside to cool.

To prepare the cauliflower, bring a saucepan of lightly salted water to a boil. Cook the cauliflower for 12 to 15 minutes, or until completely soft.

Drain the cauliflower and transfer to a clean saucepan. Add the cream and, over medium heat, mash the cauliflower with a whisk until puréed. Continue stirring for about 4 to 5 minutes to eliminate any excess moisture (otherwise the purée will be runny). Transfer to a blender and purée until very smooth. Season with salt and

white pepper, transfer to a clean saucepan, and keep warm. The texture should be light and creamy.

To prepare the sauce, bring a saucepan of salted water to a boil and blanch the watercress leaves for about 3 to 4 minutes, or until just tender. Drain and reserve ¹/₂ cup of the cooking water. Refresh the leaves under cold running water. Heat the olive oil in a small saucepan and sauté the shallot over medium-high heat for about 3 minutes, or until it turns a light golden color. Deglaze with the white wine and reduce until the pan is almost dry. Add the reserved watercress blanching water and the cream, and bring to a boil. Season with salt and pepper. Reduce the heat and simmer for 2 minutes. Add the blanched watercress leaves. Transfer to a blender and purée for 1 minute, until smooth and light. Adjust the seasonings if necessary.

Spoon a mound of cauliflower purée in the center of each serving plate. Garnish the tops with the caviar and spoon the watercress sauce all around the mounds. Stand 8 to 10 of the potato chips evenly spaced around the edge of the mounds, pressing them into the purée. Sprinkle the chives and chopped egg yolk over the caviar and serve.

# Baked Oysters on Spinach Leaves with a Zinfandel and Chive Sauce

WHEN MICHAEL Bauer, food editor of the **San Francisco Chronicle**, asked me to develop a recipe using Zinfandel wine for an article he was writing, I created this dish. It worked out so well that I put it on the menu at Fleur de Lys. It's an unusual combination because oysters are typically matched with white wine, but it just goes to show that shellfish and seafood can be successfully paired with red wines.

### CHEF'S NOTES

Allow about 45 minutes to prepare. Adding the chives to the sauce at the last minute ensures they will keep their vibrant color. Allow 6 oysters per person.

Recommended Wines: A light, peppery Zinfandel or a French Chablis, such as Premier Cru or Grand Cru Chablis.

SERVES: 4

24 fresh oysters, in their shells

ZINFANDEL AND CHIVE SAUCE

1 teaspoon virgin olive oil

1 tablespoon minced shallot

3 tablespoons Zinfandel

1/3 cup plus 1/4 cup cream

Salt and pepper to taste

2 egg yolks

2 tablespoons finely sliced fresh chives

SPINACH

3/4 tablespoon plus 1 teaspoon virgin olive oil

2 bunches fresh spinach, stemmed

Salt and pepper to taste

1/8 teaspoon ground nutmeg

2 pounds rock salt or coarse salt

3 tablespoons blanched, peeled, seeded, and chopped tomato, for garnish

Shuck the oysters, also reserving their liquor and the deeper half of each shell. Strain the liquor and set aside. Keep the oysters refrigerated.

To prepare the sauce, heat the olive oil in a small saucepan and cook the shallot over medium-high heat, or until lightly golden. Deglaze with the Zinfandel, add the reserved oyster liquor, and reduce the liquid by half, about 2 minutes. Pour in 1/3 cup of the cream and bring to a boil. Season with salt and pepper. Reduce the heat to a simmer and cook for 3 to 4 minutes, stirring occasionally.

Meanwhile, whisk the remaining 1/4 cup of cream in a mixing bowl until firm, and fold in the egg yolks. Slowly whisk the cream-egg mixture into the wine sauce. Cook over low heat, stirring continuously, until the sauce thickens. (Take care not to let the sauce boil because the egg will curdle.) Adjust the seasonings if necessary. Transfer the sauce to a double boiler and keep warm. Add the chives just before serving.

To prepare the spinach, heat 3/4 tablespoon of the olive oil in a sauté pan and cook the spinach over high heat, stirring occasionally. Season with salt and pepper. Sauté until the leaves are wilted but still bright green, about 3 to 4 minutes. Drain in a colander and let cool. When the spinach has cooled, squeeze out the excess moisture with your hands.

Heat the remaining 1 teaspoon of the olive oil in a clean sauté pan. Sauté the spinach again over medium heat, adding salt and pepper if necessary and the nutmeg, and cook for about 1 minute, or until heated through.

Fill a shallow baking dish with rock salt 1/4 inch deep. Arrange the oyster shells on top of the salt and divide the spinach among them. Top with an oyster and sprinkle with some of the chopped tomato. Spoon the sauce over each shell and broil for 1 1/2 minutes, or until the sauce browns. Serve immediately.

# The Best Crab Cakes

THIS IS another recipe that Rick Richardson, my chef de cuisine, helped develop. He certainly has the credentials—he grew up in Maryland, one of the richest sources of crabs in the world. The key to wonderful crab cakes is the quality of the crab, and in this recipe, I have given both the flavor and texture of the cakes an elegant twist by using a smooth, fluffy scallop mousseline. In addition, I've added cilantro, for which I developed a strong affinity while working in Brazil. It is most important that the scallops, egg, and cream are thoroughly chilled before blending. If they are not, the mixture might break. Ideally, the blender container should be chilled as well.

## CHEF'S NOTES

Allow about 30 minutes to prepare. For an alternative preparation, serve the crab cakes with the asparagus, greens, and Marinated Vegetable Vinaigrette from the grilled tuna salad recipe on page 84.

Recommended Wines: A medium-bodied young California Sauvignon Blanc or Alsatian Pinot Gris.

SERVES: 4

### CRAB CAKES

3 ½ ounces sea scallops

1 egg

Salt and pepper to taste

½ cup cream or half-and-half

1 pound jumbo lump crabmeat, picked through

2 tablespoons blanched, peeled, seeded, and diced tomato

1 teaspoon Dijon-style mustard

1 tablespoon minced fresh cilantro

3 drops Tabasco sauce

1 tablespoon virgin olive oil

1 tablespoon olive oil

Red Bell Pepper Coulis (page 128)

To prepare the crab cakes, place the scallops, egg, salt, and pepper in a blender and pulse until thoroughly blended. With the blender running, add the cream in a slow steady stream until incorporated.

Transfer to a large mixing bowl and add the crabmeat, tomato, mustard, cilantro, Tabasco, and olive oil. Gently mix and adjust the seasonings if necessary. Shape the crab mixture into 8 patties, about ³/₄ inch thick and 2¹/₂ inches across. Refrigerate for 15 minutes before cooking.

Prepare the coulis.

Heat the olive oil in a large heavy skillet. Sauté the crab cakes over medium-high heat for about 2¹/₂ minutes on each side, or until lightly browned. Drain on paper towels and keep warm.

Ladle the coulis in the center of each serving plate. Place 2 crab cakes, slightly overlapping, on top of the coulis and serve immediately.

# Mosaic of Tuna and Sea Scallops in Black Pepper Gelée

ACH MARBLED slice of this basic but beautiful terrine looks like an inlaid design of seafood, which is why I called it a mosaic. It's another ideal dish for entertaining as you can prepare it ahead of time and the colorful terrine will defintely impress your guests. Sea bass, salmon, or lobster can be substituted for the tuna or sea scallops (or both). Be sure to use the freshest possible sushi-grade tuna. You can add any variety of cooked vegetables to the seafood to create a diversity of flavors and colors.

### CHEF'S NOTES

Allow about 1½ hours to prepare, and 3 hours for chilling. For added touches, present the terrine with the Citrus Vinaigrette (page 79) or Chardonnay and Olive Oil Vinaigrette (page 87), garnished with chervil and served with toasted baguette bread or Nori Bread (page 37) on the side.

Recommended Wine: A rich Rhône Valley white wine such as a Hermitage.

### SERVES: 10

1 pound sushi-quality tuna, cut into 8 by ½-inch strips (about 4 pieces)

1 tablespoon virgin olive oil

Salt to taste

Coarsely cracked pepper to taste

1 pound sea scallops, washed and patted dry

BLACK PEPPER GELÉE (ASPIC)

2¼ cups finely strained Fish Broth (page 25) or Vegetable Broth (page 26)

3 tablespoons powdered gelatin

1 Bouquet Garni (page 22)

Salt to taste

Cracked pepper to taste

HERB-EGG MIXTURE

1 tablespoon finely sliced fresh chives

1 tablespoon finely minced fresh parsley

1 tablespoon finely minced fresh chervil

1 tablespoon finely minced fresh cilantro

2 hard-boiled eggs, whites only, coarsely chopped

½ teaspoon cracked black pepper

1 large tomato, blanched, peeled, seeded, and finely diced

Brush the tuna strips with ½ tablespoon of the olive oil and season with the salt and pepper. Heat a nonstick sauté pan and briefly sear the tuna over high heat, about 7 to 8 seconds on each side, or until rare. Set aside to cool.

Season the scallops with salt and pepper. Heat the remaining ½ tablespoon of olive oil in a clean nonstick sauté pan and sear the scallops over high heat, about 2 minutes on each side. Set aside to cool.

To prepare the gelée, place the broth in a saucepan over medium heat and stir in the gelatin until dissolved. Add the Bouquet Garni, salt, and pepper, and bring to a boil, stirring occasionally. Remove from the heat, cover, and set aside until cool but not set, about 20 minutes. Remove the Bouquet Garni.

In a mixing bowl, combine the ingredients for the herb-egg mixture and set aside.

Line an 8 by 4-inch terrine mold with plastic wrap. Pour one-quarter of the cooled gelée into the mold and spread one-third of the herb-egg mixture on top. Refrigerate for 15 minutes, or until set.

Remove the chilled terrine and add 2 tuna strips, placing them lengthwise. Arrange 2 lines of scallops between the tuna strips. Top with another one-third of the herb-egg mixture, spreading evenly. Sprinkle with one-third of the diced tomatoes. Add the remaining tuna strips and scallops in alternating rows. Sprinkle on the

remaining tomatoes. Top with the remaining herb-egg mixture. Pour the remaining gelée over to cover.

Cover the terrine with plastic wrap and chill for at least 3 hours, or until set. When ready to serve, dip the base of the terrine mold into hot water and invert onto a cutting board. Unmold the terrine, removing the plastic wrap, cut into 10 slices ¹/₂ inch wide, and serve.

# Vegetable Risotto with Saffron

THIS IS a lowfat recipe that I originally developed for Dr. Dean Ornish's book, **Eat More, Weigh Less,** but here I've allowed you the luxury of adding salt to taste. Most vegetarians I know enjoy the texture and earthy tones of mushrooms; the herbs and other ingredients in the risotto also contribute an array of contrasting flavors.

## CHEF'S NOTES

Allow about 45 minutes to prepare. Risottos are traditionally made with the starchier arborio rice, which gives a creamier texture. You can use it here, if you prefer.

Recommended Wine: A dry, well-balanced, and mature Riesling from Alsace.

SERVES: 4

- ½ cup diced onion
- ½ teaspoon black mustard seed
- 1 cup arborio rice
- 2 to 2½ cups Vegetable Broth (page 26)
- 1 teaspoon finely grated lime zest
- ½ teaspoon saffron threads
- 2 cloves garlic, minced
- 6 shiitake mushrooms, diced (optional)
- ¼ cup shelled fresh or frozen young green peas (petits pois)
- Salt and pepper to taste.
- 8 fresh basil leaves, chopped
- 2 tablespoons minced fresh chives
- ½ teaspoon minced fresh thyme
- 2 tomatoes, blanched, peeled, seeded, and diced

Lightly spray a nonstick saucepan with olive oil. Heat the pan, add the onion, and sauté over medium-low heat for 3 to 4 minutes, or until translucent. Add the mustard seeds, turn up the heat to medium-high, and cook for about 2 minutes, or until the seeds turn gray, sputter, and pop.

Add the rice and cook for 2 to 3 minutes, stirring continuously. Add the broth, lime zest, saffron, garlic, mushrooms, peas, salt, and pepper, and bring to a boil over high heat. Reduce the heat to a simmer and stir gently. Simmer for about 20 to 25 minutes, or until the rice is tender and fluffy, and the liquid is evaporated. During the cooking process, add more broth as needed to keep the rice covered. Gently fold in the basil, chives, thyme, and tomatoes. Cook for 2 minutes longer and serve immediately.

# Gruyère Puffs with Roasted Garlic-Tomato Sauce

THIS VEGETARIAN dish is a twist on the classic **pâte à choux** (choux paste). Choux paste is a special pastry used for profiteroles or éclairs that is made with flour, boiling water, butter, and eggs, and mixed to a sticky consistency. It puffs up as it bakes. **Pâte à choux** was a specialty that my father made at his **pâtisserie** in Alsace. As a child, there was nothing better than soaking up the aromas while watching him pull a batch from the hot oven and waiting with anticipation until he filled the puff pastry with pastry cream he'd cooled on a big marble slab. Even now, just looking at **pâte à choux** brings back fond memories of growing up over the family shop.

### CHEF'S NOTES

Allow about 1 hour to prepare. When baking the puffs, avoid opening the oven door for the first 15 minutes; a slight change in temperature or a jar to the oven may make them fall.

Recommended Wine: A light, crisp white wine, such as a Chablis or California Chardonnay.

SERVES: 4

### GRUYÈRE PUFFS

7 tablespoons butter, diced

Pinch of salt

1 cup water

1 cup flour, sifted

5 medium eggs

¾ cup freshly grated imported Gruyère cheese

### EGG WASH

1 egg yolk

½ teaspoon water

### ROASTED GARLIC-TOMATO SAUCE

1 cup Tomato and Cumin Seed Sauce (page 124), without cumin seeds

12 cloves garlic, roasted, peeled, and cut in half lengthwise

8 fresh basil leaves, minced

Salt and pepper to taste

Vegetable oil, for frying

12 fresh basil leaves, for garnish

Preheat the oven to 400°.

To prepare the puffs, combine the butter, salt, and water in a heavy-bottomed saucepan, and bring to a boil. Immediately remove from the heat and add the flour all at once. Beat the mixture vigorously with a wooden spoon, until the mixture comes away from the sides of the pan and forms a ball.

Return the pan to low heat and, stirring constantly, cook the mixture for 2 to 3 minutes longer, until the dough is shiny and does not stick to the sides of the pan. Transfer to a large mixing bowl and stir in the 5 eggs, one at a time, with a wooden spatula. Stir in ½ cup of the cheese, mixing until the dough is smooth and glossy.

Lightly butter and flour a large baking sheet. Fill a pastry bag fitted with a plain ½-inch tip with the warm dough and pipe it onto the sheet in mounds 1½ inches in diameter, spacing them about 2 inches apart. (You should have 16 to 20 mounds.) Set aside.

In a small mixing bowl, beat the egg yolk with the water and brush the egg wash over the top of each mound. Sprinkle the mounds with the remaining ¼ cup of cheese.

Bake in the center of the oven for 20 to 25 minutes, or until golden brown and crisp. Remove from the oven and let cool.

Bring the tomato sauce to a boil in a saucepan, stir in the garlic and basil, and season with salt and pepper. Keep warm.

Meanwhile, heat ½ inch of vegetable oil in a deep skillet to 325°. Fry the 12 basil leaves, two or three at a time, for 30 seconds, until they're bright green and translucent. Remove from the oil and drain on paper towels. Sprinkle lightly with salt and set aside.

Divide the sauce between 4 warm serving places. Place 4 or 5 of the puffs on each plate, garnish with the fried basil leaves, and serve immediately.

# Thinly Sliced Salmon Baked in Tender Corn Pancakes with Watercress Sauce

*I*NTRODUCED THIS appetizer onto the menu at Fleur de Lys in 1986, and it's remained ever since—a true "signature" dish. Occasionally I'll change it a little and give it a twist here or there, but it's so simple and so popular, it would be a crime to alter it too much! It's an elegant dish in terms of presentation as well as composition of flavors and textures. It has a pretty contrast of colors and a delightful taste that comes from the richness of the salmon and caviar blended with the corn and watercress.

### CHEF'S NOTES

Allow about 1 hour to prepare. This dish can also be easily turned into a vegetarian appetizer by substituting a small, thin disc of goat cheese for the salmon and caviar.

Recommended Wines: A classic match is vintage Champagne; a rich Chardonnay would work, too.

### SERVES: 6

### CORN PANCAKE BATTER

3 to 4 ears fresh young corn, husked

3 eggs

2 tablespoons flour

Salt and pepper to taste

8 ounces salmon fillet

4 tablespoons caviar, such as whitefish, salmon, or sturgeon

Salt and pepper to taste

1 teaspoon virgin olive oil

Watercress Sauce (page 102)

### GARNISH

30 blanched asparagus tips, about 3 inches long, fanned

30 ½-inch-wide slices tomato, fanned

1 teaspoon mixed black and white sesame seeds

1 tablespoon sour cream

Salt and pepper to taste

1 tablespoon minced fresh chives

To prepare the batter, bring 4 quarts of salted water to a boil in a large stockpot. Add the ears of corn and boil for 8 minutes. Quickly remove the corn and plunge into a pan of ice water. Drain thoroughly and cut the kernels from the cobs. (You should have about 2 cups.) Reserve 3 tablespoons of kernels for garnish.

Transfer the corn to a food processor and add the eggs, flour, salt, and pepper. Pulse briefly, keeping the texture of the batter a little chunky. Pour the batter into a small mixing bowl and set aside.

Slice the salmon evenly and thinly into 6 scallopines, using a very sharp knife at a 30-degree angle. Spread out the salmon on a work surface and top each scallopine with 1 teaspoon of the caviar. Fold the scallopines in half so the caviar is sealed inside the salmon. Season with salt and pepper on both sides.

Heat the olive oil in a nonstick sauté pan over medium heat. Ladle 1 ½ tablespoons of the batter into the sauté pan for each pancake, cooking 3 pancakes at a time. Top the batter with a scallopine of salmon and ladle enough additional batter over the salmon to barely cover it. Cook for about 3 minutes, or until golden brown on one side, then turn and cook for 2 to 3 minutes longer until golden brown on the other side.

Remove from the pan and keep warm while cooking the remaining 3 pancakes.

Ladle the Watercress Sauce in the center of each serving plate, spreading it into a wide circle. Place a pancake on the sauce and garnish each serving with 5 asparagus tips and 5 tomato wedges dipped in sesame seeds, arranged like spokes around the scallopine. Place 1 of the reserved corn kernels between each asparagus tip and tomato wedge. Season the sour cream with a little salt and pepper and dollop ½ teaspoon on top of each pancake. Place the remaining caviar on top of the seasoned sour cream, sprinkle with the chives, and serve.

# Sautéed Foie Gras on Braised Endives with Sauternes and Ginger Sauce

FOIE GRAS may date back to 2600 BC Egypt, but it was the Romans who brought it to Alsace. Later on, they also introduced foie gras into the Périgord region of southwest France, and these areas are still two of the major producers in the world. Until the mid-1980s, it was illegal to produce foie gras in the United States, and it could only be imported cooked and in sterilized form. Regulations have changed, and now the two leading producers in this country are June Gonzales in Sonoma, California, and Michael Ginor in New York's Hudson Valley. The recent availability of the fresh product has done wonders for its popularity. Like chocolate, foie gras is so rich and flavorful, you only need a little to please the palate. It's important not to overcook it, which compromises its delicate texture.

CHEF'S NOTES
Allow about 45 minutes to prepare.
The foie gras, endives, and leeks can all be cooked (and the ginger blanched) several hours in advance.

Recommended Wine: A young Sauternes.

SERVES: 4

1 ½ tablespoons sugar

Juice of 1 lemon

4 small Belgian endives, trimmed, and the bitter cone at the base removed

1½ tablespoons virgin olive oil

2 small leeks, split lengthwise and finely sliced

Salt and pepper to taste

2 tablespoons finely sliced fresh chives

1 teaspoon finely julienned ginger

12 ounces foie gras

½ cup Sauternes wine

1 cup Brown Chicken Broth (page 23)

2 tablespoons blanched, peeled, seeded, and finely diced tomato

Bring a saucepan of salted water to a boil and add 1 tablespoon of the sugar, the lemon juice, and endives. Reduce the heat to a simmer and cook gently until soft, 20 to 30 minutes. Drain the endives thoroughly, and set aside on a plate. Sprinkle with the remaining ¹/₂ tablespoon of sugar and let cool.

Heat ¹/₂ tablespoon of the olive oil in a small, heavy-bottomed saucepan, add the leeks, season with salt and pepper, and sauté over medium-high heat, stirring gently. When translucent, cover the pan and continue cooking until the leeks are soft but not brown. Remove from the heat, stir in 1 tablespoon of the chives, and set aside.

To reduce the sharp flavor of the ginger, blanch it in a small saucepan of boiling water for 2 minutes. Drain, refresh under cold running water, and set aside.

Using your hands, gently but firmly squeeze out the excess moisture from the endives and season with salt and pepper. Heat the remaining 1 tablespoon of olive oil in a sauté pan and when hot, sauté the endives over medium-high heat until evenly browned on each side, about 3 minutes per side. Remove the endives from the pan and cut lengthwise with a knife to within ¹/₄ inch of the top end, forming a "V." Keep warm.

Remove any membranes from the foie gras and cut crosswise into 4 slices, about ¹/₂ inch thick. With the tip of the knife, remove the thin red blood vessels that run through the foie gras. Season with salt and pepper on both sides.

Heat a nonstick sauté pan and sear the foie gras over medium-high heat until a rich golden brown on all sides, about $2^{1}/_{2}$ to 3 minutes per side; the inside should still be soft and pink. Drain on paper towels, cover with aluminum foil, and keep hot.

Pour off the fat from the sauté pan and deglaze with the Sauternes. Add the blanched ginger, bring to a boil over medium-high heat, and reduce the liquid by two-thirds. Add the broth and reduce by one-half. Season with salt and pepper and gently stir in the tomato and the remaining 1 tablespoon of chives. Keep warm.

To serve, place each V-shaped endive on a warm serving plate and spoon about 1 tablespoon of leeks in the apex of the "V." Cover the open end of the endive with a slice of foie gras. Spoon the sauce around the endive and foie gras, and serve immediately.

# Vegetarian Entrées

*I* AM PROUD of the fact that Fleur de Lys was the first upscale French restaurant—in fact, the first upscale restaurant of any kind—in the United States to offer a vegetarian tasting menu. I never imagined how much attention our vegetarian menu would attract and how popular it would become. Since we introduced it in the 1980s, the nation's awareness of the healthfulness of vegetarian food has grown significantly. Over the last two or three years especially, professional chefs have led the way in demonstrating how flavorful and resourceful meatless dishes can be.

I am glad to say that the general misconception that "vegetarian" is a euphemism for bland, limited, and unexciting food has finally been discredited, primarily because of the interest professional chefs have taken in vegetarian cuisine. Too often, though, vegetables are still prepared in an unattractive, heavy style. When I work with vegetables, I love to give them an elegance and finesse. As a result, I have relished the personal challenge of creating flavorful vegetarian dishes that are delicate or robust, exotic or familiar, and often lowfat, too.

Many of our nonvegetarian guests enjoy these dishes for their unique merits and do not insist on labeling them "vegetarian." In fact, about 80 percent of the guests who order these entrées are nonvegetarians. One of the qualities I admire in our clientele, and the American dining public in general, is that they dare to eat entirely vegetarian dinners and can appreciate the dishes' flavors and healthfulness. That attitude is inspiring and quite different than anywhere else I've been.

The success you can expect from the recipes in this chapter is directly related to the quality of the produce you use. Always take advantage of the peak growing season and resist making dishes when their star ingredients are not in season. Sometimes I am asked about the vegetarian tradition in France, and although none exists in the formal sense, the availability of produce and the emphasis placed on seasonality means that meatless dishes have always been a part of the culinary heritage.

When shopping for ingredients, take advantage of the access you now have to the beautiful premium produce—much of it organic—sold at the farmer's markets in this country. Even in more rural areas (such as Sonoma, which is northwest of San Francisco), where backyard gardens abound, the farmer's market is packed with a variety of produce that sets the pulse racing. These well-stocked farmer's markets remind me of the ones in the town squares of France, where small farmers and landholders bring whatever they grow or raise—vegetables, eggs, butter, garlic, chickens—to sell each Saturday morning. Support your local economy by shopping at a farmer's market, where the produce is likely to be extra fresh, high quality, and raised with care and integrity. One final thought: Most of these dishes are inexpensive to prepare, so I recommend you use whatever you've saved by not buying meat on upgrading the wine to accompany the meal.

# Red Cabbage, Apple, and Chestnut Casserole

*T*HIS WARM, rustic dish is traditionally served during the fall hunting season in Alsace—I've always thought this was a little ironic, considering it's a vegetarian dish. The hearty, satisfying flavors of the casserole also make it a popular side dish with pork chops. The acidity of the marinated cabbage and wine should be perfectly balanced by the sweetness of the apples and sugar, and the richness of chestnuts. I like to serve this casserole with fresh, crusty country bread.

### CHEF'S NOTES

Allow about 2½ hours to prepare. You can substitute ⅓ cup toasted pine nuts or pecans for the chestnuts, but add them at the last minute. The chestnuts can be prepared ahead of time.

Recommended Wine: A peppery red wine with soft tannins, such as Pinot Noir.

### SERVES: 4

1 quart peanut oil

20 to 25 fresh chestnuts, shelled and peeled

1 large head red cabbage

1 tablespoon red wine vinegar

1 teaspoon sugar

Salt and pepper to taste

2 tablespoons butter or virgin olive oil

1 large onion, minced

1 cup Pinot Noir, Merlot, or other red wine

2 bay leaves

2 large Golden Delicious or Rome apples, peeled, cored, and each sliced into 8 wedges

2 tablespoons finely minced fresh parsley

Heat the peanut oil in a deep skillet and fry the chestnuts over medium-high heat until crisp, about 3 to 4 minutes. Drain, and when cool, remove the thin inner layer of skin. Cover and keep refrigerated.

Discard the outer leaves of the cabbage and cut it in half lengthwise. Remove the core and shred the leaves or julienne into slices no more than ⅛ inch wide. Transfer to a mixing bowl, add the vinegar, sugar, salt, and pepper, and let marinate for 20 minutes.

Melt the butter in a casserole or a heavy-bottomed saucepan and sweat the onion over medium heat for 5 to 8 minutes, or until translucent. Add the cabbage and marinade, red wine, and bay leaves. Cover the pan and simmer gently for about 1½ hours.

Add the apples and chestnuts, stir well, cover, and simmer for 30 minutes longer. Adjust the seasonings and sprinkle with the parsley. Serve directly from the casserole or saucepan, or transfer to a serving platter.

# Stuffed Artichoke Hearts "Barigoule"

*T*HIS RECIPE is a cross between the classic **barigoule**—a traditional Provençal dish made with artichokes, wild mushrooms, and herbs added at the last minute—and **farcis Provençaux**, the stuffed vegetable dish from the same region. Both classics are examples of healthful vegan dishes that have been savored for generations (proving that healthy eating is not just a contemporary fad). I was introduced to this recipe for the first time by Roger Vergé, who used the tiny purple artichokes that are very popular in the South of France. This dish is a dynamic combination of colors and aromas.

## CHEF'S NOTES

Allow about 1 hour to prepare. In summer, this dish can be presented at room temperature, which is often how it is served in the South of France.

Recommended Wine: A light and peppery red wine with soft tannins and high acidity, such as a Pinot Noir.

### SERVES: 4

- 3½ tablespoons virgin olive oil
- 6 cloves garlic
- 1 to 1¼ pounds fresh spinach leaves
- Salt and pepper to taste
- 3 tablespoons freshly grated Parmesan cheese
- 1 quart water
- Juice of 1 lemon
- 8 artichokes
- 2 lemons, cut in half
- 1 cup thinly sliced young carrots
- 1 cup thinly sliced white onion
- 1 cup halved and thinly sliced leeks (white part only)
- 2 bay leaves
- 2 sprigs fresh thyme
- 1½ cups dry white wine
- 10 to 12 fresh basil leaves
- ¼ cup finely minced fresh parsley
- 2 tomatoes, blanched, peeled, seeded, and finely diced

Heat 1 tablespoon of the olive oil in a large saucepan over high heat. Lightly crush 1 garlic clove and add to the pan. Just before the oil begins to smoke, add the spinach. Season with salt and pepper, and stir continuously with a wooden spoon for about 5 minutes, or until the spinach is tender and the liquid is evaporated. Sprinkle with the cheese and stir well. Remove and discard the garlic, transfer the spinach to a platter, and let cool.

Mix the water and lemon juice in a bowl. Break off the stems from the artichokes (rather than cut them) so that the tough fibers will pull away from the heart. Break off 2 rows of the largest leaves from the base. Using a paring knife, trim away all the leaves and hard green skin from the artichokes. Immediately rub each artichoke with a lemon half to prevent discoloration.

Using a melon baller, scoop out the hairy choke of each artichoke. Place the artichoke bottoms in the bowl of lemon water. Divide the spinach into 8 equal amounts. Remove the artichoke bottoms from the water and fill them with the spinach.

Heat the remaining 2½ tablespoons of the olive oil in a casserole. Add the carrots, onion, and leeks and sweat over medium heat for 6 or 7 minutes, or until translucent. Arrange the artichokes in the casserole, add the bay leaves, thyme, and 3 lightly crushed garlic cloves, and season with salt and pepper. Pour in the wine and add enough water to come halfway up the artichokes. Cover the casserole and cook over medium heat for 20 to 25 minutes, or until the artichokes are tender and they can be pierced with the point of a sharp paring knife.

Meanwhile, finely mince the remaining 2 garlic cloves and transfer to a bowl together with the basil and parsley. When the artichokes are cooked, carefully transfer them to a warm serving platter and cover with aluminum foil to keep them hot. Reduce the liquid in the casserole over high heat to about 1½ cups, and then stir in the tomatoes and the garlic, basil, and parsley mixture. Adjust the seasonings if necessary.

Arrange the artichokes on warm serving plates and spoon the vegetables and liquid around. Make sure each place setting includes a spoon for the flavorful liquid.

# Ratatouille and Pure Goat Milk Cheese Wrapped in Phyllo

*A*LTHOUGH RATATOUILLE is another Provençale classic, I always associate it with my grand-mother, who did most of the cooking when I was growing up. It was a family favorite, and we all considered it exotic back then. This dish is served as a main course on the vegetarian tasting menu at Fleur de Lys. It's a recipe that incites enthusiasm and creates interest because the ratatouille is sealed inside a crispy phyllo crust, which provides a satisfying contrast to the creamy filling.

## CHEF'S NOTES

Allow about 1 hour to prepare. The calorie- or dairy-conscious can substitute roasted or sautéed garlic for the goat cheese. Although this dish is a little labor intensive, it's well worth it. Besides, it can be made ahead of time.

Recommended Wines: A white wine high in acidity, such as Sauvignon Blanc or even a light, fruity Beaujolais.

SERVES: 4

RATATOUILLE

1 tablespoon dry white wine

2 tablespoons water

½ teaspoon distilled white vinegar

1 teaspoon mustard seed

4½ tablespoons plus 4 teaspoons virgin olive oil

1 small firm eggplant, unpeeled and finely diced

Salt and pepper to taste

2 small green zucchini (about 1 inch in diameter), unpeeled and finely diced

2 small yellow zucchini (about 1 inch in diameter), unpeeled and finely diced

1 small red bell pepper, seeded and finely diced

1 onion, minced

2 cloves garlic, finely minced

1 tomato, blanched, peeled, seeded, and diced

½ teaspoon finely minced fresh thyme

6 to 8 fresh basil leaves, finely sliced

8 sheets phyllo dough, about 15 by 10 inches, covered with a damp towel to prevent drying

4½-inch-thick slices mild goat cheese, about 3 inches in diameter

GREENS AND DRESSING

4 cups loosely packed mixed baby greens (about 4 ounces)

3 tablespoons virgin olive oil

1 tablespoon freshly squeezed lemon juice

Combine the wine, water, and vinegar in a small bowl. Add the mustard seed and soak overnight. Drain, and set aside.

Heat 1 tablespoon of the olive oil in a nonstick sauté pan and sauté the eggplant over medium heat for about 2 minutes, or until soft. Season with salt and pepper, and transfer to a mixing bowl. Repeat for the zucchini and bell pepper, adding 1 tablespoon of oil to the pan each time. Add another tablespoon of oil to the pan and sauté the onion over medium heat for 2 to 3 minutes, or until translucent. Add the garlic and tomato, and season with salt and pepper. Lower the heat and simmer for 3 minutes to evaporate the liquid.

To assemble the ratatouille, add the sautéed eggplant, zucchini, and bell pepper to the pan and toss gently over medium heat for 5 minutes. Stir in the thyme, basil, and mustard seed. Adjust the seasonings if necessary, remove from the heat, and let cool.

Lay 1 sheet of the phyllo on a work surface and brush lightly with about 1/2 teaspoon of the remaining olive oil. Cover with a second sheet of phyllo and brush with another 1/2 teaspoon of the oil. With a sharp knife, cut the phyllo into 15 equal strips, 1 inch wide by 10 inches long. Lightly brush the inside of a round (non-fluted)

cookie cutter that measures about 3¼ inches across and 1¼ inches deep with olive oil (you will need about ½ teaspoon of oil to brush the cutter four times). Using the pastry cutter as a mold, lay a strip of phyllo over the middle of the cutter and gently push it down so that it lines the mold; the ends will extend outwards from the top edge of the cutter. Lay a second strip in the same way, overlapping the first. Repeat with 8 to 10 strips, so the cutter is completely lined. Spoon a layer of ratatouille into the mold, so that it comes about one-third of the way up the sides. Press it down, and top with a piece of goat cheese. Completely fill the mold with more ratatouille. Enclose the ratatouille by flipping over the ends of the phyllo strips, one by one. Gently twist the pastry cutter while lifting to remove it. Repeat to make 3 more ratatouille packages.

Preheat the oven to 450°. Spray a little olive oil into an ovenproof skillet or sauté pan, and over medium heat, brown the packages on the bottom side, about 1 minute. Flip the packages over onto the top side and place the skillet or pan in the oven. Bake for 6 to 8 minutes, or until the phyllo is golden brown. Arrange the lettuce on serving plates. Whisk together the olive oil and lemon juice, and dress the greens. Serve 1 phyllo package on top of the greens on each plate.

# Rick's Ragout of Wild Mushrooms and Caramelized Vegetables in a Potato Shell

*I* DEDICATE THIS recipe to Dr. Nair, a regular customer who enjoys our vegetarian menu and particularly loves this dish. Rick Richardson, my chef de cuisine for the past 10 years, enjoys informal, hearty dishes. This brilliant creation of his reflects that style; it's also full of delicious flavors. It's a lowfat dish that has always been a popular item on our vegetarian menu, even among nonvegetarians, who like the meaty flavor of the mushrooms and the rich, sweet caramelized vegetables.

## CHEF'S NOTES

Allow about 1½ hours to prepare (allow about 3 to 4 minutes each to hollow out potatoes). When serving, pass the pepper mill—mushrooms and freshly ground pepper complement each other.

Recommended Wine : A vibrant California Pinot Noir or a red from the Côte de Beaune.

SERVES: 4

RAGOUT

1 ounce dried porcini or black chanterelle mushrooms (or a combination)

2 cups warm water

1½ tablespoons virgin olive oil

10 shiitake, morel, or golden chanterelle mushrooms (or a combination), stemmed and diced

2 tablespoons finely minced shallots

Salt and pepper to taste

1 small onion, thinly sliced

1 small carrot, thinly sliced

1 small leek, white part only, julienned

2 tablespoons Spanish sherry vinegar

8 fresh basil leaves, coarsely chopped

2 tablespoons minced fresh parsley

1 teaspoon minced garlic

2 tablespoons soy sauce

2 tablespoons finely sliced fresh chives

1 tomato, blanched, peeled, seeded, and diced

4 russet potatoes (about 12 ounces each)

4 sprigs fresh thyme, for garnish

Place the dried mushrooms in a mixing bowl and add the warm water. Let soak for 30 minutes to 1 hour. Remove the mushrooms and strain the liquid to remove any grit or impurities. Set the liquid aside. Dice the rehydrated mushrooms.

Heat ½ tablespoon of the olive oil in a nonstick sauté pan and sauté the rehydrated mushrooms, fresh mushrooms, and shallots over medium heat, for 5 to 7 minutes, or until the shallots just begin to turn color. Season the mushrooms with salt and pepper. Remove the pan from the heat and set aside.

To complete the ragout, heat the remaining 1 tablespoon of olive oil in a heavy-bottomed saucepan and sauté the onion, carrot, and leek over medium-high heat for 8 to 10 minutes, or until browned and caramelized. Deglaze the pan with the vinegar. Add the mushroom soaking liquid, basil, parsley, garlic, soy sauce, salt, and pepper, and bring to a boil. Lower the heat and simmer for 12 to 15 minutes. Transfer the mixture to a food processor or blender and purée until smooth. Strain into a small saucepan, add the sautéed mushrooms, the chives, and tomato, and bring to a boil. Reduce the heat to low, adjust the seasonings if necessary, and keep warm.

Cut a ½ inch slice off the ends of each (unpeeled) potato. With a melon baller, hollow out the potatoes from one end, taking care not to break through the skin or the other end. Discard the scooped-out flesh, or use for soup or another purpose (store in water to prevent discoloration). Bring a large saucepan of salted water to a boil and add the potato shells. Lower the heat and simmer gently for 8 to 10 minutes, or until tender. Remove the potatoes and drain well. Place the potato shells on a serving platter and fill with the ragout. Spoon the remaining ragout around the potatoes. Garnish with the thyme and serve.

# Succulent Truffled Potato Stew in a Sealed Casserole

*A*HH, TRUFFLES—what a miracle! This recipe was inspired by the traditional Alsatian dish **baeckeoffe** (page 180), but without the meat. All the ingredients meld together wonderfully, making this one of my favorite vegetarian dishes of all. Ideally, for this recipe, you will need an ovenproof earthenware tureen or casserole with a matching lid; the pastry seal around the lid makes an impressive presentation.

## CHEF'S NOTES

Allow 1 to 1¼ hours to prepare. You may substitute wild mushrooms for the truffles in this stew.

Recommended Wines: An intense California Merlot or a rich and earthy red Bordeaux such as a Pauillac.

SERVES: 4

3 pounds Yukon gold or other yellow potatoes, peeled and sliced into ⅛-inch-thick rounds

2 cloves garlic, finely minced

1 onion, minced

3 tablespoons coarsely chopped carrot

3 tablespoons coarsely chopped celery

1 small leek, white part only, finely julienned

1 sprig fresh thyme

1½ ounces fresh truffles, julienned

Salt and pepper to taste

1 cup dry white wine

1 quart Vegetable Broth (page 26) or water

PASTRY SEAL

1 cup flour

½ cup water

1½ tablespoons canola oil

Preheat the oven to 400° and lightly spray or brush a large ovenproof earthenware tureen or casserole dish with olive oil.

Combine the potatoes, garlic, onion, carrot, celery, leek, thyme, and truffles in a large mixing bowl. Season with salt and pepper, and gently toss together. Transfer to the prepared tureen and pour in the white wine. Add the broth (you should have just enough to cover the top of the potatoes) and cover with the lid.

Mix all the pastry seal ingredients together in a mixing bowl and form into a rope shape. Remove the lid of the tureen. Press the dough onto the rim of the tureen. Replace the lid, pressing down so the dough forms a complete seal. This seal will prevent any of the cooking liquid from evaporating.

Bake the stew in the oven for 45 minutes to 1 hour, or until the potatoes are tender. Remove from the oven and cut through the pastry seal. Lift off the lid, and serve directly from the tureen or casserole.

# Vegetable Ragout Accented with Herbed Broth

T HE FRENCH word **ragoûter** means "to stimulate the appetite," and traditionally, a ragout is a thick, hearty meat or fish stew. Usually, it contains less expensive, often fatty but flavorful cuts of meat that require long, slow cooking. Typically, vegetables are added to contribute flavor and bulk, but here, they take center stage. I have kept the style of a hearty ragout by flavoring tender young vegetables with intensely aromatic herbs. When a dish like this is executed well, it becomes a kaleidoscope of distinct, exciting, yet delicate flavors that will please any palate.

### CHEF'S NOTES

Allow about 1½ hours to prepare. The mixture of vegetables can be varied. Try using pearl onions, mushrooms, fava beans, artichoke hearts, cauliflower, or whatever's in season.

Recommended Wine: A mature, golden Hermitage Blanc from the Rhône Valley.

SERVES: 4

2 quarts Vegetable Broth (page 000)

8 baby beets, with stems trimmed to 1 inch

12 to 16 baby carrots

4 small blue potatoes, cut into quarters

8 baby turnips

4 ounces tender haricots verts and yellow wax beans, trimmed

8 to 12 broccoli florets

8 ears baby corn

8 baby yellow or green zucchini

12 to 16 asparagus tips, 3 inches long

12 to 16 snow peas, trimmed

12 cherry tomatoes

8 to 10 basil leaves, finely sliced

3 tablespoons finely minced fresh parsley

1 tomato, blanched, peeled, seeded, and finely diced

1 tablespoon olive oil

Salt and pepper to taste

In a large saucepan, bring the broth to a boil. Add the beets and boil for 4 minutes. Add the carrots, blue potatoes, and baby fennel, and boil for 8 minutes. Add the turnips, green beans, broccoli, and corn, and boil for 5 minutes longer. Add the zucchini, asparagus, and snow peas, and boil for 4 minutes.

When the vegetables have cooked, drain carefully, reserving the broth. Arrange the vegetables in 4 shallow, warm soup plates. Add the cherry tomatoes, basil, parsley, and diced tomato to the broth, stir, and adjust the seasonings if necessary. Spoon the broth over the vegetables and drizzle the olive oil over the top. Sprinkle with salt and pepper and serve immediately.

# Ecuadorian Quinoa and Wild Rice Wrapped in Cabbage with a Tomato and Cumin Seed Sauce

*T*HIS SATISFYING, lowfat recipe was inspired by the traditional French stuffed cabbage leaves; every region of France has its own version. In the South of France, the leaves are stuffed with olives and roasted garlic; in Alsace, simpler stuffings of smoked meat and cumin seeds are popular; in the Southwest, foie gras and truffles are preferred; and in Brittany, seafood stuffings are common. Cabbage leaves keep their shape nicely and retain moisture well, providing a great medium for quinoa, a relatively unknown grain. When properly cooked, quinoa has a springy, crunchy, caviarlike texture. I like to toast the quinoa, which makes it lighter and more flavorful for this recipe.

## CHEF'S NOTES

Allow about 1½ hours to prepare. For more about quinoa, see page 220.

Recommended Wine: A rich white wine such as a California Chardonnay.

SERVES: 4

### STUFFING

¾ cup quinoa

Salt and pepper to taste

¼ cup wild rice

2 teaspoons virgin olive oil

2 tablespoons finely minced shallots

½ teaspoon finely minced garlic

3 tablespoons raisins

½ cup water

1 head savoy or green cabbage (about 2½ pounds), cored and darker outside leaves removed

Salt and pepper to taste

### TOMATO AND CUMIN SEED SAUCE

1 tablespoon virgin olive oil

1 onion, minced

2 cloves garlic, minced

2 pounds tomatoes, blanched, peeled, seeded, and coarsely chopped

1 sprig fresh thyme, leaves only

1 bay leaf

Pinch of sugar

Pinch of cumin seeds

Salt and pepper to taste

3 tablespoons water

2 tablespoons finely sliced chives, for garnish

To prepare the stuffing, place the quinoa in a saucepan and toast over medium-low heat, shaking the pan constantly for about 3 minutes, until the grains turn a light tan color. Be careful not to let them burn. Add enough water to the pan to cover the quinoa by ½ inch.

Bring the water to a boil and season lightly with salt and pepper. Cover the pan, lower the heat, and simmer for about 15 minutes, without stirring, until the liquid has been absorbed, the white filaments of the quinoa uncoil, and the grains become translucent. Remove from the heat and let rest briefly. Fluff with a fork, and set aside.

Meanwhile, rinse the wild rice in a strainer under cold running water for 1 to 2 minutes. Heat the olive oil in a saucepan and sauté the shallots and garlic over medium-low heat for about 5 minutes, or until translucent and golden. Add the rice and stir for about 30 seconds. Add enough water to cover the rice by ¼ inch, season lightly with salt and pepper, and bring to a boil. Lower the heat and simmer for 50 to 55 minutes, adding water if necessary, or until the rice is tender. Take care not to overcook it. Remove from the heat and set aside.

Meanwhile, soak the raisins in the water for 15 to 20 minutes to dilute their sweetness.

Separate the cabbage leaves, taking care to keep them whole and undamaged, leaving the heart of the cabbage intact (use for another purpose). Bring a large saucepan of salted water to a boil. Plunge the leaves into the boiling water and blanch for 6 to 8 minutes, in batches if necessary, until they are limp and flexible, but not mushy. Drain and refresh the leaves in a large bowl of cold water. Drain once again and spread the leaves out on paper towels to dry. Cut out the thick stem in the center of each leaf.

In a large mixing bowl, combine the quinoa and wild rice, and the raisins, salt, and pepper. Line 4 round coffee cups with pieces of plastic wrap 10 by 10 inches. Then line with one or two of the cabbage leaves, so the plastic wrap is covered.

Spoon the quinoa mixture into the cups and fold the leaves and plastic wrap over the filling, completely enclosing it. Twist the ends of the plastic wrap tightly. Then unwrap the plastic to yield firm, round, stuffed cabbage leaves. Set aside.

To prepare the sauce, heat the olive oil in a saucepan and sauté the onion and garlic over medium-low heat for about 5 minutes, or until translucent and golden. Add the tomatoes, thyme, bay leaf, sugar, cumin seeds, salt, and pepper, and simmer for 20 to 25 minutes, stirring occasionally, until the sauce thickens.

Preheat the oven to 350°.

Take a casserole just large enough to hold the stuffed cabbage leaves and brush lightly with olive oil. Arrange the stuffed cabbage leaves side by side in the dish. Pour the warm sauce over and around the leaves and add the water. The water and sauce should come halfway up the sides of stuffed leaves (add more water if necessary).

Cover the dish and bake in the oven for 20 minutes. Remove, sprinkle with the chives, and serve at the table directly from the dish.

# Braised Sweet Bell Peppers Stuffed with Rice and Vegetables

*H*ERE'S ANOTHER recipe influenced by the cuisine of the South of France (stuffed bell peppers are typical Provençale fare). It's both versatile and convenient—it can be prepared ahead of time, easily reheated, or served at room temperature as a summer meal. You can use yellow or even orange sweet bell peppers, if you can find them, and you can vary the curry to taste or leave it out entirely if you prefer.

## CHEF'S NOTES

Allow about 1¼ hours to prepare. As an elegant option, you can cook ¼ cup diced black chanterelle or button mushrooms with the rice. For a more rustic presentation, serve the peppers at the table in an attractive tureen or earthenware dish.

Recommended Wine: A flinty, fruity wine such as a Pouilly-Fumé from the Loire Valley.

SERVES: 4

1 tablespoon virgin olive oil

¼ cup finely diced onion

1 teaspoon curry powder, or to taste

1 cup long-grain white rice

4 cups Vegetable Broth (page 26)

¼ cup fresh corn kernels

¼ cup shelled young fresh peas or petits pois

2 to 3 tablespoons grated Gruyère or Swiss cheese (optional)

Juice of 1 lemon

¼ cup black olives, such as kalamata, pitted and coarsely minced

8 to 12 fresh basil leaves, sliced

3 tablespoons finely sliced fresh chives or young scallions

Salt and pepper to taste

2 large sweet red bell peppers

2 large sweet green bell peppers

Heat ½ tablespoon of the olive oil in a nonstick saucepan and sauté the onion over low heat for 5 minutes, stirring frequently with a wooden spoon until soft and translucent. Stir in the curry powder.

Add the rice and continue to stir gently for 1 or 2 minutes. Pour 2 cups of the broth over the rice, stir only once, and bring to a boil. Lower the heat, cover the pan, and cook until the rice is al dente, about 14 to 15 minutes. Remove from the heat.

Meanwhile, blanch the corn in a saucepan of boiling salted water for 3 minutes. Add the peas, and blanch for 2 minutes longer. Drain and set aside.

Preheat the oven to 350°

When the rice has absorbed the liquid, transfer to a mixing bowl and fluff with a fork. Stir in the cheese, lemon juice, olives, corn, peas, basil, and chives. Season with salt and pepper, and add 1 or 2 tablespoons of broth to the rice mixture if it is too dry.

Cut the peppers lengthwise, and remove the core and seeds. Fill each half pepper with the rice mixture. Lightly coat a shallow baking dish (just large enough to hold the peppers) with olive oil. Set the stuffed peppers in the dish. Pour the remaining broth, or enough to come halfway up the sides of the peppers, into the dish.

Cover the dish tightly and bake in the oven for 30 to 40 minutes, or until the rice is puffy and tender, but not crusty. Baste the peppers periodically with the broth in the baking dish. Serve immediately.

# Sundried Tomato, Fresh Herb, and Fettucine Pancakes

*I* FIRST CREATED this dish at La Cuisine du Soleil in Brazil as an accompaniment for chicken breasts. I've expanded it since then, so that it stands on its own as a main course. The pancakes are fluffy and almost quichelike (but without the dough), and they're best served right out of the pan. This recipe also makes an ideal brunch dish, and in the summer it makes a wonderful picnic item.

## CHEF'S NOTES

Allow 30 to 35 minutes to prepare. I recommend using two small nonstick sauté pans no larger than 7½ inches in diameter for cooking the pancakes. This recipe doubles well, so don't hesitate to make extra! Serve with a colorful mesclun salad and the Red Bell Pepper Coulis (page 128), if desired.

Recommended Wine: A fruity white wine such as a Loire Valley Pouilly-Fumé.

SERVES: 4

- 1 tablespoon virgin olive oil
- 4 ounces fresh fettucine, or 2½ ounces dried
- 5 ounces spinach leaves (about ½ bunch), stemmed
- Salt and pepper to taste
- 3 eggs
- ½ cup milk
- ¼ cup cream
- 4 to 5 tablespoons freshly grated Parmesan cheese
- Pinch of freshly ground nutmeg
- 2 tablespoons diced dry-packed sundried tomatoes
- 10 to 12 fresh basil leaves, finely sliced
- 3 tablespoons finely minced fresh parsley
- 1 teaspoon butter

Preheat the oven to 325°.

Bring a large saucepan of salted water to a boil and add ½ tablespoon of the olive oil (to prevent the pasta from sticking). Add the fettucine and boil over high heat for 3 minutes (if using fresh pasta), or about 8 minutes (for dried pasta). Drain immediately in a colander, and refresh under cold running water. Drain again and set aside.

Meanwhile, heat the remaining ½ tablespoon of olive oil in a skillet over high heat. Just before the oil begins to smoke, add the spinach, salt, and pepper, and cook for 5 to 6 minutes, or until the spinach is wilted and tender and all the liquid is evaporated. Remove from the heat, mince coarsely, and set aside.

In a mixing bowl, combine the eggs, milk, cream, cheese, and nutmeg. Stir in the fettucine, sundried tomatoes, basil, parsley, and cooked spinach. Season to taste and set aside.

Heat the butter in each of 2 small ovenproof nonstick sauté pans over medium heat. As the butter melts, tilt the pans in all directions so the bottom and the sides of the pans are completely covered. Add about ⅔ cup of the fettucine mixture to each pan and transfer to the oven. (Alternatively, cook one pancake at a time.) Cook for 15 to 17 minutes, or until golden brown.

Turn the pancake over and transfer to a warm serving platter. Cut the pancake into 4 wedges and cover with aluminum foil to keep warm. Cook the remaining pancakes. Serve 1 pancake per person.

# Black Pepper Polenta with Red Bell Pepper Coulis and Shiitake Mushrooms

*L*IKE OYSTERS and tomatoes, polenta was something I didn't much care for when I was growing up. Perhaps it was because my grandmother would serve it with tomato sauce (and I disliked tomatoes) or because she would make a polenta porridge for us when we were sick or had upset stomachs—guilt by association, in either case! However, as time went by, I learned to appreciate polenta's wholesome, rich, and hearty qualities. I created this balanced, filling recipe for Dr. Dean Ornish's book, **Eat More, Weigh Less,** and although I've added cheese here, you can omit it or substitute diced or shredded nonfat Parmesan, Cheddar, Swiss, or mozzarella.

## CHEF'S NOTES

Allow about 1¼ hours to prepare. For best results, eat the polenta as soon as you've made it. The coulis can be made up to a day ahead and freezes well. As an optional serving suggestion, offer your guests freshly grated Parmesan cheese on the side and serve with a salad of mixed greens.

Recommended Wines: A light Pinot Noir from Oregon or a young, rich, and fruity Beaujolais.

SERVES: 4

### RED BELL PEPPER COULIS
- 1½ tablespoons virgin olive oil
- 1 small onion, minced
- 2 cloves garlic, minced
- 3 large red bell peppers, roasted, peeled, seeded, and diced
- 3 large tomatoes, blanched, peeled, seeded, and finely diced
- ¼ teaspoon minced fresh thyme
- 6 fresh basil leaves
- 1 teaspoon honey
- Salt and pepper to taste

- 10 to 12 shiitake mushrooms, stemmed and minced
- 1 tablespoon water

### POLENTA
- 5 cups Vegetable Broth (page 26)
- 1¼ cups coarse cornmeal
- ¼ cup freshly grated Parmesan cheese
- 1 teaspoon coarsely ground pepper
- 3 tablespoons butter, diced (optional)

- 1½ tablespoons sliced fresh chives or young scallions, for garnish

Preheat the broiler.

To prepare the coulis, heat 1 tablespoon of the olive oil in a saucepan. Sauté the onion over medium heat for 5 minutes, stirring occasionally, until translucent. Add the garlic, bell peppers, tomatoes, thyme, basil, honey, salt, and pepper. Cover the pan and cook gently for 15 minutes until the mixture thickens slightly. If the mixture thickens too quickly, thin with 1 to 2 tablespoons of water. Transfer to a blender and purée, in batches if necessary, until completely smooth. Transfer to a clean saucepan, adjust the seasonings if necessary, and keep warm.

Heat the remaining ½ tablespoon of olive oil in a small sauté pan or skillet and sauté the mushrooms over medium heat for 2 minutes. Add the water and cook for 3 to 4 minutes, or until all the liquid is evaporated. Season with salt and pepper, and set aside.

To prepare the polenta, bring the broth to a boil in a large heavy saucepan over high heat. While whisking, add the cornmeal in a thin stream to prevent it from becoming lumpy. Reduce the heat to low and whisk continuously for 25 to 30 minutes, or until the mixture begins to thicken. Stir in the cheese, pepper, and butter, and season with salt to taste.

When the polenta has a smooth and soft but ridged texture, spoon it onto warm serving plates. Spoon the coulis around the polenta and top the polenta with the sautéed mushrooms. Sprinkle with the chives and serve immediately.

# A Rich Potato, Shallot, and Fresh Herb Pie

*T*HIS RECIPE is based on a traditional Alsatian recipe, **tourte d'Alsacienne**, a classic potpie stuffed with meat and a creamy quichelike custard, and cooked in a decorated terra cotta mold. I've simplified it by adding the custard before cooking the pie (rather than adding it as it cooks, as called for with **tourte d'Alsacienne**), and I've given it a vegetarian twist.

## CHEF'S NOTES

Allow about 1¹/₂ hours to prepare. This pie is easier to serve if you let it rest after cooking, and it reheats well. I recommend serving it with a spinach or frisée salad.

Recommended Wines: A rich California Chardonnay or a white Burgundy, such as Corton-Charlemagne or Chassagne-Montrachet.

SERVES: 4 TO 6

1 recipe Pastry Dough (page 92), flattened into a disc and chilled

2 pounds Yukon gold, Bintje, or other yellow potatoes, peeled

¹/₂ tablespoon virgin olive oil

³/₄ cup minced shallots

Salt and pepper to taste

3 eggs

³/₄ cup cream or half-and-half

³/₄ cup freshly grated Swiss cheese (optional)

1 teaspoon finely minced fresh thyme

2 tablespoon finely minced fresh parsley

2 tablespoons finely sliced fresh chives

2 cloves garlic, finely minced

EGG WASH

1 egg yolk

¹/₂ teaspoon water

Preheat the oven to 375°.

Roll out the chilled pastry dough in a circle about ¹/₁₆ inch thick. Place in a 9-inch pie pan, bringing the dough up the sides and trimming off. Prick the bottom of the pastry dough at ¹/₂-inch intervals with a fork.

Lightly butter the shiny side of a 12-inch square of aluminum foil and line the pastry shell with it, shiny side down. Cover the foil with about 1¹/₂ cups of dry beans or pastry weights.

Bake the pastry shell in the oven for 20 to 25 minutes. Remove from the oven and discard the beans (or remove the weights) and the foil. Bake for a few minutes longer, or until the pastry shell turns a light golden color. Remove from the oven and place on a wire rack to cool.

Place the potatoes in a large saucepan, cover with salted water, and bring to a boil. Reduce the heat and simmer for about 15 to 20 minutes, until just tender. Drain and let cool.

Heat the olive oil in a small skillet and add the shallots, salt, and pepper. Sweat over medium heat for 8 to 10 minutes, stirring frequently, until soft (add 1 tablespoon of water if the skillet becomes too dry). Remove from the heat and set aside.

Reheat the oven to 375°.

Beat the eggs in a mixing bowl for 1 minute. Add the cream, cheese, thyme, parsley, chives, garlic, and cooked shallots, and stir well. Adjust the seasonings if necessary.

Slice the boiled potatoes into ¹/₈-inch rounds. Line the bottom half of the pastry shell with the potato slices. Ladle half of the cream mixture over the potatoes, and then add another layer of potatoes. Fill with the remaining cream mixture.

Roll out a thin layer of the leftover pastry dough into a circle large enough to cover the pie. Whisk the egg yolk and water together and brush this egg wash over the dough and the rim of the pie shell. Then place the dough on top of the potatoes and cream, egg wash side up, and pinch the dough against the rim of the shell to form a seal (cut off any excess dough with scissors or a knife). Cut out a small hole in the center of the lid, to allow the steam from the pie to escape.

Bake the pie in the middle of the oven for 30 to 40 minutes. Remove and let rest for 10 minutes before serving.

# Mushroom and Spinach Saint-Honoré with Glazed Pearl Onions

*M*Y FATHER used to make the classic Saint-Honoré dessert (named after the patron saint of French bakers) in the family **pâtisserie**, which is why I was particularly fascinated by a savory version created by Jacques Maximin. I worked for Maximin for about a year at Le Chantecler restaurant in Nice's Negresco Hotel in the late 1970s, and I was inspired by his innovative approach. He adapted the traditional Saint-Honoré as a side dish for rabbit, using spinach filling instead of the usual pastry cream and glazed pearl onions instead of cream puffs.

### CHEF'S NOTES
Allow about 1 1/4 hours to prepare. This sophisticated dish makes an elegant centerpiece for any special occasion.

Recommended Wine: An herbal Cabernet Sauvignon from California.

### SERVES: 4

- 10 to 20 small white pearl onions
- 3 tablespoons butter
- 1 tablespoon sugar
- 1 cup Vegetable Broth (page 26) or water
- Salt and pepper to taste
- 12 ounces white mushrooms, trimmed and minced
- 2 eggs plus 1 egg white, lightly beaten
- 1/2 cup milk
- 1/2 cup plus 3 tablespoons cream
- 4 pounds young fresh spinach, stemmed
- Pinch of freshly ground nutmeg
- 2 tablespoons sliced almonds, toasted

Place the pearl onions in a saucepan just large enough to hold them in a single layer, and combine with 1 tablespoon of the butter and the sugar. Add the broth to just cover the onions (add more if needed), and season with salt and pepper. Bring to a simmer, cover, and cook for 20 to 25 minutes, or until the onions are tender and the liquid is reduced to a syrup that coats them.

Preheat the oven to 350°.

Melt 1 tablespoon of the butter in a skillet and sauté the mushrooms over medium heat for 6 to 8 minutes, or until the pan is dry. Season with salt and pepper. Transfer the mushrooms to a blender and purée. Pour into a mixing bowl and stir in the eggs and egg white. Add the milk and 1/2 cup of cream, mix well, and season with salt and pepper. Line a 7- or 8-inch sponge cake pan with parchment paper greased on both sides. Transfer the mushroom mixture to the prepared pan; it should be about 3/4 inch thick. Set the cake pan in a water bath and bake in the oven for 20 to 25 minutes.

Bring 3 quarts of salted water to a boil in a large saucepan. Add the spinach leaves and cook for 2 to 3 minutes. Drain immediately and plunge into a bowl of ice water. Drain again and squeeze out as much moisture as you can with your hands. Transfer the spinach to a blender and purée until very smooth and creamy.

In a skillet, heat the remaining 3 tablespoons of cream and 1 tablespoon of butter, and the spinach purée, mixing gently until hot. Season with salt, pepper, and nutmeg.

When the mushroom cake is cooked, turn it out onto a large round plate. Arrange the glazed onions in a circle on the cake around the edge. Place the spinach mixture in a pastry bag fitted with a medium star tip and pipe it on the top of the cake, in a rosette pattern. Garnish with the toasted almonds. Reheat in a hot oven for a few seconds, if necessary, and serve.

# Stuffed and Braised Potatoes with Julienned Vegetables

*Y*OU DON'T have to be a vegetarian to love stuffed potatoes, and here is an interesting and unusual way to serve them. Stuffing the hollowed-out potatoes from one end so they keep their shape makes for an attractive rustic effect, and cooked this way, the vegetable filling does not dry out inside the potato. Served cold and sliced, this dish makes a great potato salad starter or buffet item, drizzled with a fresh herb vinaigrette.

## CHEF'S NOTES

Allow about 1 hour 45 minutes to prepare. If you use small enough potatoes you can also adapt this recipe to make a side dish with meat.

Recommended Wine: A medium-bodied, fresh and delicate Chardonnay.

2 tablespoons virgin olive oil

1/2 cup thinly sliced onion

1 cup julienned leeks, white part only

1 cup julienned carrots

1 cup julienned celery

Salt and pepper to taste

2 tablespoons cream

1 teaspoon finely minced fresh thyme

2 tablespoons finely minced fresh parsley

1 egg yolk

8 russet potatoes (about 10 ounces each), peeled

3 cloves garlic, lightly crushed

1 1/2 cups Vegetable Broth (page 26)

1 tablespoon finely sliced fresh chives, for garnish

Heat 1 tablespoon of the olive oil in a heavy-bottomed saucepan. Add the onion and sweat over medium heat for 5 or 6 minutes, stirring occasionally, or until soft and translucent. Add the leeks and cook for 4 to 5 minutes longer, taking care not to brown the vegetables. Add the carrots, celery, salt, and pepper. Stir for 1 minute, reduce the heat to medium-low, and cover the pan with a lid. Cook for 5 to 6 minutes, or until the vegetables are tender.

Add the cream to the mixture and bring to a boil over medium-high heat. Cook for 2 to 3 minutes, stirring frequently, until the cream thickens. Remove the pan from the heat and stir in 1/2 teaspoon of the thyme, the parsley, and egg yolk. Set aside to cool.

Preheat the oven to 400°.

Trim the potatoes so that they are all the same height. Using a melon baller, hollow out the potatoes from one end. Discard the scooped-out flesh, or use for soup or another purpose (store in water to prevent oxidation).

Using a small spoon, fill the cavities with the vegetable mixture. Season the potatoes with salt and pepper. Heat the remaining 1 tablespoon of olive oil in a large sauté pan. Place the stuffed potatoes in the pan and brown them on all sides over medium-high heat, about 5 minutes.

Transfer the potatoes to an attractive baking dish just large enough to hold them. Add the garlic cloves and add enough of the broth to come halfway up the sides of the potatoes. Sprinkle with the remaining 1/2 teaspoon of thyme, and cover the dish tightly with a lid or aluminum foil.

Bake in the oven for 30 to 40 minutes, or until the potatoes are tender when pierced with a knife; only about 1 cup of the braising liquid should remain in the dish. Remove the lid or foil, sprinkle with the chives, and serve at the table.

# Couscous with Mixed Vegetables and Harissa

 COUSCOUS, MADE from semolina (granular durum wheat), is a traditional North African staple, and it's usually served with meat as a hearty stew. As this recipe proves, it can just as easily make a satisfying main course served with vegetables. My partner at Fleur de Lys, Maurice Rouas, spent his childhood in Algeria and was almost weaned on couscous—it's still one of his favorite ingredients. Of course, his family never used instant couscous, but made it from semolina, which is an acquired skill.

### CHEF'S NOTES

Allow about 2 hours to soak the garbanzos and $1^1/2$ hours to prepare. You can add or substitute other vegetables, such as fava beans, artichokes, potatoes, eggplant, chanterelle mushrooms, fennel, and peas, as well as almonds or raisins. If time is pressing, you can used canned garbanzos; just add them to the broth in the last 10 minutes of cooking.

**Harissa** is a traditional spicy puréed chile sauce served with couscous in Tunisia. You can also use it to perk up all kinds of other dishes; it will keep for up to 5 weeks in the refrigerator.

Recommended Wines: A fresh, crisp, and light Rosé from southern France.

SERVES: 4 TO 5

½ cup dried garbanzo beans, rinsed

HARISSA

4 ounces dried chile peppers (preferably red New Mexican or Anaheim), stemmed and seeded

5 to 6 cloves garlic

3 tablespoons ground cumin

3 tablespoons ground coriander

2 tablespoons ground caraway

2 tablespoons dried mint

Salt to taste

3 tablespoons virgin olive oil

2 tablespoons virgin olive oil

1 cup minced onions

$1^1/2$ cups sliced small carrots

VEGETABLES

$1^1/2$ cups sliced small turnips

1 quart Vegetable Broth (page 26)

Pinch of cayenne pepper

4 tomatoes, blanched, peeled, seeded, and finely diced

Salt to taste

$1^1/2$ cups sliced unpeeled zucchini

1 cup haricots verts, cut in half crosswise

COUSCOUS

$2^1/2$ cups water

Pinch of salt

Pinch of saffron threads (optional)

½ teaspoon virgin olive oil

2 cups medium-grain instant couscous

3 tablespoons finely minced fresh parsley

2 tablespoons finely minced fresh cilantro

Place the garbanzos in a saucepan and cover with cold water. Boil for 2 to 3 minutes. Remove from the heat, cover, and soak for 2 hours. Drain the cooking liquid and add cold water. Bring to a boil, skim off any impurities, cover, and simmer for 45 to 50 minutes, or until tender but not mushy. Drain and set aside. To prepare the harissa, soak the chiles in hot water until soft, 20 to 30 minutes. Transfer to a blender and add the remaining harissa ingredients. Purée to a paste, transfer to a jar, and add the olive oil to cover. Refrigerate. To prepare the vegetables, heat the olive oil in a large heavy-bottomed saucepan. Add the onions and sweat over medium heat, stirring occasionally, for 5 minutes, or until translucent. Add the carrots and turnips and cook for 2 minutes, stirring occasionally. Add the broth, cayenne, tomatoes, and salt. Cover and simmer for 15 minutes. Add the zucchini, haricots verts, and garbanzos. Cover and simmer for 10 minutes. To prepare the couscous, place the water, salt, and saffron in a saucepan and bring to a boil. Add the olive oil and couscous, stir once, and remove from the heat. Cover and let stand for 10 minutes. Fluff the couscous with a fork and transfer it to a platter. Add the parsley and cilantro to the broth and adjust the seasonings if necessary. Spoon the vegetables around the couscous, and serve.

# Braised Celery Hearts with Roasted Shallots and Wild Mushrooms

 ELERY IS an underused vegetable, so here's a recipe that showcases it in an attempt to redress the balance. The rustic flavors of the slow-braised celery and shallots and the meaty wild mushrooms marry well to create a hot dish that's perfect for fall or winter. In the summer, you can serve this dish at room temperature.

## CHEF'S NOTES

Allow 35 to 45 minutes to prepare. If serving at room temperature, use the braising liquid as a base for a vinaigrette—just add some oil, vinegar, and chopped fresh herbs.

Recommended Wine: A hearty Zinfandel.

### SERVES: 4

1 pound unpeeled shallots

Salt and pepper to taste

1/4 teaspoon finely minced fresh thyme

4 bunches celery

2 1/2 cups Vegetable Broth (page 26)

1/2 tablespoon virgin olive oil

12 ounces mixed wild mushroom caps, finely diced

1 1/2 tablespoons finely minced fresh chives or scallions

Preheat the oven to 375°.

Place the shallots in a large bowl of water and let soak for 1 to 2 minutes. Remove the shallots from the water and trim off the tops and root ends. Place in a dry roasting pan and roast in the oven for 30 to 35 minutes.

Remove the shallots from the oven and let cool. When cool enough to handle, squeeze the pulp from the skins by pressing firmly with your thumb and index finger. Set aside.

Lower the temperature of the oven to 350°.

Lightly oil a 10 by 6-inch baking dish with olive oil. Spread out the shallot pulp to evenly cover the bottom of the dish. Season with salt and pepper, and sprinkle with the thyme.

Remove the outer stalks from the celery and reserve for another use. Set any celery leaves aside for garnish. Cut off the tops of the remaining celery stalks, leaving the celery hearts and about 5 inches of the attached stalks. Arrange celery hearts side by side on top of the shallots, and season with salt and pepper. Pour enough of the broth over the celery to cover by two-thirds. Cover the dish with a sheet of parchment paper or aluminum foil cut to size.

Transfer to the oven and braise for 35 to 45 minutes, or until the celery is very tender but still holding its shape.

Meanwhile, heat the 1/2 tablespoon of olive oil in a skillet. Add the mushrooms and sauté over medium heat for 4 to 5 minutes, or until tender. Season with salt and pepper, and set aside.

When the celery hearts have cooked, transfer them and the shallots to a hot serving platter, and keep warm. Place the braising liquid in a saucepan and quickly reduce over high heat until it reaches a syrupy consistency. Stir in the sautéed mushrooms and the chives. Spoon the sauce over the celery hearts. Garnish the platter with the celery leaves, and serve immediately.

# Fish and Seafood Entrées

OVER THE course of my professional career, working with fish, from selecting and buying to filleting and preparing, has been my favorite assignment. I have always enjoyed the diversity and versatility of fish and seafood, as well as the challenge of combining them with other ingredients to create a delicate balance of flavor and texture. I feel that somehow it's easier to be more flexible with fish than with meat, and I find myself thinking along less traditional lines when developing new dishes.

While growing up in Alsace, I always considered fish a big treat. Following religious tradition, every Friday we had fish—cod, eel, carp, or trout that our local miller raised as a sideline—rather than meat. Occasionally, we ate salmon. This explains why as an apprentice at L'Auberge, I was immediately impressed by the wide array of unfamiliar fish, especially ocean fish and shellfish. Chef Haeberlin worked the fish station in the kitchen, and spending time alongside him was a special experience for me. He introduced me to the exciting possibilities of combining fish and seafood in imaginative ways to accentuate differences in flavor and texture; he taught me many lessons I have never forgotten.

When I arrived in the South of France, I found a completely different style of fish cuisine. It was my introduction to a varied collection of delicious soups and stews, of which only bouillabaisse was well known at the time. In the South of France, fish are commonly prepared and served whole, which I was not used to, and of course, I also encountered a whole new range of Mediterranean fish and shellfish, such as the **poissons des roches**, little minnows that were sold still flapping in wooden boxes and used as a base for stews.

In Brazil, the variety was even more dramatic as I found myself working with Amazon River fish (such as **bicuda**), ocean fish (such as **dorado**), and warm water shellfish (such as spiny lobsters). When I moved to San Francisco, I was able to make the most of the city's location as a major fish center for Pacific catch, especially from Hawaiian, Alaskan, and Chilean waters, and spectacular seafood of all kinds. Although I acknowledge that all of us in San Francisco are spoiled by the selection of fresh fish and shellfish available here, these days fresh fish and seafood are also available in regions of the United States that are hundreds—or thousands—of miles from the nearest ocean.

Fish have undergone a tremendous growth in popularity over the last twenty years, partly because they are perceived (and rightly so) as more healthful than meat. Most of the recipes in this chapter follow in this vein, offering lowfat presentations with little or no dairy content. This differs from traditional French cuisine, which often pairs the natural delicacy of fish with rich cream sauces. Those combinations can be spectacular, but I strive to show that there are other equally interesting and delicious possibilities.

# Whole Red Snapper on Celery Leaves with Orange, Lemon, and Fennel

ROASTING WHOLE fish on the bone is the best way to preserve all the delicate juices and flavors of moist fish. Roasting fish on celery leaves is a traditional method of preparation in the South of France. The celery leaves infuse the fish with additional flavor, while the sweetness and citric acidity of the simple dressing gives the dish a Mediterranean touch. Farmer's markets are the best places to buy celery leaves (look for crisp, firm ones) if your produce store cannot get them for you; alternatively, you can use celeriac tops.

## CHEF'S NOTES

Allow about 45 minutes to prepare. Be sure to use the celery stalks for another purpose, such as stock. If snapper is unavailable, use skinless whole monkfish, large trout, or sea bass. Serve with freshly sautéed spinach, ratatouille, or Stuffed and Braised Potatoes with Julienned Vegetables (page 132), if desired. The dressing can also be used as a last-minute drizzle for grilled or panfried scallops, or fish fillets.

Recommended Wine: A well-balanced white wine such as Alsatian Riesling

SERVES: 4

### DRESSING

1 orange, peeled and sectioned

2 lemons, peeled and sectioned

1/2 teaspoon fennel seeds

Salt and pepper to taste

1/4 cup virgin olive oil

4 whole red snapper (about 1 pound each), scaled, cleaned, with heads and skin

Salt and pepper to taste

1 1/2 tablespoons virgin olive oil

3 bunches leafy celery, leaves only, stalks cut off

To prepare the dressing, cut the orange sections in half and place in a nonreactive saucepan. Add the whole lemon segments, fennel seeds, salt, pepper, and olive oil, and gently stir together. Set aside.

Preheat the oven to 425°.

To prepare the snapper, season the skin and stomach cavity of each fish with salt and pepper, and rub with 1 tablespoon of the olive oil.

Spread out the celery leaves on the bottom of a lightly oiled roasting pan, and place the snapper on top of them. Sprinkle the fish with the remaining 1/2 tablespoon of olive oil and transfer to the oven.

Bake the snapper for 10 to 14 minutes, or until a small section of the back fin comes out fairly easily when pulled away from the flesh.

Meanwhile, warm the dressing over very low heat for 2 or 3 minutes.

Using two spatulas or one long spatula, transfer the snapper and bed of celery leaves to a large serving platter, just the way it was cooked. Serve with the warm dressing on the side.

# Snapper Topped with Roasted Bell Peppers Drizzled with Black Olive Essence

HERE'S A summertime dish that evokes memories of the South of France and the Mediterranean. The striking olive sauce brings the whole dish together and proves once again that French cuisine does not depend on heavy, dairy-based sauces for spectacular and delicious results.

## CHEF'S NOTES

Allow about 1 hour to prepare. The roasted peppers will keep for several days and are useful to have on hand, so make more than you think you might need and enjoy them with salads or pasta, as garnish, and with any other fish. An ideal side dish would be mashed potatoes. This recipe works equally well with sturgeon, grouper, or salmon. If you'd like to add a crunchy texture to the fish, dredge the fillets in ¼ cup cornmeal mixed with ½ teaspoon hot paprika and a pinch of cayenne before panfrying.

Recommended Wine: A rich Chardonnay.

SERVES: 4

### BELL PEPPER TOPPING

1 red bell pepper, roasted, peeled, and seeded

1 green bell pepper, roasted, peeled, and seeded

1 yellow bell pepper, roasted, peeled, and seeded

½ tablespoon virgin olive oil

¼ teaspoon finely minced garlic

1 bay leaf

¼ teaspoon minced fresh thyme

Salt and pepper to taste

### FISH

½ tablespoon virgin olive oil

4 skinless red snapper fillets (6 to 7 ounces each)

Salt and pepper to taste

### BLACK OLIVE ESSENCE

½ tablespoon virgin olive oil

¼ teaspoon finely minced garlic

2 tablespoons sweet sherry

½ cup Brown Chicken Broth (page 23)

2 small anchovies packed in oil, drained

⅓ cup niçoise or other small black olives, pitted

2 fresh mint leaves

Salt and pepper to taste

2½ tablespoons finely sliced fresh chives, for garnish

Cut the bell peppers into a fine julienne, about ¹/₁₆ inch wide. Heat the olive oil in a skillet and sauté the garlic over medium-high heat until golden brown, stirring continuously to prevent burning, about 2 to 3 minutes. Gently stir in the bell peppers, bay leaf, thyme, salt, and pepper, and cook for 2 minutes. Keep warm until needed (or let cool and reheat just before serving).

To prepare the fish, heat the olive oil in a large nonstick skillet over medium-high heat. Season both sides of each snapper fillet with salt and pepper, and sauté for 3 to 4 minutes on each side. Transfer the fillets to a warm platter, cover loosely with aluminum foil, and keep warm.

To prepare the essence, pour out the oil remaining in the skillet, wipe with a paper towel, and heat the olive oil. Sauté the garlic over medium-high heat, stirring constantly, until it turns golden. Add the sherry, cook for 30 seconds, and then add the broth, anchovies, olives, salt, and pepper. (Use salt sparingly as the anchovies may be salted.) Bring the mixture to a boil, reduce the heat to a simmer, and cook for 2 minutes longer. Transfer the essence to a blender, purée until smooth, and pass through a fine strainer into a clean skillet. Adjust the seasonings if necessary and keep warm.

To serve, place a snapper fillet in the center of each warm serving plate, and top with the warm bell pepper mixture. Spoon the essence around the fillets, sprinkle with the chives, and serve immediately.

# Fillet of Sea Bass in a Golden Potato Crust with Rhubarb Coulis

F ISH AND rhubarb may seem an odd combination, but they really work together, as our guests at Fleur de Lys will attest. The light acidity of the rhubarb accents the sea bass, in the same way that freshly squeezed lemon juice is commonly paired with fish to highlight its natural flavor. At the same time, the sweetened rhubarb is offset by its inherent tartness, making an intriguing counterpoint. The potato crust provides an interesting textural contrast to the delicate, moist fish. Good substitutes for the sea bass are snapper, grouper, Alaskan halibut, and even salmon.

### CHEF'S NOTES

Allow about 1 hour to prepare. The coulis can be made in advance and stored in the refrigerator for up to 3 days. This recipe doubles and freezes well. I also recommend serving it with roasted venison, snapper, grouper, or halibut. Tender corn pancakes (page 110) go well with this dish. To cook plain corn pancakes (without salmon), flip when golden after about $1^1/2$ minutes, and cook for 1 to $1^1/2$ minutes longer.

Recommended Wine: A full-bodied Chardonnay.

### SERVES: 4

### RHUBARB COULIS

4 cups diced young rhubarb ($1^1/2$ to 2 pounds)

$^1/2$ tablespoon butter

1 cup port

3 tablespoons sugar

Salt and pepper to taste

### POTATO CRUST

2 large russet potatoes (about 12 ounces each), peeled

1 quart canola oil, for deep frying

Salt to taste

### FISH

3 teaspoons virgin olive oil

1 thick skinless fillet of sea bass (about $1^1/4$ pounds), boned and cut into 4 equal portions

Salt and pepper to taste

1 small bunch fresh chervil, minced, for garnish

To prepare the coulis, place the rhubarb, butter, and port in a nonreactive saucepan, stir together, and cover with a lid. Bring the mixture to a simmer over medium heat and cook for 5 to 7 minutes, or until the rhubarb is soft. Remove the lid, stir in the sugar, and cook for 2 more minutes. Transfer the mixture to a blender and purée until smooth. Season with salt and pepper and keep warm.

To prepare the crust, julienne the potatoes with a mandoline into $^1/16$-inch-thick strips, and rinse in cold water to remove the starch. Drain and pat dry.

Pour the canola oil into a large, deep skillet to a depth of 2 inches, and heat to 325°. When the oil is hot, add the potatoes in 2 or 3 batches and fry for 8 to 10 minutes, or until golden brown. Carefully remove the potatoes from the oil with a slotted spoon, and drain on paper towels. Season with salt, transfer to a work surface, and coarsely chop. Transfer to a mixing bowl, and set aside.

Preheat the oven to 375°.

To prepare the fish, lightly brush a small roasting pan with olive oil. Season the fish with salt and pepper. Coat the fish on both sides with 2 teaspoons of the olive oil. Dredge the fish, on one side only, in the chopped potatoes to coat generously.

Place the coated fillet slices, crust side up, in the roasting pan, and sprinkle with the remaining 1 teaspoon of olive oil. Bake in the oven for 6 to 8 minutes, depending on the thickness of the fish; it should be barely cooked through and moist, and the crust should be crisp and golden.

Spoon about $1^1/2$ tablespoons of the Rhubarb Coulis in the center of each warm serving plate. Spread the coulis into a 4- or 5-inch circle. Carefully place the fish on top of the coulis, sprinkle with the chervil, and serve immediately.

# Crusted Fillet of Sea Bass with a Beet and Sherry Vinegar Sauce

*S*EA BASS is one of my favorite fish. There are several different types, but I prefer the delicate, moist striped bass and Chilean sea bass, which is a little fattier and flakier, making it perfect for roasting. In this recipe, the combination of the rustic beets and the sherry vinegar makes an intriguing combination. The earthy, hearty, and sweet yet acidic flavors of the sauce contrast perfectly with the delicate fish, and the vibrant colors—the pink sauce, crisp herb-flecked golden crust, white-fleshed fish, and green chervil garnish—make a striking presentation.

## CHEF'S NOTES

Allow about 45 minutes to prepare. Served with the Sundried Tomato, Fresh Herb, and Fettucine Pancakes (page 127), this dish has become a trademark main course at Fleur de Lys.

Recommended Wine: A light and peppery red wine with soft tannins, such as a Pinot Noir.

SERVES: 4

### BEET AND SHERRY VINEGAR SAUCE

2 beets (about 8 ounces), peeled and diced

Salt and pepper to taste

1/2 teaspoon sugar

1/2 tablespoon Spanish sherry vinegar

1 tablespoon butter

### CRUST

1/2 cup fresh fine white bread crumbs

1 teaspoon finely sliced fresh chives

1 teaspoon finely minced fresh parsley

4 to 5 fresh basil leaves, finely sliced

1 thick skinless fillet of sea bass (about 1 1/4 pounds), cut into 4 equal portions

Salt and pepper to taste

2 tablespoons virgin olive oil

4 sprigs fresh chervil, for garnish

To prepare the sauce, place the beets in a small saucepan and cover with water. Bring to a boil and reduce the heat to a simmer. Add the salt, pepper, and sugar, and continue cooking for 15 to 20 minutes, or until the beets are tender. Remove the beets with a slotted spoon and set aside.

Reduce the cooking liquid over medium-high heat until 2 tablespoons remain. Transfer to a blender, add the beets and sherry vinegar, and purée until smooth.

Transfer the beet purée to a clean small saucepan. Over medium heat, slowly whisk in the butter (this will turn the color from rich ruby red to pink). Adjust the seasonings if necessary; you want a balance between the sweetness of the beets and the acidity of the sherry vinegar. Keep warm.

Preheat the oven to 450°.

To prepare the crust, mix the bread crumbs and herbs together in a shallow dish or bowl. Season the bass portions with salt and pepper on both sides and brush generously on one side with 1 tablespoon of the olive oil. Dip only the oiled side of the fish into the bread crumb mixture and press lightly to coat evenly with the crust.

Lightly brush a small roasting pan with olive oil. Place the bass in the pan with the crust side up. Drizzle the remaining 1 tablespoon of olive oil over the fish. Bake in the oven for 4 to 6 minutes, depending on the thickness of the fish; it should be barely cooked through and moist, and the crust should be crisp and golden.

Spoon about 1 1/2 tablespoons of the beet sauce in the center of each warm serving plate. Spread the sauce into a 4- to 5-inch circle. Carefully place the fish on top of the sauce, garnish with the chervil, and serve immediately.

# Roasted Swordfish on a Bed of Fingerling Potatoes and Onions

R OASTING MEAT with vegetables in a casserole and serving it family style may be an accepted way of cooking meat, but it's an unusual presentation for fish. The firm texture and moistness of swordfish makes it ideal for this preparation, as it has a meatlike quality, similar to veal loin. (This texture also makes swordfish appropriate for grilling, barbecuing, and roasting.) The juices mingle to give this dish remarkable flavor—it's an ideal dish for informal entertaining.

## CHEF'S NOTES

Allow at least 6 hours for marinating and about 45 minutes to prepare. It's important to use fresh swordfish, as it tends to dry out once it has been frozen and thawed. Halibut can also be substituted.

Recommended Wine: A full-bodied Chardonnay.

SERVES: 4

### FISH

- 1 1/2 to 1 3/4 pounds skinless, boneless swordfish
- 1 1/2 tablespoons virgin olive oil
- 1/2 teaspoon crushed black peppercorns
- 1/2 teaspoon crushed red peppercorns
- 4 large basil sprigs, leaves only
- Salt to taste

### POTATO-ONION BED

- 1 1/2 pounds very small fingerling, yellow Finn, or Yukon gold potatoes
- 12 pearl onions
- 1 tablespoon virgin olive oil
- Salt and pepper to taste
- 5 cloves garlic
- 2 bay leaves
- 1 cup hot Fish Broth (page 25) or Brown Chicken Broth (page 23)
- 8 fresh basil leaves, sliced

Place the swordfish on a large piece of plastic wrap. Brush generously with 1 tablespoon of the olive oil and sprinkle with both peppercorns. Rub the basil leaves between your fingers to bruise them and release the oils, and cover the swordfish with them. Wrap up the plastic tightly to make a sealed package, transfer to a plate, and refrigerate for at least 6 hours, but preferably overnight.

Preheat the oven to 400°.

Unwrap the swordfish and bring to room temperature. Remove the basil leaves and season with salt. Heat the remaining 1/2 tablespoon of olive oil in a skillet over high heat. When hot, sear the fish quickly, for about 2 minutes on the first side and 1 minute on the second. Remove the swordfish from the pan and reserve.

To prepare the potato bed, bring a saucepan of salted water to a boil. Add the potatoes and onions, boil for 5 minutes, and drain. When cool enough to handle, toss the potatoes and onions with the 1 tablespoon of olive oil, salt, and pepper.

Brush an ovenproof baking dish just large enough to hold the swordfish and potato mixture with olive oil. Add the potatoes and onions, garlic cloves, and bay leaves. Pour in the broth, and place the swordfish on top of the vegetables.

Roast in the oven, uncovered, for 15 to 20 minutes until the fish is only just cooked through and still moist. Baste the fish frequently and toss the surrounding potatoes and onions. Remove the baking dish from the oven and transfer the fish to a warm plate. Cover with aluminum foil and keep warm. Return the dish to the oven and roast for 10 to 15 minutes longer, or until the potatoes are very tender, lightly browned, and almost no liquid remains in the dish. Remove the baking dish from the oven. Mix the sliced basil leaves into the vegetables. Adjust the seasonings if necessary. Cut the swordfish into 1/2-inch thick slices, and place in the middle of a warm serving platter. Arrange the roasted vegetables around the fish and serve immediately.

# Broiled Grouper on a Fondue of Endives with Red Wine Sauce

*I* HAVE ADAPTED this straightforward recipe from a dish we prepared at L'Auberge de L'Ill using freshwater carp, but here I use the lean, firm-fleshed grouper. I've given it an elegant twist with the addition of endives and roasted garlic. The garlic not only adds flavor but also binds the sauce, another cooking technique that makes cream unnecessary. Meanwhile, the slight bitterness of the endive balances the sweetness of the roasted garlic, contrasting nicely with the delicate fish.

### CHEF'S NOTES

Allow about 45 minutes to prepare. You can use large trout, halibut, or swordfish instead of the grouper. Serve with a mesclun or frisée side salad, if desired.

Recommended Wine: A fragrant, silky red wine, such as a Volnay from Burgundy.

### SERVES: 4

**RED WINE SAUCE**

- ¹/₂ tablespoon virgin olive oil
- 3 tablespoons minced shallots
- 2 cup Pinot Noir or other red wine
- 1 cup port
- 1 teaspoon minced fresh thyme
- 1¹/₂ cups Brown Chicken Broth (page 23)
- 2 heads garlic, roasted and peeled
- 1 tablespoon butter
- Salt and pepper to taste
- 2 slices bacon, sliced into ¹/₄-inch pieces (optional)

**FONDUE OF ENDIVES**

- 4 endives, trimmed and bitter cone at the base removed
- ¹/₂ tablespoon virgin olive oil
- 1 tablespoon freshly squeezed lemon juice
- 1 tablespoon sugar
- Salt and pepper to taste
- 1¹/₂ tablespoons finely sliced chives

**FISH**

- 4 thick grouper fillets (about 7 ounces each), with skin
- Salt and pepper to taste
- 1 tablespoon virgin olive oil
- 24 whole sprigs fresh chervil, for garnish

To prepare the sauce, heat the olive oil in a saucepan and cook the shallots for 5 minutes over medium-high heat, stirring frequently. Add the red wine, port, and thyme, and reduce until ¹/₄ cup remains. Add the broth and reduce to ¹/₂ cup. Add half of the roasted garlic. Transfer to a blender and blend until smooth. Strain the sauce and return to a clean saucepan over low heat and stir in the butter. Add the remaining garlic cloves, salt and pepper, and keep warm. If the sauce is too thick, stir in a little water to thin.

Sauté the bacon in a skillet until crisp. Drain on paper towels and set aside.

To prepare the fondue, slice each of the endives lengthwise, and then cut crosswise into 1-inch slices. Heat the olive oil in a sauté pan and sauté the endives over medium-high heat for 5 minutes, until almost soft. Stir in the lemon juice, sugar, salt, pepper, and chives, and keep warm.

Season both sides of the grouper with salt and pepper. Heat the olive oil in a nonstick sauté pan and sauté the grouper over medium heat for 3 or 4 minutes, or until the skin is crisp and light colored. Carefully turn over the fish and cook for another 3 to 4 minutes, depending on the thickness of the fish.

Place the Fondue of Endives in the middle of each warm serving plate, creating a bed for the fish. Stir the bacon into the sauce (adding it at the end keeps it crisp) and spoon the sauce around the endives. Place a grouper fillet, skin side up, on top of the endives, fan 4 of the whole garlic cloves from the sauce and place one on top of each fillet. Garnish with the chervil and serve immediately.

# Braised Grouper Topped with Paper-Thin Cucumber Slices on a Bed of Caramelized Onions

*I* CREATED THIS elegant dish while I was in Brazil. The idea is to spread a **mousseline** on the grouper to seal it and keep it moist during the braising process. The cucumber slices overlapping on the **mousseline** simulate scales. The whole process is rather involved, but the impressive presentation is satisfying. Once again, the fish features an array of delicious contrasts—the delicate grouper, herbal vermouth, subtly assertive tarragon, and the sweet, lusty boost of caramelized onions.

### CHEF'S NOTES

Allow about 1 hour to prepare. You can substitute sea bass, salmon, or snapper for the grouper. In preparing the **mousseline**, it is important that all the ingredients are chilled, including the mixing bowl, so the mixture does not break.

Recommended Wines: An Alsatian Riesling, a Muscat, or a Chenin Blanc, such as Vouvray, from the Loire Valley.

SERVES: 4

**MOUSSELINE**

4 ounces grouper fillet

1 egg white, chilled

Salt to taste

White pepper to taste

1/4 cup cream, chilled

**CARAMELIZED ONIONS**

1/2 tablespoon virgin olive oil

2 cups thinly sliced onions

Salt to taste

White pepper to taste

3 tablespoons sugar

3 tablespoons Spanish sherry vinegar

**FISH**

4 skinless, boneless grouper fillets (about 5 ounces each)

Salt to taste

White pepper to taste

1 tablespoon finely minced shallot

1 small English cucumber, thinly sliced and blanched for 30 seconds

1 tablespoon dry vermouth

1 cup Fish Broth (page 000) or clam juice

**VERMOUTH AND TARRAGON SAUCE**

3 tablespoons dry vermouth

1 tablespoon finely minced shallot

1 tablespoon finely minced fresh tarragon

2 tablespoons blanched, peeled, seeded, and finely diced tomato

Salt to taste

White pepper to taste

1/2 teaspoon virgin olive oil

2 tablespoons diced tomato, for garnish

To prepare the mousseline, place the grouper in a food processor. Process until finely ground, then chill in the bowl of the food processor. Add the egg white to the chilled grouper and process with several pulses. Add the salt and white pepper, and pulse 2 or 3 more times. With the food processor running, slowly add the cream through the feed tube. Adjust the seasonings if necessary and transfer to a chilled mixing bowl. Cover with plastic wrap and refrigerate for at least 15 to 20 minutes.

To prepare the onions, heat the olive oil in a heavy-bottomed saucepan. Add the onions, salt, and white pepper, and cook over low heat for about 10 to 15 minutes, stirring constantly, until soft and golden brown.

Place the sugar and 1 tablespoon of the vinegar in a small heavy-bottomed saucepan and cook over medium heat until golden, about 3 to 4 minutes. Remove from the heat and stir in the remaining 2 tablespoons of vinegar. Return to the heat, bring to a boil, and immediately stir into the onions. Simmer for 3 minutes, then let cool.

Preheat the oven to 350°. Season the grouper fillets on both sides with salt and white pepper. Generously

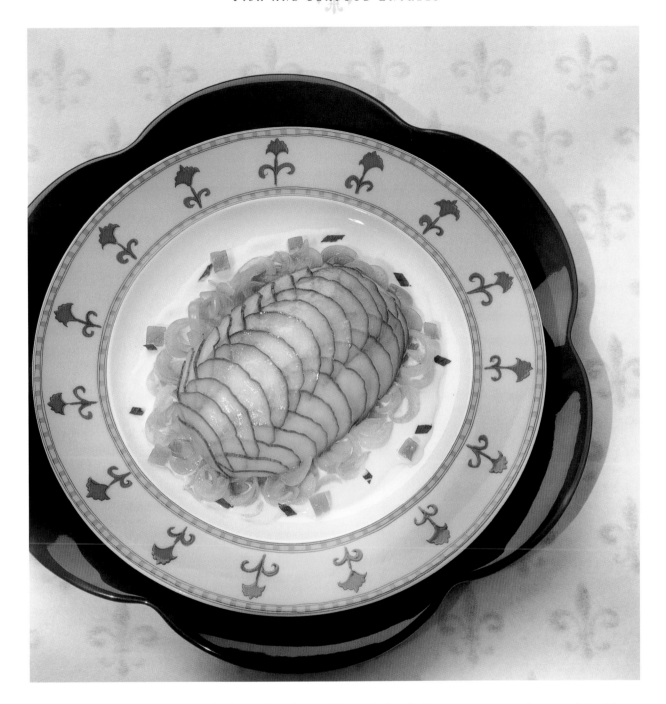

brush the bottom of a casserole with olive oil, and sprinkle with the shallots. Using a spatula, spread 2 tablespoons of the mousseline over each fillet. Arrange the cucumber slices on top of the mousseline, overlapping them to resemble fish scales. Place the fillets in the casserole and add the vermouth and broth so there is at least $1/2$ inch of liquid in the casserole. Cover with aluminum foil and bake in the oven for 12 to 15 minutes.

Reheat the caramelized onions.

To prepare the sauce, place the vermouth and shallot in a small saucepan and bring to a boil. Reduce over medium-high heat until the liquid is almost evaporated. When the grouper is done, add the cooking liquid from the casserole to the vermouth reduction (keep the fish covered and warm). Bring the sauce to a boil over medium heat, stir in the tarragon, and reduce to $3/4$ cup. Stir in the tomato, and add the salt and white pepper. Arrange the caramelized onions in the center of each warm serving plate. Lightly brush the cucumber "scales" on the fish with the $1/2$ teaspoon of olive oil. Place the fillets on top of the caramelized onions and spoon the sauce around them. Garnish the sauce with the diced tomatoes and serve immediately.

# Skate Served on Spinach Leaves with Julienned Vegetables and a Lemon-Oil Dressing

*S*KATE, A member of the ray family, is very popular in France and, fortunately, it is also widely available in the United States. It has a subtle, sweet flavor and a firm, delicate texture, which is why this recipe does not contain strong or assertive flavors that might overwhelm those qualities.

## CHEF'S NOTES

Allow 45 minutes to 1 hour to prepare. It will really make a difference if you use a top-quality, fruity olive oil for this recipe; extra virgin olive oil will also work well. If you want to eliminate the oil entirely, simply steam the spinach and vegetables without sautéing them first. Sea scallops, sea bass, or even salmon can be substituted for the skate.

Recommended Wine: A mature white Hermitage or a white wine from the South of France.

SERVES: 4

**SPINACH**

1 tablespoon virgin olive oil

2 cloves garlic, lightly crushed

2½ pounds spinach leaves

Salt to taste

White pepper to taste

**VEGETABLES**

½ tablespoon virgin olive oil

½ cup julienned red bell pepper

½ cup julienned celery

½ cup julienned carrots

½ cup julienned yellow (or green) zucchini

Salt to taste

White pepper to taste

**LEMON-OIL DRESSING**

3 tablespoons virgin olive oil

2 tablespoons freshly squeezed lemon juice

Salt to taste

White pepper to taste

8 to 10 fresh basil leaves, finely sliced

3 tablespoons blanched, peeled, seeded, and finely diced tomato

¼ teaspoon green peppercorns (optional)

**FISH**

2 skate wings with bones (about 1 pound each), 2 inches thick at the widest point

Salt to taste

White pepper to taste

1 bunch fresh dill, or 1 cup celery leaves

To prepare the spinach, heat the olive oil in a large high-sided sauté pan over high heat. Add the garlic, and just before the oil begins to smoke, add the spinach. Season with the salt and white pepper. Stirring continuously with tongs, sauté for 4 to 5 minutes, or until wilted and no liquid remains. Remove from the heat and discard the garlic. Transfer the spinach to a small platter and let cool. Squeeze out the excess moisture from the spinach with your hands and set aside. To prepare the vegetables, heat the olive oil in a sauté pan and sauté the bell pepper, celery, and carrots over medium-high heat for 2 minutes. Add the zucchini, salt, and white pepper, and sauté for another 2 minutes. Set aside to cool. To prepare the dressing, combine the olive oil, lemon juice, salt, and white pepper in a mixing bowl, and whisk until well blended. Stir in the basil, tomato, and peppercorns, and set aside. To prepare the fish, bring water to a boil in a stackable 2-part steamer or a roasting pan with a wire rack inside. Season the fish on both sides with the salt and white pepper. Spread the dill over the bottom of the steamer and place the skate on top. Cover and steam for 20 to 25 minutes. Remove from the heat and discard the dill. Transfer the dressing to a small saucepan and warm slightly over low heat. Warm the spinach and vegetables in the steamer. Peel the skin from one side of each skate wing. Slide a flat spatula between the flesh and bone to loosen and push the meat off the bone. Transfer the meat to a warm plate. Turn the skate over and repeat for the other side. Arrange the spinach in the middle of a warm serving platter and place the skate, slightly overlapping, on top. Spoon the julienned vegetables on top, drizzle the dressing all around the platter, and serve.

# Sea Scallops Served on Lentils with Celery and Ginger Sauce

*A*LTHOUGH YOU usually find lentils in rustic stews and hearty dishes, they are versatile and have a delicate side, which makes them a good partner for most types of seafood. I also like to pair lentils with lobster and smoked salmon.

## CHEF'S NOTES

Allow 45 to 50 minutes to prepare. If you prefer, you can quickly panfry the scallops in a nonstick pan over high heat until just medium done; be careful not to overcook them. It's best to buy fresh sea scallops that are sold loose, not plastic-wrapped (especially frozen ones). Before buying scallops, ask to smell them and avoid any that smell of ammonia or that are floating in a milky liquid (added to preserve and make them heavier). Scallops should be firm and dry (or a little sticky) and not soft.

Recommended Wine: A simple, earthy Chardonnay.

SERVES: 4

### LENTILS

1 1/2 cups dried green or French lentils, picked through and rinsed

5 cups cold water

1 carrot

1 small onion

1 bay leaf

Salt to taste

White pepper to taste

1 tablespoon virgin olive oil

2 tablespoons finely diced onion

### CELERY AND GINGER SAUCE

1/2 tablespoon virgin olive oil

2 tablespoons finely diced onion

1/2 cup thinly sliced celery

2 teaspoons minced ginger

2 tablespoons peeled, cored, and finely diced Golden Delicious or other sweet apple

1/4 cup dry vermouth

1/4 cup Fish Broth (page 25) or clam juice

1/4 cup cream

Salt to taste

White pepper to taste

8 large sea scallops, about 1 1/2 inches wide, cut in half crosswise (into medallions)

1 teaspoon virgin olive oil

Salt to taste

White pepper to taste

2 tablespoons finely sliced chives, for garnish

Place the lentils in a saucepan with the cold water and bring to a boil. Add the carrot, onion, bay leaf, salt, and pepper. Reduce the heat to low, cover, and simmer for about 35 minutes, until tender. Stir the lentils occasionally to prevent them from sticking. Drain the lentils, reserve the carrot, and discard the onion and bay leaf. When cool, dice the carrot finely and set aside.

Heat the olive oil in a saucepan and sweat the diced onion over low heat for about 5 minutes, or until translucent. Gently add the lentils and diced carrot to the saucepan, and adjust the seasonings if necessary. Keep warm.

To prepare the sauce, heat the olive oil in a saucepan. Add the diced onion, and sauté over medium heat for 2 minutes. Add the celery, ginger, and apple, and sauté for 3 minutes longer. Add the vermouth and reduce until the liquid has almost evaporated. Add the broth and cream. Season lightly with salt and white pepper, and reduce by half.

Transfer the mixture to a blender and purée until very smooth. Return the mixture to a clean saucepan, adjust the seasonings if necessary, and keep warm.

Prepare a very hot grill. Brush the scallops lightly with the olive oil. Place on the hot grill and cook quickly for 1 to 1 1/2 minutes on each side. Transfer to a warm serving platter and season with salt and pepper.

To serve, spoon the lentils onto the center of warm serving plates. Spoon the sauce evenly around the lentils and top the lentils on each plate with 4 scallop medallions. Sprinkle with the chives and serve immediately.

# Salmon Steak on Mashed Potatoes Accented with Saffron Broth

*S*ALMON IS one of my favorite fish because it's so versatile. Its essential flavorful, meaty qualities come through, whether you grill, panfry, steam, or roast it, and yet each cooking method will yield different enough results to always keep it interesting. It's important not to overcook salmon, or it will dry out. The Atlantic variety is fattier than Pacific salmon, which means it takes a little longer to cook and is less prone to losing its moisture. I recommend cooking the salmon so the interior is just medium and still lightly translucent.

## CHEF'S NOTES

Allow about 1 hour to prepare. I prefer using saffron threads rather than powder because the latter can sometimes be a blend rather than a pure product. When saffron is old, it loses its color and dries out. Try to buy loose saffron so you can feel its texture; the threads should not fall apart and should be bright. For variations, substitute trout for the salmon or flavor the mashed potatoes with a fine purée of sautéed leeks, using a two-to-one ratio.

Recommended Wines: A mature white Hermitage or an Alsatian Pinot Gris.

SERVES: 4

- 1 pound russet or other baking potatoes, unpeeled
- ½ cup milk
- 2 tablespoons butter, diced
- Salt to taste
- White pepper to taste

- 4 skinless salmon fillets (6 to 7 ounces each), sliced about 2 inches wide and 1 inch thick
- Salt to taste
- White pepper to taste

- 2 tablespoons finely minced shallots
- 1 sprig fresh thyme, leaves only, finely minced
- ⅓ cup dry white wine
- ⅓ cup water
- 1 small apple, peeled, halved, cored, and diced
- Pinch of saffron threads
- ½ tablespoon cream
- 1 tablespoon finely sliced fresh chives
- 1 tomato, blanched, peeled, seeded, and diced

Place the potatoes in a stockpot and cover with at least 1 inch of salted water. Bring to a boil, reduce the heat, and gently simmer for 20 to 30 minutes, until tender.

While the potatoes are cooking, sprinkle both sides of the salmon fillets with salt and white pepper. Lightly brush the bottom of a casserole with olive oil and add the shallots and thyme. Place the salmon in the dish, add the wine and water, and cover with aluminum foil.

Peel the potatoes as soon as they cool. Process through a food mill or mash with a handheld mixer or heavy whisk. Bring the milk to a boil in a saucepan and gradually whisk into the potatoes until thoroughly incorporated. Add 1½ tablespoons of the butter, a little at a time, and continue mixing until the potatoes are light and fluffy. Season with salt and white pepper. If the mashed potatoes seem too firm, stir in a little more milk. Set aside and keep hot.

Preheat the oven to 325°. Braise the salmon in the oven for 12 to 15 minutes, or until medium in the center and still moist.

Meanwhile, heat the remaining ½ tablespoon of butter in a sauté pan and sauté the apple over medium-high heat for about 2 to 3 minutes, or until tender. Remove from the heat and set aside.

When the salmon is done, pour the cooking broth into a saucepan, add the saffron and cream, and simmer for 2 minutes. Gently stir in the sautéed apple, the chives, and tomato, and season with salt and white pepper.

Spoon the mashed potatoes onto the center of each warm serving plate and gently place the salmon on top. Spoon the saffron broth all around the mashed potatoes and serve immediately.

# Paper-Thin Sliced Salmon with an Oyster and Chive Sauce

BROILING THE salmon directly on serving plates is a unique presentation that never fails to provide a conversation piece. It's important for the heat to be as high as possible, so the fish will sear and the sauce will turn a brown tint. If not cooked over high heat, the salmon would overcook and the sauce would break. For this reason, the fattier Atlantic salmon is preferable as it is less likely to dry out. Be sure to use fresh salmon for this recipe, rather than frozen, because the quality is superior and frozen salmon is more difficult to slice finely. The salmon and sauce can be prepared ahead (make the sauce without the cream and eggs, then add them when ready to assemble the dish), which makes it a good dish for entertaining. The final steps are quick and easy to execute.

### CHEF'S NOTES

Allow about 30 minutes to prepare. For an optional garnish, place a bouquet of chives, or a teaspoon of caviar, or both, on top of the salmon. Serve with the Sundried Tomato, Fresh Herb, and Fettucine Pancakes (page 127), if desired.

Recommended Wine: A rich, dry, earthy white wine, such as a Chassagne-Montrachet from Burgundy.

### SERVES: 4

1 ¼ to 1 ½ pounds boneless salmon fillet, with skin

Salt to taste

White pepper to taste

OYSTER AND CHIVE SAUCE

½ teaspoon virgin olive oil

1 tablespoon minced shallot

3 tablespoons sparkling wine or Champagne or Chardonnay

6 freshly shucked oysters, chopped, with liquor strained and reserved

½ cup plus 1 tablespoon cream

Salt to taste

White pepper to taste

2 egg yolks

1 ½ tablespoons sliced fresh chives

Holding a very sharp filleting knife at a 30-degree angle, cut the salmon fillet diagonally into 4 slices, separating them from the skin (the slices should be as thin and transparent as smoked salmon). If preparing in advance, keep the slices separated between sheet of plastic wrap in the refrigerator. Season with salt and white pepper.

To prepare the sauce, heat the olive oil in a small saucepan and sauté the shallot over medium heat for 2 to 3 minutes, or until light golden. Deglaze the pan with the sparkling wine and add the oyster liquor. Reduce the mixture by half. Add 5 tablespoons of the cream and bring to a boil. Reduce the heat and simmer for 3 to 4 minutes. Season with salt and white pepper.

Meanwhile, in a small mixing bowl, whisk the remaining 4 tablespoons of cream until stiff. Fold in the egg yolks. Pour this mixture into the saucepan while whisking over low heat. Stir continuously with a small whisk until the sauce thickens; do not let it boil or the egg yolk will curdle. Adjust the seasonings if necessary. Remove the saucepan from the heat and add the oysters and chives.

Preheat the broiler to high.

Cover each warm serving plate with the sauce. Lay the salmon slices on top of the sauce. When the broiler is hot, broil the salmon for 45 seconds to 1 minute, until the sauce is browned and the salmon is just opaque. Serve immediately.

# Tuna Steak on a Fondue of Scallions with Beets and Fresh Corn

*M*OST PEOPLE think of a fondue as a cheese dip, but in classic French cuisine the term also refers to a mixture of diced or minced vegetables that have been cooked slowly until they are completely soft. This visually striking dish is another that was developed by Fleur de Lys's chef de cuisine Rick Richardson. The meaty tuna stands up to the other assertive flavors—curry oil, ginger, scallions, and beets. When these flavors are combined, a slightly sweet, slightly acidic, and pleasingly aromatic dish emerges.

## CHEF'S NOTES

Allow at least 2 days to infuse the oil and about 40 minutes to prepare the dish. Tuna and beets may seem like an unusual pairing, but they are very effective together. The mildness of the tuna is complemented by the assertiveness of the beets, which introduce a sweet and sour element. The smooth tuna and firm beets also create a wonderful contrast of textures. I think beets are underrated and overlooked because they are inexpensive, uncomplicated, and always available. This recipe showcases them well. Use the curry oil to drizzle over scallops, grilled fish, or chicken. The oil will keep for up to 1 month in the refrigerator.

Recommended Wines: A soft and fruity Merlot or a fine Gewürztraminer from Alsace.

SERVES: 4

### CURRY-INFUSED OIL
3 1/2 tablespoons curry powder

1 1/2 tablespoons water

2 cups grapeseed oil

1 large ear fresh corn, husks and silk removed

### BEETS
3 beets, peeled and finely diced

2 tablespoons sugar

1 tablespoon Spanish sherry vinegar

Salt and pepper to taste

1 teaspoon water

1/2 teaspoon cornstarch

### FONDUE
2 teaspoons virgin olive oil

24 scallions, white and tender green parts only, cut on the bias into 1/4-inch-thick slices

1/2 teaspoon finely minced ginger

2 tablespoons cream

Salt and pepper to taste

2 tablespoons blanched, peeled, seeded, and diced tomato

### FISH
1 tablespoon virgin olive oil

4 sushi-quality tuna steaks (6 to 7 ounces each), about 1 inch thick

Salt and pepper to taste

1 1/2 tablespoons finely sliced fresh chives, for garnish

To prepare the curry oil, mix the curry powder and water in a bowl until a smooth paste forms (add more water if the paste forms solid chunks). Transfer the paste to a canning jar or wide-mouthed glass bottle and add the oil. Tightly seal and shake well. Let the curry oil sit at room temperature for at least 2 days. During the first day, shake the jar vigorously a couple of times to help develop a more intense flavor. After the second day, strain the oil through a coffee filter. Discard the solids and store the oil in the refrigerator.

Place the corn in a saucepan of boiling salted water. Boil for about 8 minutes, then shock in a bowl of cold water. Using a sharp knife, cut twenty 1 1/2-inch-long sections of corn kernels off the cobs and reserve.

Place the beets, sugar, and vinegar in a nonreactive saucepan and add enough water to just cover. Season with

salt and pepper and bring to a boil. Reduce the heat, cover, and simmer for 25 to 30 minutes, or until tender. Combine the water and cornstarch in a small bowl and stir into the beets. Adjust the seasonings, and set aside.

To prepare the fondue, heat the olive oil in a sauté pan or skillet and sauté the scallions over medium-high heat for 2 or 3 minutes, or until just barely tender. Add the ginger, cream, salt, and pepper, and continue cooking for 3 or 4 minutes, or until the cream thickens. Stir in the tomato, and adjust the seasonings if necessary. Set aside.

To prepare the fish, heat the olive oil in a heavy-bottomed skillet over high heat. Season both sides of the tuna with salt and pepper, and sear for 2 to 3 minutes on each side, or until browned but still rare. Keep warm.

Reheat the scallions and beets. To serve, gently warm the corn sections in a small sauté pan with $1/2$ teaspoon of the curry oil, and season with salt and pepper. Set 5 sections of corn around the edge of each warm serving plate, spacing them equally apart. Drizzle each corn mound with a few drops of the curry oil. Arrange the reheated scallions in the center of each plate, and spoon the reheated beets and their cooking broth between the corn sections. Place the tuna on top of the scallions and sprinkle with the chives. Serve immediately.

# Seared Tuna on Lightly Creamed Spinach with Sesame Oil Vinaigrette

THIS IS a very popular dish at Fleur de Lys, and it's easy to make at home. I recommend cooking tuna between rare to medium-rare; if it's cooked longer, it dries out and loses its distinctive flavor. The vinaigrette gives a slightly exotic touch and goes equally well with other fish, lobster, or poultry. It also makes a flavorful marinade for scallops, so you might consider making up a large batch and keeping it on hand.

## CHEF'S NOTES

Allow about 40 minutes to prepare. This is my favorite spinach recipe. I hope it will become your favorite one, too. You can reduce the quantities in the recipe by half and serve this dish as an appetizer. Alternatively, you can serve the tuna and vinaigrette over mixed lettuces as a salad. You can also serve this dish with Black Pepper Polenta (page 128), if you like.

Recommended Wines: A bone-dry California sparkling wine or an Alsatian Riesling.

SERVES: 4

### SESAME OIL VINAIGRETTE

- 1 tablespoon unseasoned rice vinegar or cider vinegar
- 1 tablespoon soy sauce
- 1 tablespoon freshly squeezed lemon juice
- $1/2$ teaspoon finely minced garlic
- $1/2$ teaspoon finely minced ginger
- Salt and pepper to taste
- $5 1/2$ tablespoons sesame oil

- 4 sushi-quality tuna steaks (6 to 7 ounces each), about 1 inch thick
- Salt and pepper to taste

### SPINACH

- 3 bunches spinach, stemmed (about 1 pound leaves)
- 1 teaspoon butter
- Salt and pepper to taste
- Pinch of sugar
- Pinch of freshly grated nutmeg (optional)
- 3 tablespoons cream

- $1/2$ teaspoon virgin olive oil
- $1/2$ teaspoon toasted black sesame seeds (optional)
- $1/2$ teaspoon toasted white sesame seeds (optional)

To prepare the vinaigrette, place the vinegar, soy sauce, lemon juice, garlic, ginger, salt, and pepper in a mixing bowl and whisk together. Whisk in the sesame oil until thoroughly incorporated. (Alternatively, combine all the ingredients in a food processor or blender and mix until incorporated.) Set aside.

Trim any dark oily portions from the tuna and discard. Season the tuna with salt and pepper and brush both sides liberally with some of the vinaigrette (reserve the remaining vinaigrette). Set the tuna aside on a plate in the refrigerator while preparing the spinach.

Bring a large saucepan with 2 or 3 quarts of salted water to a boil. Add the spinach to the water and cook for about 5 minutes. Drain, and when cool enough to handle, squeeze out the excess moisture with your hands. When the spinach is as dry as possible, chop finely. Melt the butter in a separate heavy saucepan over medium-high heat and stir in the chopped spinach, salt, pepper, sugar, and nutmeg. Cook for 1 minute, stir in the cream, and simmer for 2 to 3 minutes. Reduce the heat the low to prevent the spinach from sticking to the pan, cover, and keep warm while cooking the tuna.

Heat the olive oil in a heavy skillet or nonstick sauté pan over high heat. Sear the tuna for 2 to 3 minutes on each side, or until browned on the outside but still rare; turn only once.

Place the creamed spinach in the center of warm serving plates. Slice each of the tuna steaks into four equal pieces and arrange on top of the spinach with the rare sides facing up. Spoon the remaining vinaigrette all around the spinach, sprinkle with the sesame seeds, and serve immediately.

# Maine Lobster Macaroni and Cheese "Au Gratin"

WHAT BETTER food to match with lobster than the good old everyday macaroni and cheese? The inspiration for this dish came from Jacques Maximin, with whom I worked at Le Chantecler in Nice. I made it once for Roger Vergé in Brazil, and he enjoyed it so much, he often asked for it after that, which was the ultimate compliment. This is the only recipe in this chapter that contains plenty of calories and is this rich, but making an exception to the rule once in a while is good for the soul!

## CHEF'S NOTES

Allow about 1 hour to prepare. Some connoisseurs believe that female lobsters taste a little richer. I invite you to test this theory for yourself. Whatever the gender, lobster is best stored in the refrigerator, in a tightly wrapped damp newspaper, **Le Monde**, perhaps.

Recommended Wines: A great white Burgundy, such as Corton Charlemagne or Chassagne Montrachet.

SERVES: 4

3 tablespoons white wine vinegar

4 live Maine lobsters (about 1 pound each)

Salt to taste

White pepper to taste

1 tablespoon butter

⅓ cup finely minced shallots

¼ cup very finely diced carrots

¼ cup very finely diced celery

1 tablespoon cognac

2 tablespoons port

1½ cups plus 2½ tablespoons cream or half-and-half, chilled

1 Bouquet Garni (page 22)

1 egg yolk

8 ounces elbow macaroni or small pasta shells

3 tablespoons freshly grated Gruyère cheese

To prepare the lobster, bring 1½ gallons salted water to a boil in a large stockpot. Add the vinegar and then add 2 of the lobsters, head first. Cover tightly with a lid, and cook for 3 minutes. Remove the lobsters, drain, and set aside to cool. Repeat with the remaining 2 lobsters. Break the lobsters in two where the tail meets the body. Using scissors, cut the underside of the tail and remove the meat in one piece. Break off the claws, carefully crack the shells, and remove the claw meat in a single piece. Cut the bodies in half lengthwise, and remove and discard the greyish, milky sand sacks located near the eyes. Remove the soft green strip of tomalley and dark green coral and reserve.

Season the lobster meat with salt and white pepper. Heat the butter in a large nonstick skillet, and gently sauté the lobster meat over medium heat for 2 minutes. Remove the claw meat and continue to sauté the rest of the lobster meat for 1 to 2 minutes. Transfer the lobster meat to a work surface and let cool slightly. Cut the meat into ¼-inch-thick slices and set aside.

In the same skillet, sweat the shallots, carrots, and celery over medium heat for 3 minutes. Add the cognac, port, 1½ cups of the cream, the Bouquet Garni, salt, and pepper. Reduce the heat to a simmer, and cook for 5 to 7 minutes. Cover the skillet, remove from the heat, and set the sauce aside.

Whisk the remaining 2½ tablespoons of cream in a small mixing bowl until thick. Fold in the egg yolk and keep refrigerated.

Cook the macaroni in a large saucepan of boiling water until just tender, about 10 minutes. Drain in a colander and set aside.

Preheat the broiler. Return the sauce to low heat and warm gently. Whisk the reserved lobster tomalley and coral into the sauce, and then stir in the cheese, lobster meat, and macaroni. Increase the heat to high and quickly bring to a boil. Adjust the seasonings if necessary.

Divide the mixture equally between individual warm gratin dishes. Pour the reserved cream-egg mixture over the macaroni, and place the gratin dishes under the broiler until golden brown. Serve immediately.

# Sautéed Santa Barbara Shrimp with Chanterelles and Fresh-Picked Almonds

FOR TWO or three summer months, fresh-picked almonds and chanterelle mushrooms are both available. This recipe, in which the contrasting but complementary flavors and textures of the almonds and chanterelles are a perfect combination, gives you an undeniable excuse to use them. Fresh-picked almonds tend to be overlooked, but they are so tender and flavorful, it's a sin not to take advantage of them when you can, especially with great seafood. The tender, sweet Santa Barbara shrimp are similar to the European **langoustines**, or prawns, but spot prawns or other shrimp can be used interchangeably.

## CHEF'S NOTES

Allow about 1½ hours to prepare. The broth can be prepared ahead of time, and any unused can be frozen. Fresh-picked almonds are available in late summer and early fall. Alternatively, buy blanched mature almonds and reblanch for 5 minutes, or until they become tender.

Recommended Wine: A full-bodied Chardonnay.

SERVES: 4

**SHRIMP BROTH**

24 fresh Santa Barbara or other extra-large shrimp (about 2 pounds with heads on)

½ tablespoon virgin olive oil

3 tablespoons finely diced carrot

3 tablespoons finely diced onion

2 tablespoons finely diced celery

3 tablespoons finely diced leek

1 cup dry white wine

1 tomato, blanched, peeled, seeded, and finely diced

1 teaspoon minced garlic

½ tablespoon minced fresh tarragon

1 sprig fresh thyme

Salt and pepper to taste

1 tablespoon virgin olive oil

8 ounces small chanterelle mushrooms

24 fresh-picked almonds, peeled, or reblanched blanched almonds

1 tablespoon finely minced shallot

½ teaspoon minced fresh tarragon

1 small tomato, blanched, peeled, seeded, and diced

1 tablespoon butter

½ cup finely julienned carrot, blanched, for garnish

1 large handful fresh chives (with buds attached, if possible), cut into 1-inch slices, for garnish

To prepare the broth, remove the heads, shells, and veins from the shrimp and reserve. Keep the shrimp refrigerated. Heat the olive oil in a heavy-bottomed saucepan and sauté the carrot, onion, celery, and leek over medium heat for 6 or 7 minutes, stirring often, until just golden brown.

Add the shrimp heads and shells, and cook for 6 or 7 minutes longer. Add the wine, tomato, garlic, tarragon, and thyme, and cook for 5 minutes longer. Add enough water to just cover the shells, and bring to a simmer. Lightly season with salt and pepper, and gently cook, uncovered, for 45 minutes.

Strain the broth through a fine sieve into a large bowl, pressing down hard on the solids to extract all the liquid and flavors. Discard the solids and reserve the broth.

Season the reserved shrimp with salt and pepper. Heat ½ tablespoon of the olive oil in a large sauté pan and sauté the shrimp over high heat for 1 or 2 minutes on each side, or until just cooked through. Transfer to a warm

platter, cover with aluminum foil, and keep warm.

Immediately heat the remaining $^1/_2$ tablespoon of olive oil in the same pan. Add the mushrooms and sauté over high heat, tossing occasionally, for 2 to 3 minutes. Season with salt and pepper, and add the almonds and shallot. Cook for 2 minutes longer, tossing occasionally. Transfer to a warm platter, cover with aluminum foil, and set aside.

Over high heat, deglaze the pan with $1^1/_4$ cups of the reserved Shrimp Broth, and reduce by half. Stir in the tarragon, tomato, and butter, and season with salt and pepper. Keep warm.

Arrange 5 shrimp in the shape of a pinwheel in the center of each warm serving plate, with 1 additional shrimp positioned vertically in the middle of the pinwheels. Place the chanterelle mixture in the center. Spoon the broth over and around the shrimp, and sprinkle the carrot over the shrimp. Garnish with the chives, and serve immediately.

# Poultry and Meat Entrées

ALSACE IS famous for its meat products and is especially renowned for the quality and flavor of its pork, which is featured prominently in the region's rich gastronomic history, dating all the way back to ancient Roman times. In addition to different cuts of fresh pork, the meat is used for charcuterie—sausages, terrines, hams, and various smoked cuts. Other popular meats in Alsace are rabbit and chicken, and it is common to find these animals being kept and fattened up in backyards, even in the towns of the region. Duck and geese are also popular, for their meat as well as for the delicacy that Alsace is also famous for—foie gras. During hunting season, the Vosges Mountains are a prolific source of wild game, such as venison, wild boar, pheasant, and partridge. Although I am fond of them all, I crave venison, beef, veal chops, and chicken the most.

Most of these meats are also available in the United States, and while some of them are perfect candidates for formal restaurant-style dishes, other meats are more suited to home cooking. Because I like cooking with all kinds and cuts of meats, whether they lend themselves to formal or informal preparations, I have included recipes that range from the casual and rustic dishes Chantal and I like to make at home to the elegant and refined dishes we serve at Fleur de Lys. They are all interesting in some way, and none of them is difficult to execute.

At the restaurant, we serve as much meat as fish, which is perhaps surprising. The 6- or 7-ounce fillets we serve are modest portions by traditional American standards, but a much more healthful way to enjoy meat. The days of oversized slabs of red meat are thankfully numbered. We also tend to serve lean cuts that are enhanced by side dishes, garnishes, and other ingredients rather than elaborate or calorific sauces. We find that even our most health-conscious customers order meat dishes as a result.

In the United States as well as France, the consumption of meat has always depended on geographical location. In San Francisco, I have the privilege of creating dishes for customers who are an exception to the rule—our guests order fish **and** meats with enthusiasm.

# Chicken and Spinach Wraps with Hazelnut Sauce

*I*N JULY 1993, I was invited to the White House with Dr. Dean Ornish to demonstrate some lowfat and vegetarian recipes and to discuss some of the techniques that I use to promote healthfulness and heighten flavor. I developed this lowfat dish for that occasion, and the **New York Times** printed the recipe in their coverage of the visit. It's based on a classic dish, **poularde en vessie**, a cleaned and cognac-rinsed pig's bladder stuffed with chicken and truffles and poached in a consommé, that Paul Bocuse is famed for serving. This is a much simpler version that uses humble plastic wrap instead of a bladder; the juices are sealed in just the same, and it's a healthy cooking technique that can also be used for fish, veal, rabbit, and squab. Adding hazelnut oil to the reduced sauce creates an explosion of flavor, without the calories of nuts or a dairy-based sauce.

## CHEF'S NOTES

Allow 35 to 40 minutes to prepare. You can serve this dish hot, warm, or cold, and whole or sliced. The rolls can be prepared up to 1 day in advance, making it a perfect buffet or potluck dish. Stuffed and Braised Potatoes (page 132), or Braised Celery Hearts (page 135) make good accompaniments to this dish.

Recommended Wine: A sturdy red wine, such as a Santenay from Burgundy.

SERVES: 4

2 teaspoons virgin olive oil

1 clove garlic, lightly crushed

1¼ pounds young spinach leaves

Salt and pepper to taste

4 skinless and boneless chicken breast halves (about 5 ounces each), trimmed

HAZELNUT SAUCE

2 tablespoons port

2 cups Brown Chicken Broth (page 23)

2 teaspoons cornstarch

1½ tablespoons hazelnut oil

1 small tomato, blanched, peeled, seeded, and finely diced

1 tablespoon minced fresh parsley

Salt and pepper to taste

Heat the olive oil in a large sauté pan over high heat. Add the garlic, and just before the oil begins to smoke, add the spinach. Season with salt and pepper, and sauté, stirring constantly with a wooden spoon, for about 4 or 5 minutes, or until the spinach is wilted and all the liquid has evaporated. Remove the garlic clove and discard. Transfer the spinach to a platter and let cool. When the spinach has cooled, squeeze out the excess moisture with your hands. Divide the spinach into 4 equal portions, and set aside.

Using the blade of a large knife or cleaver, lightly flatten the chicken breasts until ½ to ⅔ inch thick. (Alternatively, cover the chicken breast with plastic wrap and lightly pound with the bottom of a heavy sauté pan or skillet.) Season with salt and pepper. Lay a 12 by 12-inch square piece of plastic wrap on a work surface. Place a flattened chicken breast in the center of the plastic wrap and add a line of spinach in the center of the chicken. Lift up the plastic wrap so the chicken flips over in a roll, sealing the spinach inside. Without rolling the plastic wrap inside the chicken, roll the chicken into a cylinder and seal with the wrap. Tie both ends of the plastic wrap with kitchen twine and repeat for the remaining chicken. Keep refrigerated.

To prepare the Hazelnut Sauce, place the port in a saucepan and reduce by half over medium-high heat. Mix the broth and cornstarch in a bowl, increase the heat to high, add the broth mixture, and reduce again by half. Vigorously stir in the hazelnut oil until emulsified. Gently stir in the tomato and parsley, season with salt and pepper, and keep warm.

Bring 1 gallon of water to a boil in a large saucepan or stockpot. Reduce the heat to a simmer, and slowly lower the wrapped chicken breasts into the water. Poach for 10 to 12 minutes, remove from the water, and place on a platter. Cut one end off the plastic wrap, and holding the tied end, squeeze out the chicken breasts. Slice each breast, on the bias, into 4 or 5 slices. Fan out the slices on warm serving plates, and spoon the Hazelnut Sauce over the top of the chicken. Serve immediately.

# Brazilian Chicken with Shrimp and Peanut Sauce

WHEN I moved to Sao Paulo to open La Cuisine du Soleil, I started taking cooking classes to learn as much as I could about Brazilian cuisine. This was one of the recipes I studied that's popular in the northern part of the country. The combination of chicken and shrimp is typically Brazilian. I find the flavors of the whole dish exotic and exciting.

## CHEF'S NOTES

Allow about 1 hour 15 minutes to prepare. Serve with long-grain rice, pasta, or mashed potato. The Brazilian name for the dish, **xinxin**, is a Portuguese word, pronounced "shin shin."

Recommended Wine: A rich Alsatian Gewürztraminer, Pinot Gris, or peppery Pinot Noir.

1 free-range chicken (about 3 to 4 pounds), at room temperature, rinsed, patted dry, and cut into 8 pieces (4 breast pieces, 2 thighs, and 2 legs)

4 tablespoons freshly squeezed lime juice

2 teaspoons finely minced garlic

Salt and pepper to taste

$1\frac{1}{2}$ tablespoons virgin olive oil

1 onion, finely minced

1 green bell pepper, seeded and finely diced

4 tomatoes, blanched, peeled, seeded, and finely diced

$\frac{1}{3}$ cup ground toasted peanuts

1 jalapeño chile, seeded and minced

2 bay leaves

$\frac{1}{2}$ cup Brown Chicken Broth (page 23)

$1\frac{1}{2}$ cups canned unsweetened coconut milk

12 extra-large Gulf shrimp (about 12 ounces), peeled and deveined

2 tablespoons minced fresh cilantro

Place the chicken in a large mixing bowl and add 3 tablespoons of the lime juice and $1\frac{1}{2}$ teaspoons of the garlic. Season with salt and pepper, and mix thoroughly. Refrigerate for 15 minutes.

In a large casserole, heat the olive oil and sauté the onion over medium-high heat for 4 to 5 minutes, or until translucent, stirring frequently. Add the bell pepper and cook for 2 minutes longer. Stir in the tomatoes, peanuts, jalapeño, bay leaves, salt, and pepper, and cook for a further 8 to 10 minutes more, stirring occasionally, until the mixture thickens.

Stir in the chicken and the marinade, and continue cooking for 5 minutes, turning the chicken pieces once. Add the broth and coconut milk, cover the casserole, and simmer for 25 to 30 minutes, or until the chicken is cooked through.

Meanwhile, place the shrimp in a mixing bowl and add the remaining 1 tablespoon of lime juice and $\frac{1}{2}$ teaspoon of garlic. Season with salt and pepper, and mix thoroughly. Refrigerate for 5 to 8 minutes at the most (the lime juice will begin to "cook" the shrimp after that).

Stir the shrimp and marinade into the casserole and cook for 4 to 5 minutes, or until the shrimp turn pink and begin to curl (be careful not to overcook the shrimp or they will be tough). Adjust the seasonings if necessary.

Stir in the cilantro just before serving; the sauce should be thick. Spoon onto serving plates.

# Roasted Turkey with Wild Mushroom, Fresh Herb, and Chestnut Stuffing

THIS IS a typical French recipe for Christmas turkey (chestnut stuffing is very popular back home). I developed this version for an article on Thanksgiving dinner at Michael Bauer's request for the **San Francisco Chronicle**. Whether you prepare this delicious fare for Thanksgiving, Christmas, or another special celebration, you will be delighted by the hearty, satisfying flavors of this recipe. Chestnuts have a uniquely dense texture that's almost vegetablelike. I don't use canned chestnuts for this recipe because their quality and texture are inferior. Instead, you can substitute 1 pound of water chestnuts or brussels sprouts blanched for 10 minutes.

## CHEF'S NOTES

Allow about 1 hour 15 minutes to prepare and about 1 hour 45 minutes to 2 hours for roasting.To remove the shell and bitter skin of chestnuts, make an incision on the flat side, place on a baking sheet, and roast in the oven at 425° for 20 to 25 minutes. This will make the shell crack and facilitate its removal. Serve with Stuffed and Braised Potatoes (page 132), or roasted parsnips. When the next opportunity to serve American-style gravy arises, try using this light, flavorful sauce for a Provenal touch.

Recommended Wine: A meaty California Pinot Noir or red Burgundy such as Chambertin.

### SERVES: 10 TO 12

### STUFFING

1 ½ pounds fresh pork fat

1 ½ pounds boneless veal loin or boneless and skinless chicken breasts

8 ounces chicken livers

2 tablespoons virgin olive oil

¼ cup minced shallots

3 cloves garlic, finely minced

8 ounces assorted wild mushrooms, stemmed and finely diced

½ cup finely diced celery

Salt and pepper to taste

2 tablespoons port

¼ cup cognac

3 eggs

1 tablespoon minced fresh rosemary needles

1 ½ tablespoons minced fresh thyme

2 tablespoons finely sliced fresh chives

2 tablespoons minced fresh parsley

1 ½ pounds fresh chestnuts, roasted and peeled (see Chef's Note)

¼ cup pistachios (optional)

### TURKEY

1 (12-pound) free-range turkey

Salt and pepper to taste

3 tablespoons virgin olive oil

### SAUCE

1 tablespoon minced fresh rosemary needles

3 tablespoons minced shallots

1 cup port

4 cups Brown Chicken Broth (page 23)

1 tablespoon cornstarch

2 tablespoons water

2 bunches watercress, for garnish

To prepare the stuffing, mince together the pork fat, veal loin, and chicken livers in a meat grinder.

Heat the olive oil in a sauté pan or skillet, and sauté the shallots over high heat for about 4 minutes, or until translucent. Add the garlic, mushrooms, and celery, and cook for 5 minutes, stirring continuously. Stir in the ground meat and cook for 5 minutes, still stirring continuously. Season with salt and pepper, and stir in the port and cognac. Remove from the heat and transfer to a large mixing bowl to cool.

When the mixture has cooled, thoroughly mix in the eggs and all of the herbs. Adjust the seasonings if necessary, and gently stir in the chestnuts and pistachios, being careful not to break the nuts. Refrigerate for 20 minutes.

Preheat the oven to 350° (about 30 minutes before you are ready to roast the turkey).

Thoroughly rinse the turkey inside and out, and pat dry with paper towels. Season the cavity with salt and pepper. Loosely stuff the neck cavity first by placing the turkey breast side down. Pull the neck skin over the filling and secure it to the back bone with 1 or 2 skewers.

Turn the turkey breast side up, and fill the main cavity with the stuffing. Place a double layer of aluminum foil over the exposed filling, and tie the drumsticks together with kitchen twine.

Rub the turkey with the olive oil and season the outside with salt and pepper. Place the turkey, breast side up, in a roasting pan.

Roast the turkey in the oven for about 1 hour 45 minutes to 2 hours, or until the internal temperature reaches 165°. If the turkey begins to brown too much, cover loosely with aluminum foil. Remove the roasted turkey from the oven and allow to rest for 20 minutes before carving.

To prepare the sauce, combine the rosemary, shallots, and port in a saucepan and bring to a boil. Reduce the mixture to $1/3$ cup over high heat. Add the broth and simmer for 10 to 15 minutes. Combine the cornstarch and water in a small bowl, stir into the sauce, and simmer for 2 minutes. Adjust the seasonings if necessary and keep warm.

Transfer the turkey to a warm platter, and garnish with the watercress. Carve and serve with the sauce.

# Roasted Chicken Breasts on Leeks with Truffle Sauce

THIS RECIPE uses lacelike caul fat, a thin pork membrane, to hold the stuffing around the chicken breasts, keeping them moist and juicy. Using caul fat in this way is a traditional French technique. The caul fat melts away during the cooking process. If you prefer not to use it, or if you just want to take a shortcut with this recipe, omit the mousseline step, sauté the chicken in olive oil, and serve on a bed of the leeks, topped with the truffle sauce.

## CHEF'S NOTES

Allow about $1^{1}/_{2}$ hours to prepare. You can order caul fat from your butcher; it freezes well. For a more colorful presentation, serve with cooked baby carrots or roasted cherry tomatoes.

Recommended Wine: A sweet Merlot or red Burgundy, such as a Morey-St-Denis.

SERVES: 4

### CHICKEN-VEGETABLE MOUSSELINE

- 1 skinless and boneless large chicken breast half (about 6 ounces), finely diced
- 2 egg whites
- Pinch of salt and pepper
- 2 tablespoons cream
- 1 tablespoon virgin olive oil
- 3 tablespoons finely minced carrot
- 3 tablespoons finely minced onion
- 3 tablespoons finely minced celery
- 2 teaspoons finely minced garlic
- 1 sprig fresh thyme, finely minced
- 4 large skinless and boneless chicken breast halves (about 6 ounces each), trimmed
- Salt and pepper to taste

- 1 teaspoon virgin olive oil
- 8 to 12 ounces pork caul fat

### LEEK FONDUE

- $^{1}/_{2}$ tablespoon virgin olive oil
- 4 leeks, white and tender green parts only, cut in half lengthwise and sliced crosswise
- $^{1}/_{2}$ teaspoon finely minced garlic
- Salt and pepper to taste

### TRUFFLE SAUCE

- 1 truffle (about 1 ounce), julienned
- 2 tablespoons port
- 1 cup Brown Chicken Broth (page 23)
- 1 teaspoon cornstarch
- Salt and pepper to taste

- 1 tablespoon finely sliced fresh chives, for garnish

Thoroughly chill all the ingredients for the mousseline (to prevent the mixture from breaking). To prepare the mousseline, process the diced chicken in a food processor, pulsing about 5 times. Add the egg whites, season with salt and pepper, and pulse again to mix. With the machine running, slowly pour the cream through the feed tube and blend until thoroughly incorporated. Transfer to a chilled mixing bowl, and chill thoroughly.

Heat the olive oil in a sauté pan or skillet and sauté the carrot, onion, celery, and garlic over medium-high heat for 3 to 4 minutes. Add the thyme, season with salt and pepper, and transfer to a mixing bowl. Chill thoroughly.

When both mixtures are chilled, fold the vegetables into the cream mixture until thoroughly combined. Keep refrigerated.

Season the chicken breasts with salt and pepper. Heat the olive oil in a sauté pan or skillet and sear the chicken breasts over high heat for 1 minute. Remove and set aside.

Lay out the caul fat and divide into 4 rectangles, 5 by 7 inches. Using half of the mousseline, spread a thin layer in the center of each rectangle, approximately the same size as the chicken breast. Lay the seared chicken breasts on top, and cover with the remaining mousseline. Fold the long side of the caul fat (as if wrapping a package with paper) over to firmly cover and enclose the chicken and filling. Keep refrigerated.

To prepare the fondue, heat the olive oil in a heavy-bottomed saucepan. Add the leeks and garlic, season with salt and pepper, and sweat over medium heat for 8 to 10 minutes, stirring occasionally, until soft but not brown. Keep warm.

Preheat the oven to 375°.

Place the chicken wrapped in caul fat in an ovenproof pan or skillet and roast in the oven for about 10 minutes. Transfer the chicken to a platter, cover with aluminum foil, and keep warm.

To prepare the sauce, pour out the excess grease and particles from the ovenproof pan or skillet in which the chicken roasted, and add the truffle. Sauté for 1 minute over medium-high heat. Deglaze the pan with the port, scraping loose any particles that have adhered to the pan, and simmer for 1 minute.

Combine the broth and cornstarch in a bowl, and stir into the truffle mixture. Reduce the mixture by half over medium high heat, about 5 minutes. Adjust the seasonings if necessary, and keep warm.

Place the leeks in the center of warm serving plates. Slice the chicken breasts on the bias into 4 or 5 slices each, and arrange on top of the leeks. Spoon the Truffle Sauce around the leeks and sprinkle the chives over the top of the dish. Serve immediately.

# Roasted Quail Stuffed with Swiss Chard and Pine Nuts with a Red Wine–Thyme

QUAIL IS a popular game bird in France, just as it is here in the United States. I use this precooked stuffing because the delicate, lean quail cooks so fast, it becomes tough if it's in the oven long enough to cook a raw stuffing. The red wine reduction provides a twist—you might expect white wine to best match the quail, but not so in this case. The reduction substantially contributes to the rich flavors of this simple, comforting dish.

## CHEF'S NOTES

Allow about 1 hour to prepare. The stuffing can be prepared ahead of time and the birds are quick to stuff, so this dish is ideal for entertaining. If you wish, roast wholegarlic cloves, shallots cut in half, and carrots cut in 1-inch rounds with the quail and serve the birds on a bed of the roasted vegetables.

Recommended Wine: A soft, fruity Pinot Noir.

### SERVES: 4

### STUFFING

1 tablespoon currants

1 or 2 slices bacon, chopped into ¼-inch strips

3 tablespoons minced onion

1 small clove garlic, finely minced

1½ pounds leafy, young Swiss chard, stalks removed, cut into ½-inch-wide strips

Salt and pepper to taste

1 tablespoon pine nuts

4 large boneless quail

½ tablespoon virgin olive oil

Salt and pepper to taste

1 small carrot, diced

1 small onion, diced

### RED WINE–THYME REDUCTION

½ cup Pinot Noir or Cabernet Sauvignon or other red wine

2 sprigs fresh thyme

1½ cups Brown Chicken Broth (page 23) or Vegetable Broth (page 26)

1 bunch fresh thyme, for garnish

Preheat oven to 375°. Place the currants in a small bowl, cover with warm water, and let soak for 10 minutes. Drain and reserve.

Place the bacon in a large sauté pan or skillet and sauté until crisp. Remove the bacon and drain on paper towels. Drain off all but 1 tablespoon of the bacon fat, add the onion, and sauté over medium-high heat for 3 minutes, until translucent. Add the garlic, increase the heat to high, and add the Swiss chard. Season with salt and pepper, and sauté for about 5 or 6 minutes, or until the leaves are wilted but still green, and the liquid has evaporated. Remove from the heat and let the stuffing cool. Stir in the bacon, pine nuts, and currants. Adjust the seasonings if necessary.

Fill each of the quail with the stuffing, brush with the olive oil, and season with salt and pepper. Place the quail on their sides in a small roasting pan (this promotes even cooking and coloring), and arrange the diced carrot and onion all around them. Roast the quail in the oven for 4 minutes, then turn them breast side up, and roast for 4 to 5 minutes longer. Cover with aluminum foil, and keep warm.

To prepare the reduction, drain off the excess fat from the roasting pan and place the pan on top of the stove over medium-high heat. Deglaze the pan with the red wine, add the thyme, and bring to a boil. Reduce the mixture to 2 tablespoons, add the broth, and simmer for 5 to 6 minutes. Adjust the seasonings if necessary and strain through a fine sieve into a gravy boat.

Place the quail on warm serving plates and spoon the reduction over them. Garnish with the thyme sprigs, and serve.

# Squab Breasts Baked in Puff Pastry–Capped Potato Shells

*I*N CLASSICAL French cooking, preparing meat à l'étuvé involves placing it on a bed of vegetables in a casserole, covering with a lid, and braising very slowly without adding any cooking liquid. I thought it would be interesting to recreate this method with squab breast, using a potato sealed with puff pastry instead of a casserole. This way, the natural juices infuse the meat, integrating the flavors of the whole dish.

## CHEF'S NOTES

Allow about 4 to 6 hours to marinate the squab and about 1 hour to prepare. This is another good dish for entertaining as it can mostly be prepared ahead of time. The potato shells can be made up to 1 day ahead. Just store the baked shells upside down on a damp towel. If you wish, serve the squab with cooked baby vegetables, arranged around the potato shells, garnished with fresh thyme.

Recommended Wine: A relatively mature red Burgundy or California Pinot Noir.

SERVES: 4

4 large skinless and boneless squab breast halves (about 2¹/₂ ounces each) or double quail breasts, or 2 single chicken breasts, cut in half

MARINADE

¹/₂ cup minced onions

¹/₄ cup peeled and finely diced carrot

1 clove garlic

1 Bouquet Garni (page 22)

¹/₂ tablespoon juniper berries, crushed

¹/₂ tablespoon cracked pepper

1 cup Pinot Noir or Cabernet or other robust red wine

4 russet potatoes (about 12 ounces each), unpeeled

¹/₂ tablespoon virgin olive oil

2 small leeks, white part only, split in half lengthwise and thinly sliced

1 teaspoon finely minced garlic

Salt and pepper to taste

2 tablespoons finely sliced fresh chives or minced fresh basil

4 ounces puff pastry dough

1 egg yolk, whisked

1 teaspoon tomato paste

2 cups Brown Chicken Broth (page 23)

2 teaspoons cornstarch

Place the squab breasts in a nonreactive baking dish and add the onions, carrot, garlic, Bouquet Garni, juniper berries, and pepper. Pour the wine over the squab, cover the dish, and marinate in the refrigerator for 4 to 6 hours.

Cut a ³/₄-inch slice from the end of each potato. Using a melon baller, hollow out the potatoes from one end, taking care not to break through the skin or the other end. Discard the scooped-out flesh, or use for soup or another purpose (store in water to prevent oxidation).

Bring a large saucepan of salted water to a boil and add the potato shells. Lower the heat and simmer gently for 8 to 10 minutes, or until tender. Carefully remove the potato shells and drain.

Heat the olive oil in a small heavy-bottomed saucepan, add the leeks and garlic, and season with salt and pepper. Cover and sauté over medium-high heat, stirring occasionally, for 5 to 8 minutes, or until soft but not brown. Stir in 1 tablespoon of the chives, remove from the heat, and let cool.

Preheat the oven to 375°.

Drain the marinade from the squab breasts, scraping off the vegetables and herbs back into the marinade and reserve. Season the breasts on both sides with salt and pepper.

Cover a baking sheet with parchment paper and stand the potato shells up on the baking sheet. Fill each potato shell with about 1 tablespoon of the leek mixture, and place a squab breast over the leeks. Cover the squab with about ¹/₂ tablespoon of the leek mixture, spreading it out evenly; the leeks should not come up higher than the edge of the potatoes.

Roll out the pastry dough on a lightly floured work surface to a thickness of ¹/₁₆ inch. With a knife, cut out 4 ovals just a little larger than the top of the potatoes. Brush the dough and the edge of the potatoes with the egg yolk. Lay the dough over the filling, and press very lightly to form a seal. Place the potatoes in the oven and cook for 12 to 14 minutes, or until the pastry dough is golden brown.

Meanwhile, strain the marinade into a saucepan, and add back the Bouquet Garni. Bring the mixture to a boil and stir in the tomato paste. Reduce by half. Combine the broth and cornstarch in a bowl, and add to the pan. Simmer over medium heat until reduced to ³/₄ cup. Remove the Bouquet Garni, adjust the seasonings if necessary, and stir in the remaining 1 tablespoon of chives. Place the potatoes in the center of warm serving plates, spoon the broth around, and serve immediately.

# Lamb Chops Wrapped in Julienned Potatoes with a Rich Merlot and Vanilla Bean Sauce

*I* FIRST MADE this entrée for a dinner held at Fleur de Lys for Andy Lawlor, a prominent wine collector and gourmet. It has since become a signature dish, and the sauce elicits more comments and compliments than any other. I created it because Merlot is often described as having vanilla tones, and I was curious to see if adding vanilla would pull out distinct but subtle flavors. Voila! It worked well.

### CHEF'S NOTES

Allow about 45 minutes to prepare. The technique of wrapping the lamb in potato to seal in the flavor works equally well for chicken breasts, salmon, and most seafood. Serve with a frisée salad, if desired.

Recommended Wine: A big, intense, spicy California Merlot.

### SERVES: 4

**MERLOT AND VANILLA BEAN SAUCE**

- 1/2 teaspoon virgin olive oil
- 2 tablespoons finely minced shallots
- 1 clove garlic, finely minced
- 1/2 cup Merlot
- 1 1/2 cups Brown Chicken Broth (page 23)
- 1 1/2 teaspoons cornstarch
- 1 tablespoon port
- 1/3 vanilla bean
- Salt and pepper to taste

**LAMB**

- 3 tablespoons plus 1 teaspoon virgin olive oil
- 8 cloves garlic, blanched
- Salt and pepper to taste
- 8 lamb chops (3/4 to 1 inch thick, about 1 1/2 to 1 3/4 pounds), trimmed
- 4 russet potatoes (about 8 ounces each), peeled
- 4 sprigs watercress, for garnish
- 8 cloves roasted garlic, for garnish

To prepare the sauce, heat the olive oil in a saucepan and sweat the shallots over medium heat for 5 to 6 minutes. Add the garlic and cook for 1 minute. Stir in the wine and simmer for 5 minutes, or until almost dry. Mix the broth, cornstarch, and port in a bowl, add to the pan, and deglaze. Split the vanilla bean in half lengthwise and scrape the seeds into the saucepan. Add the vanilla bean pod, and simmer very gently for 8 to 10 minutes. Season with salt and pepper and keep warm.

Preheat the oven to 375°. To prepare the lamb, heat 1 teaspoon of the olive oil in a small sauté pan and sauté the garlic over medium-high heat for 2 to 3 minutes, or until golden brown. Season with salt and pepper, and set aside. Season the lamb chops with salt and pepper on both sides. Make an incision in the side of each chop large enough to hold a garlic clove, and insert the cooked garlic. Using a mandoline, julienne the potatoes into very fine strips. (Do not rinse them; the starch is needed to bind them together.) Season with salt and pepper and toss to coat. Gently squeeze out all the moisture from the strips. Working quickly so that the potatoes do not oxidize, lay out a thin layer of strips the size of a lamb chop on a work surface. Place a chop on top of the potatoes and cover with another thin layer of potatoes, making sure that the chop is completely encased (except for the bone). Squeeze the covered chop firmly between your hands to extract any remaining moisture and to compact and bind together the potatoes. Quickly repeat for the remaining chops. Immediately heat the remaining 3 tablespoons of olive oil in a large ovenproof sauté pan or skillet. Sear the chops over medium-high heat for 3 minutes, or until the potatoes are golden on one side. Turn the chops and place the pan in the oven for 8 to 9 minutes for medium-rare; adding more oil to the pan if necessary. Transfer the chops to a warm serving platter. Garnish with the watercress. Serve immediately (before the crust becomes soggy), with the sauce and roasted garlic on the side.

# Whole Grain Mustard–Glazed Lamb Loin with a Tarragon Infusion

*L*AMB IS one of our most popular entrées at Fleur de Lys, and although many people enjoy eating it in restaurants, few cook it at home. This is a shame, but I understand how it happens because good cuts of lamb are not always available in supermarkets. When purchasing lamb, buy cuts that have a layer of fat, then trim after cooking. Marbled or fattier cuts are more tender and give the meat flavor that remains even after the fat has been trimmed. Tarragon, like rosemary and thyme, seems particularly suited to lamb.

## CHEF'S NOTES

Allow at least 6 hours (and up to overnight) for marinating and about 35 minutes to prepare. The Mustard Glaze complements the lamb perfectly, but it's optional, especially if you are concerned about using cream or eggs. Marinating meat by seasoning and sealing it in plastic wrap requires less oil than the traditional method of marinating, and I think the direct contact with the herbs and spices results in a more intense flavor. The Vegetable Ragout accented with an Herbed Broth (page 123) makes a perfect accompaniment for this dish.

Recommended Wines: A rich, earthy California Cabernet Sauvignon or a red Bordeaux, like Graves.

SERVES: 4

2 lamb loins, or rib eyes from 2 racks, trimmed (about 10 ounces each)

1 1/2 tablespoons virgin olive oil

4 large sprigs fresh tarragon

### MUSTARD GLAZE

3 tablespoons cream, chilled

1 egg yolk

1/2 tablespoon whole-grain or Dijon-style mustard

Salt and pepper to taste

1 tablespoon virgin olive oil

### TARRAGON INFUSION

1 onion, cut in half then into 1/2-inch slices

2 carrots, cut into 1/2-inch-thick slices

2 cloves garlic, lightly crushed

1 sprig fresh thyme

1/2 cup Merlot, Cabernet Sauvignon, or other red wine

2 cups Brown Chicken Broth (page 23)

2 teaspoons cornstarch

1 1/2 tablespoons sliced fresh tarragon, or to taste

Place the lamb on a large piece of plastic wrap, and brush with the olive oil. Rub the tarragon between your fingers to bruise it and release the oils, and place on the lamb. Enclose tightly in the plastic wrap, and refrigerate for at least 6 hours and preferably overnight. To prepare the glaze, whisk the cream in a chilled bowl until stiff. Fold in the egg yolk and mustard, and refrigerate. Preheat the oven to 425°. Unwrap the lamb and bring to room temperature. Discard the tarragon sprigs, and season the lamb with salt and pepper. Heat the olive oil in a large, heavy, ovenproof skillet over high heat. Add the lamb and sear both sides, about 2 minutes per side; remove and reserve. To prepare the infusion, place the onion, carrots, garlic, and thyme in the large skillet, and sauté over medium-high heat for 3 to 4 minutes. Place the seared lamb on top of the sautéed vegetables, using them as a bed. Transfer the skillet to the oven for 7 to 8 minutes for medium-rare. Remove from the oven and place the lamb on a small plate inverted on a larger plate (so the juices run off and the lamb stays crisp). Cover with aluminum foil and keep warm. Return the skillet and vegetables to the stovetop, and add the wine. Reduce over high heat until almost dry. Combine the broth and cornstarch in a bowl, add to the skillet with half of the sliced tarragon, and bring to a boil. Lower the heat to medium and reduce by half. Strain into a clean saucepan, add the remaining tarragon, and any lamb juices from the plate. Adjust the seasonings if necessary and keep warm. Preheat the broiler. Slice each of the lamb loins into 6 slices. Place the slices on a baking sheet, and top each with about 1/2 teaspoon of the glaze. Place under the hot broiler for 1 1/2 minutes, or until the glaze turns golden brown. Place 3 lamb slices in the center of each warm serving plate, and spoon the infusion around the lamb. Serve immediately.

# Oven~Roasted Curried Pork Loin on Green Lentils with Sautéed Apples

*I* CREATED THIS dish using veal (instead of pork) for the annual ladies' dinner of the International Wine and Food Society of San Francisco, which is regularly held at Fleur de Lys.

### CHEF'S NOTES

Allow about 1 hour 45 minutes to prepare. You can substitute veal loin for the pork if you prefer. This is another home-style pork dish whose components can be prepared ahead of time. The curried lentils add an exotic touch, and their mild heat is matched by the sweetness of the apples, which in turn are a classic partner for pork.

Recommended Wine: An earthy Alsatian Gewürztraminer.

2 to 2$^1/_2$ pounds boneless top loin pork roast, trimmed and tied, at room temperature

Salt and pepper to taste

2 teaspoons curry powder

1 tablespoon virgin olive oil

1 onion, halved and cut into $^1/_2$-inch slices

2 carrots, cut into $^1/_2$-inch slices

2 cloves garlic, lightly crushed

2 Golden Delicious apples, peeled, cored, and finely diced with peel and core reserved

$^1/_2$ cup dry white wine

2 cups Brown Chicken Broth (page 23) or water

$^1/_2$ tablespoon butter

1$^1/_2$ cups dried green or French lentils, rinsed

5 cups cold water

1 carrot, peeled

1 small onion

1 bay leaf

1 tablespoon virgin olive oil

2 tablespoons finely minced onion

2 teaspoons curry powder

3 to 4 tablespoons cream

4 small zucchini, cut into matchsticks

2 tablespoons finely sliced chives, for garnish

Preheat the oven to 350°. Season the pork with salt, pepper, and curry powder. Heat olive oil in a casserole and sear pork on the stovetop over medium-high heat for about 10 minutes, turning frequently until brown on all sides. Stir in the onion, carrots, garlic, apple peel and cores, and cook for 3 minutes longer. Transfer the casserole to the oven and roast for 30 minutes, turning the pork every 10 minutes. Add the wine and cook for 15 minutes. Add the broth, cover the casserole loosely and roast for 30 minutes longer. When the meat is tender, remove the casserole from the oven, cover tightly, and keep warm. Strain the drippings from the casserole into a small saucepan and reduce over medium-high heat to $^1/_2$ cup. (If necessary, add water to make $^1/_2$ cup.) Set aside.

Heat the butter in a skillet and sauté the apples over medium-high heat for 2 to 3 minutes, or until tender. Set aside. Place the lentils and water in a saucepan and bring to a boil. Add the carrot, onion, bay leaf, salt, and pepper. Reduce the heat to low, cover, and simmer, stirring occasionally, for 35 minutes, or until tender. Drain the lentils, reserve the carrot, and discard the bay leaf and onion. Finely dice the carrot and set aside. Heat $^1/_2$ tablespoon of the olive oil in a saucepan and sauté the minced onion and curry powder over low heat for 6 minutes, or until the onion is translucent. Stir in the cream, lentils, and reserved diced carrot, and adjust the seasonings, if necessary. Keep warm. Heat the remaining $^1/_2$ tablespoon of olive oil in a sauté pan and sauté the zucchini over high heat for 3 minutes, or until tender. Season with salt and pepper, and keep warm. Place the curried lentils in the center of a warm serving platter. Slice the roasted pork loin into $^1/_4$-inch-thick slices and arrange them, overlapping, in a circle over the lentils. Place the sautéed apples over the pork, and spoon the sauce all around the lentils. Scatter the sautéed zucchini over the sauce and garnish with the chives. Serve immediately.

# Thick Pork Chops Façon Grand'mere

*P*ORK IS very popular in Alsace, so much so that the noble animal is affectionately referred to as **seigneur cochon**—Lord Pig! Pork is an affordable and vastly underrated meat that is best-suited to home cooking because it is bred so lean these days that it is easy to overcook, especially in the professional kitchen where there are so many distractions. As a result, I rarely serve it at Fleur de Lys. This is a flavorful rustic dish with many separately cooked components, served (as the translated name declares) "Grandma style."

### CHEF'S NOTES

Allow about $1^1/4$ hours to prepare. This dish features a classic combination of flavorful ingredients that are elevated by the simple addition of black pepper.

Recommended Wine: A delicate, fruity red wine, such as Savigny-lès-Beaune, from Burgundy.

SERVES: 4

$2^3/4$ tablespoons virgin olive oil

1 tablespoon sugar

12 small onions

$1/2$ cup Brown Chicken Broth (page 23)

Salt and pepper to taste

8 cloves garlic, blanched

5 ounces shiitake mushrooms, stemmed and cut in half

12 small asparagus tips (about 2 inches long)

2 slices rindless bacon, finely diced

4 pork loin chops, about $1^1/2$ inches thick, trimmed

SAUCE

$1/4$ cup dry white vermouth

$1^1/2$ cups Brown Chicken Stock (page 23)

$1/4$ teaspoon finely minced fresh rosemary needles

$1/4$ teaspoon cracked pepper

2 tablespoons finely sliced fresh chives

12 ounces small round red-skinned potatoes, quartered, rinsed, and patted dry

4 rosemary sprigs, for garnish

Combine $1/2$ tablespoon of the olive oil, the sugar, and onions (in one layer) in a sauté pan. Add $1/2$ cup of the broth, season with salt and pepper, and bring to a simmer. Cover, and cook for 20 to 25 minutes, or until the onions are tender and coated by a syrupy liquid. Set aside. Heat $1/4$ tablespoon of the olive oil in a small sauté pan and sauté the blanched garlic over medium-high heat for 2 to 3 minutes, or until tender and golden brown. Season with salt and pepper, and set aside. Heat $1/2$ tablespoon of the olive oil in a clean sauté pan and sauté the mushrooms over medium heat for about 5 minutes. Remove from the heat, season with salt and pepper, and set aside. Bring a small saucepan of salted water to a boil and blanch the asparagus tips for 3 to 5 minutes, or until tender. Drain and refresh in ice water. Drain again and set aside. Place the bacon in a large sauté pan or skillet and sauté until crisp; drain on paper towels.

Heat $1/2$ tablespoon of the olive oil in a sauté pan. Season the pork chops with salt and pepper and sauté over medium-high heat for 6 to 7 minutes on the first side, until golden. Turn the pork chops over, reduce the heat to medium, and cook for another 6 to 7 minutes, or until just cooked through but not dry. Transfer to a serving platter, cover loosely with aluminum foil, and keep warm.

Pour out the fat from the sauté pan and return it to high heat. To prepare the sauce, deglaze the pan with the vermouth and reduce until almost dry. Add the remaining $1^1/2$ cups of broth, the rosemary, and pepper, and reduce to 1 cup. Adjust the seasonings if necessary and add the chives. Keep warm.

Heat the remaining 1 tablespoon of olive oil in a large sauté pan over medium-high heat. Add the potatoes and sauté for 15 minutes, or until tender, brown, and slightly crisp. Add the reserved onions, garlic, mushrooms, asparagus, and bacon to the potatoes, and lower the heat to medium. Toss gently and adjust the seasonings if necessary. Spoon the vegetable mixture over and around the chops. Garnish with the rosemary sprigs, and serve with the sauce on the side.

# Marinated Venison Chops with a Horseradish Crust and Currant Sauce

WITH THE growing popularity of venison, it is relatively easy to buy it fresh in the United States, and it is also a popular game meat in many parts of France. Like lamb, venison seems to be in demand in restaurants far more than at home, and we serve plenty of venison at Fleur de Lys. In this recipe, the spicy horseradish crust makes an interesting combination with the fruity sauce, and both contribute flavors that complement the venison.

## CHEF'S NOTES

Allow 24 hours to marinate and about 35 minutes to prepare. I recommend serving venison medium-rare, when it is pink and juicy. Serve the chops a bed of braised leeks (page 90), if desired, with asparagus or freshly cooked fettucine tossed with a high-quality extra virgin olive oil.

Recommended Wine: A full-bodied, ripe vintage red Burgundy, such as Pommard, or the same Cabernet or Pinot Noir used for the marinade.

SERVES: 4

MARINADE

1 tablespoon virgin olive oil

1 small carrot, coarsely chopped

1 small onion, coarsely chopped

2 cloves garlic, coarsely chopped

1 celery stalk, coarsely chopped

2 tablespoons red wine vinegar

2 1/2 cups Cabernet Sauvignon or Pinot Noir or other robust red wine

12 juniper berries, lightly crushed

1 Bouquet Garni (page 22)

12 peppercorns, cracked

1 rack (4 double chops) venison (about 2 pounds), well trimmed

Salt and pepper to taste

1 tablespoon dried currants

1 large tomato, blanched, peeled, seeded, and coarsely chopped

2 cups Beef Broth (page 24)

1 1/2 tablespoons virgin olive oil

2 teaspoons drained prepared horseradish

1/4 cup fresh bread crumbs

To prepare the marinade, heat the olive oil in a large skillet and sauté the carrot, onion, garlic, and celery over medium-high heat for 6 to 8 minutes. Stir in the vinegar, red wine, juniper berries, Bouquet Garni, and peppercorns, and bring to a boil. Lower the heat and simmer for 10 minutes. Transfer the marinade to a large bowl and let cool. Season the venison with salt and pepper, place in the marinade, cover, and refrigerate for 24 hours.

Place the currants in a bowl and add warm water to cover well. Rehydrate for 10 minutes, drain well, and set aside.

Remove the venison from the marinade, dry well with paper towels, and keep refrigerated. Strain the marinade into a saucepan and bring to a boil. Add the tomato and reduce to 1 cup. Add the broth and reduce to 1/2 cup. Strain the mixture through a fine-mesh sieve into a small saucepan, add the currants, and return to a boil. Lower the heat and simmer for 2 to 3 minutes. Remove from the heat, cover, and keep the sauce warm. (Alternatively, let cool and reheat to serve.) Preheat the oven to 375°. Place the venison rack on a work surface and cut into 4 double chops. Trim the "eye" of the rib meat, and scrape the bones clean. Season the venison with salt and pepper on both sides. Heat 1 tablespoon of the olive oil in a large skillet over medium-high heat. When very hot, but not smoking, add the venison, and sear for 2 1/2 to 3 minutes on each side, or until brown. Transfer the venison to a baking sheet. Spread a thin layer of the horseradish on top of each chop, and sprinkle generously with the bread crumbs. Drizzle the remaining 1/2 tablespoon of olive oil over the chops. Place the baking sheet on the top oven rack and roast for 4 minutes, or until the crust is golden brown and the meat is pink and juicy. Arrange the venison on warm serving plates, spoon the currant sauce around the chops, and serve.

# Morel-Filled Puff Pastries with Veal Sweetbreads on Cream of Basil and Petits Pois

*S*WEETBREADS, CALLED **ris** in French, are the thymus glands of calves or lamb, and their delicate flavor and firm texture are highly prized by epicures. I often serve them with other meats, such as veal medallions or lamb loin. The beautiful sauce balances and integrates the sweetbreads and morels, without overpowering either one. The morel-filled puff pastries and the sauce also work well as a vegetarian appetizer.

## CHEF'S NOTES

Allow at least 6 hours for the sweetbreads to soak and about 1 1/2 hours to prepare. Buy sweetbreads that are rounded and pink; avoid those that appear bruised or blood stained. Do not keep uncooked sweetbreads longer than 24 hours. If possible, select small morels. If using dried morels, rehydrate them for 3 to 4 hours in 2 quarts of warm water, or overnight in cold water, refrigerated.

Recommended Wines: A Cabernet Franc wine from California or a Chinon or Bourgueil from the Loire Valley.

SERVES: 4

### SWEETBREADS

1 1/4 to 1 1/2 pounds veal sweetbreads (about 3 pieces)

1 small onion

1 Bouquet Garni (page 22)

Salt and pepper to taste

### PUFF PASTRY

6 ounces puff pastry dough

1 egg yolk

1/2 teaspoon water

### MORELS

12 ounces fresh morels, or 4 ounces dried, or other seasonal wild mushrooms

1 teaspoon virgin olive oil

1 tablespoon finely minced shallot

Salt and pepper to taste

1 tablespoon port

### CREAM OF BASIL AND PETITS POIS

1 1/4 cups shelled fresh young peas, or frozen petits pois

1/2 teaspoon virgin olive oil

2 tablespoons minced shallots

2 tablespoons plus 1/3 cup cream

Salt and pepper to taste

2 egg yolks

6 fresh basil leaves, finely sliced

Salt and pepper to taste

Flour, for sprinkling

1 1/2 tablespoons virgin olive oil

Soak the sweetbreads in cold water for at least 6 hours and preferably overnight. Keep refrigerated. Drain the sweetbreads, place in a saucepan, and cover with fresh cold water. Add the onion, Bouquet Garni, salt, and pepper, and bring to a boil. Lower the heat and simmer for 8 minutes. Remove the sweetbreads and discard the cooking liquid, onion, and Bouquet Garni. Clean the sweetbreads by peeling off any membranes, veins, or fat, and cut each one into 4 equal slices. Keep refrigerated.

Preheat the oven to 400°. On a lightly floured surface, roll out the pastry dough to a thickness of 1/8 inch. Using a sharp knife, cut out 4 rounds, 2 1/2 inches in diameter. Moisten a baking sheet with a little water. Place the rounds on the baking sheet. Whisk the egg yolk and water together in a small bowl, and brush the pastry rounds with the eggwash. Using a fork, score the top of the rounds. Bake in the oven for 8 to 10 minutes, or until golden brown. Remove from the oven and let cool. When cool, carefully cut the rounds in half through the middle (the top halves will be the lids.) Using a fork, hollow out the interior of the baked pastry rounds. Set aside.

Rinse the morels and dry them on paper towels. Heat the olive oil in a sauté pan or skillet and sauté the shallot for 1 to 2 minutes over high heat, stirring continuously. Add the morels, season lightly with salt and pepper, cover, and cook for 3 to 4 minutes. Uncover, stir in the port, cook for 1 to 2 minutes longer, and then set aside.

Bring a saucepan of salted water to a boil. Add the peas and blanch for about 3 minutes, or until tender (if using frozen peas, blanch for 1 minute). Drain in a colander and refresh in an ice water bath. Drain again and set aside.

Heat the olive oil in a saucepan and cook the shallots over medium-high heat for 3 minutes, stirring continuously. Stir in 2 tablespoons of the cream, the blanched peas, salt, and pepper, and simmer for 1 minute. Transfer the mixture to a blender or food processor, and purée until smooth. Return to the saucepan and keep warm. Whisk the remaining 1/3 cup of cream in a mixing bowl until firm. Gently fold in the egg yolks. Slowly whisk the cream and egg mixture into the warm pea mixture. Add the basil and cook for 2 minutes, stirring continuously; do not let the sauce boil or the egg will curdle. Adjust the seasonings if necessary.

Season the blanched sweetbreads with salt and pepper, and coat lightly with the flour, shaking off any excess. Heat the olive oil in a heavy-bottomed sauté pan or skillet, and sauté the sweetbreads over medium heat, turning occasionally, for 5 to 6 minutes, or until browned and crisp. Ladle sauce on the center of each warm serving plate. Set a pastry bottom over the sauce on each plate and fill with the morels. Top the morels with the pastry lids. Arrange 3 slices of the sweetbreads and the remaining morels around the pastries, and serve immediately.

# Braised Veal Shank in White Wine and Orange Sauce

THIS IS the kind of dish I enjoy eating for dinner at home on Sunday, my day off. It is satisfying and resonates with flavor, and the veal shank is a welcome change from the more elegant cuts of meat. However, it can sometimes be difficult to find, so you might need to order it from your butcher. The shank must be well cooked; it's at its best when the meat is just falling off the bone. If it's undercooked, the meat will be stringy and disappointing, so err on the side of longer cooking. The fresh citrus flavor intensifies with the slow braising process, bringing the sauce to a wonderful crescendo. This is a plan-ahead dish that's ideal for informal dinner parties.

## CHEF'S NOTES

Allow about 2 hours to prepare. This recipe can also be made with lamb shanks (cooking time is the same if lamb shanks are the same weight as veal shanks). It's an easy dish to reheat, and it will keep in the refrigerator for at least 2 or 3 days. Accompany with steamed white long-grain rice, mashed potatoes, or sautéed Swiss chard.

Recommended Wine: A white Burgundy, such as Mersault or Chassagne-Montrachet.

SERVES: 4

- 2 veal shanks (about 2 pounds each), trimmed
- Salt and pepper to taste
- 1 tablespoon virgin olive oil
- 12 pearl onions
- 2 small carrots, cut into $1/4$-inch slices
- 1 stalk celery, cut into $1/4$-inch slices
- 2 cups dry white wine
- $1/2$ cup freshly squeezed orange juice
- 2 cups Beef Broth (page 24)
- 1 Bouquet Garni (page 22)
- Zest of 2 oranges
- Zest of 1 lemon
- 4 ounces haricots verts
- 2 tomatoes, blanched, peeled, seeded, and finely diced
- 3 tablespoons finely minced fresh parsley

Preheat the oven to 375°.

Season the veal shanks with salt and pepper. Heat the olive oil in a large, deep ovenproof skillet and sear the shanks over medium heat for 10 to 12 minutes, or until brown on all sides. Transfer the shanks to a platter and set aside.

Add the onions, carrots, and celery to the hot skillet, and cook for 5 minutes, stirring continuously. Deglaze the pan with the wine. Add the orange juice, broth, Bouquet Garni, orange and lemon zests, and season with salt and pepper.

Return the seared veal shanks to the skillet, and bring to a simmer. Cover the skillet and transfer to the oven for 35 to 45 minutes, turning the shanks once after about 20 minutes.

Remove the skillet from the oven, and using a slotted spoon, transfer the vegetables to a bowl. Return the skillet to the oven and continue cooking for 35 to 40 minutes longer, or until the shanks are tender. Place them on a warm serving platter, cover with aluminum foil, and keep warm.

Remove the Bouquet Garni from the skillet and discard. There should be about $2^1/2$ cups of sauce remaining in the skillet; if there is more, reduce the liquid over medium-high heat to $2^1/2$ cups.

Add the haricots verts and tomatoes to the skillet, and simmer over medium heat for 5 to 6 minutes, or until the beans are tender. Stir in the parsley and the reserved cooked vegetables. Adjust the seasonings if necessary. Uncover the veal shanks, arrange the vegetables around them, and spoon the sauce over the top. Serve immediately.

# Beef Tenderloin à la Ficelle with Mixed Vegetables

FICELLE, WHICH means "string" in French, refers to the classic technique of attaching the poached, tied tenderloin to the saucepan handle with kitchen twine so that it can be retrieved easily and without stirring up the cooking broth. Poaching beef is an uncommon but healthful preparation, because no fat or oil is used. Your guests will be dazzled by the unique presentation. Using coarse sea salt to sprinkle over the meat is an important touch—the texture will awaken the palate. Don't use regular table salt, which would give entirely different results. If you prefer, you can leave out the salt.

## CHEF'S NOTES

Allow about 1 hour to prepare. Ask your butcher to remove any skin and fat from the tenderloin and then tie the meat with string. Serve with fresh toasted country bread on the side. The leftover beef broth can be frozen and reused for soups, stews, and sauces. You can use the same technique with chicken, using Brown Chicken Broth (page 23) instead of the Beef Broth.

Recommended Wine: A distinguished red Burgundy, such as Pommard.

SERVES: 4

2½ quarts Beef Broth (page 24)

2 bay leaves

2 sprigs fresh thyme

4 small leeks, white and tender green parts only, tied in a bundle

2 pounds center-cut beef tenderloin, about 3 inches in diameter, tied

Salt and pepper to taste

1 large carrot, cut into ½-inch slices

12 pearl onions

1 stalk celery, cut into ¼-inch slices

2 small turnips, peeled and cut into ¼-inch slices

12 asparagus tips

¼ teaspoon coarse sea salt

12 sprigs fresh chervil, for garnish

Bring the broth to a boil in a large saucepan. Reduce the heat to a simmer and add the bay leaves, thyme, and leeks.

Season the beef with salt and pepper, and attach one end of a 10-inch length of string to the tied tenderloin. Carefully lower the tenderloin into the simmering broth, and tie the other end of the string to the handle of the saucepan. (Make sure the rest of the string is inside the pan and not hanging down outside.) To cook the tenderloin rare, allow 12 to 15 minutes; for medium-rare, 20 minutes; for medium, 20 to 25 minutes; and 30 to 35 minutes for well done.

Remove the tenderloin from the broth and keep warm. (It's important to let the meat sit before serving so the juices will be distributed evenly, thus making the meat more tender.)

Return the broth to a boil and add the carrot and pearl onions. Boil for 5 minutes, then add the celery, and continue boiling for 3 minutes longer. Add the turnips and boil for 5 minutes, then add the asparagus and continue boiling for 4 more minutes.

Drain the vegetables over a large mixing bowl and reserve the broth. Arrange the cooked vegetables in a warm, deep serving platter. Slice the tenderloin into ½-inch-thick slices and place on top of the vegetables in the center of the platter. Cover generously with the reserved broth, sprinkle the meat with the coarse salt, and garnish with the chervil.

Serve in soup plates, and make sure each place setting includes both a fork and a spoon for the flavorful broth.

# Beef, Lamb, and Pork Baeckeoffe

AECKEOFFE IS far and away my favorite traditional Alsatian dish. In the local dialect, **baeck-eoffe** means "bakers oven," and this is an oven-baked meat-and-potato stew that Alsatians began serving for Monday lunch centuries ago. The womenfolk would prepare this dish in a special earthenware crock on Sunday and drop it off with the baker on Monday morning on their way to wash their clothes in the river. The baker would seal the crocks with leftover dough and cook it in his wood-burning oven as it cooled off after early morning bread baking. On their way back home with the clean wash, the women would pick up their crocks and a loaf of bread to serve with the stew.

## CHEF'S NOTES

Allow at least 12 hours, and preferably overnight, to marinate and about 30 minutes to prepare. The tureen or casserole should be large and wide, and it must have a small hole or vent in the lid, so the steam can escape. You can substitute one type of meat by doubling up on another. The pig's "trotters" are optional, but they give the stew a suitably gelatinous consistency. Serve with a frisée salad and fresh rustic bread, such as Black Olive Bread (page 36) or San Francisco Sourdough (page 34), if desired.

Recommended Wine: An Alsatian Riesling.

SERVES: 6 TO 8

### MARINADE

- 2 onions, minced
- 2 small leeks, white and tender green parts, julienned
- 1 carrot, cut into $1/8$-inch-thick slices
- 2 or 3 cloves garlic, finely minced
- 2 bay leaves
- 1 teaspoon juniper berries
- 1 sprig fresh thyme
- 3 tablespoons finely minced fresh parsley
- 3 cups dry white wine (such as Alsatian Riesling)
- Salt and pepper to taste

### MEATS

- 1 pound beef chuck roast, cut into $1^{1}/4$-inch cubes
- 1 pound boneless pork butt, trimmed and cut into $1^{1}/4$-inch cubes
- 1 pound boneless lamb shoulder, trimmed and cut into $1^{1}/4$-inch cubes
- 1 pound pigs' feet (optional)

- 3 pounds Yukon gold or other yellow potatoes, peeled and cut into $1/8$-inch thick slices
- Salt and pepper to taste

### PASTRY SEAL

- $3/4$ cup flour
- 5 tablespoons water
- 1 tablespoon canola oil

Place the marinade ingredients in a nonreactive bowl. Add all the meats and toss gently. Cover, and refrigerate overnight.

Preheat the oven to 350°.

Season the potatoes with salt and pepper, and lightly spray a large earthenware ovenproof tureen or casserole (see Chef's Notes) with olive oil. Cover the bottom of the tureen with half of the potato slices. Remove the meats and vegetables from the marinade and reserve the marinade. Arrange the mixed meats over the potatoes, and then place the vegetables in a layer over the meats. Cover with a layer of the remaining potato slices and pour the marinade over them. Add enough additional white wine or water to just cover the top of the potatoes. Place the lid on the tureen or casserole.

Mix all the pastry seal ingredients together in a mixing bowl and form into a rope shape long enough to wrap around the tureen's rim. Press the dough onto the rim of the tureen. Place the lid on top of the dough and press to seal completely. This seal will prevent any of the cooking liquid from evaporating.

Place the dish in the oven and cook for about $3^{1}/2$ hours. Remove the dish from the oven, and bring to the table. Cut under the lid to break the pastry seal and remove the lid. Serve the baeckeoffe out of the tureen on warm serving plates.

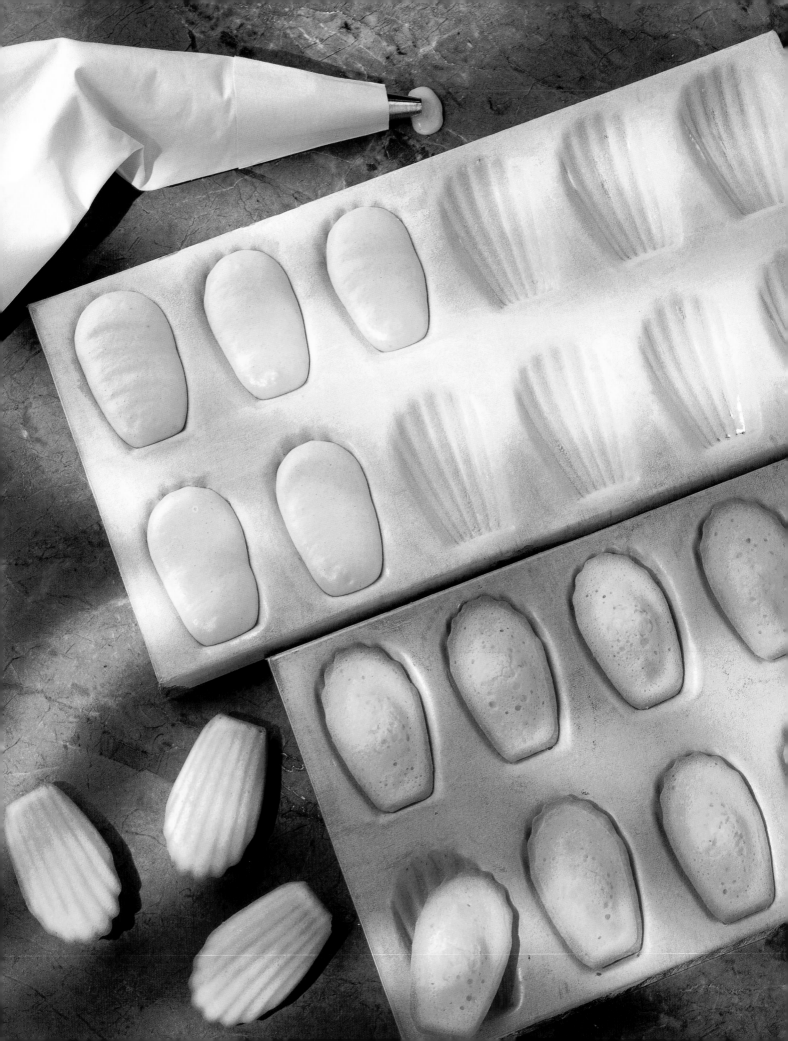

# Desserts

ALL TOO often, the last course of a meal is underemphasized. Desserts should be the crowning finale of an enjoyable dinner. Don't just take my word for it—our discriminating guests at Fleur de Lys often tell me the same thing. Because desserts give the last impression, I aim to make them colorful, beautiful, and delicious. Even our health-conscious customers seem to loosen up when it comes to desserts. I'd estimate that about 90 percent of our guests indulge their sweet tooth—a far higher percentage than you'll find at other restaurants. I take that as a compliment, and I'm sure it has a lot to do with presentation. When desserts float through the dining room, guests who are intent on their meals make a mental note to save some room. Never underestimate the magnetic power of an attractive dessert!

I think of desserts as falling into three categories: homey and satisfying, usually made the same day and often baked; "restaurant" desserts, cooked to order or ahead of time, with a last-minute touch to underscore their freshness; and store-bought pastries or desserts that are made ahead of time but that score high on presentation, appearance, and shelf life. Although my father was a **pâtissier** and I grew up surrounded by store-bought pastries, the recipes in this chapter are either homey or restaurant-style (all of which can be made at home in a similar style and spirit). Some are favorites at the restaurant.

I learned a lot growing up around the **pâtisserie** and helping out occasionally. Another important early influence on how I viewed desserts and their presentation was Marc Janodet, Vergé's young pastry chef at Moulin de Mougins. His creations were visually festive, and he enjoyed combining different flavors (and even different desserts) on the same plate—techniques that have stayed with me through the years. Another formative influence was Gaston Lenôtre, one of the leading pastry chefs in France and an acknowledged genius in the field. Both Paul Haeberlin and Roger Vergé sent me to work with him in his production kitchen just outside Paris, where I was immediately struck by his creativity, imagination, and impeccable sense of organization. I have never forgotten the value of the visual appeal and quality of the prodigious master's pastries and desserts.

In my early days at Fleur de Lys, my wife, Chantal, was our pastry chef. Although I trained her, she also demonstrated a natural talent. She started off making our trademark **petits fours** before graduating to desserts, which she made for four years. She found it fun and established the character and high standard that we have proudly maintained in our desserts ever since. (In later years, Chantal became our operations manager. Now a full-time pastry chef prepares the desserts.)

Before you set off to make the sumptuous recipes that follow, please remember that astries and desserts require more meticulous preparation than other courses. Measure ingredients carefully, and be patient and careful when making a recipe for the first time. Then, experiment with proportions and flavors and let your creativity guide you.

# Orange-Flavored Brûlée with Roasted Apples

CRÈME BRÛLÉES have become tremendously popular on both sides of the Atlantic Ocean over the last twenty years. I enjoy traditional plain brûlées, but based on the popularity of our Chocolate Crème Brûlée, I started experimenting with other flavorings. This is one of the recipes that evolved. I drew the inspiration for it from an apple pie filled with lots of creamy custard that my father used to make. (See the picture on page 187.)

### CHEF'S NOTES

Allow about 1 hour to prepare.

For another delicately flavored brûlée, substitute the orange and lemon zests with 1 teaspoon of fresh or dried organic lavender flowers. (Don't use the perfumed kind; for ordering information, see page 222.) Or for a pumpkin brûlée, use $1^{1}/_{4}$ cups of cream, $^{1}/_{4}$ teaspoon ground cinnamon, $^{1}/_{3}$ teaspoon finely grated ginger, $1^{1}/_{4}$ cups of pumpkin purée, 3 egg yolks, and $^{1}/_{3}$ cup of sugar, and follow the directions given in this recipe. Serve in a soup plate or ramekin.

Recommended Wine: A young Sauternes.

### SERVES: 6

- 3 cups cream or half-and-half
- Zest of 1 orange, finely minced
- Zest of 1 lemon, finely minced
- 8 egg yolks
- $^{1}/_{3}$ cup plus 2 tablespoons sugar
- 2 Golden Delicious, Gala, or Rome apples, peeled, cored, and quartered
- 1 tablespoon melted butter

Preheat the oven to 250°.

Place the cream in a saucepan and bring just to a boil. Remove from the heat, add the orange and lemon zests, cover, and let infuse for 15 minutes.

Meanwhile, whisk together the egg yolks and $^{1}/_{3}$ cup of the sugar in a large mixing bowl, until slightly thickened and lemon colored. Return the cream mixture to a boil, remove from the heat, and whisking continuously, slowly pour into the egg mixture. Set aside for 2 minutes. Skim off any foam that may rise to the surface of the custard.

Place 6 soup plates in 2 large baking pans, and evenly pour the custard mixture into the plates. Pour enough hot water into the pan to come halfway up the outside of the soup plates and carefully place the water bath on the middle rack of the oven.

Bake for 40 to 45 minutes, or until the custards are set but still trembling in the center. Remove the water baths from the oven, take out the soup plates, and let cool. Refrigerate if not serving immediately, but for no longer than 8 hours.

Preheat the broiler to high.

Slice each apple quarter into 3 wedges (making a total of 24 wedges). Grease a baking pan lightly with 1 teaspoon of the melted butter and add the apple slices in a single layer. Drizzle with the remaining melted butter and place under the broiler for 5 to 8 minutes, or until the apples are lightly browned and tender. Remove from the broiler and set aside. Keep the broiler hot.

Fan out 5 apple wedges on top of each crème brûlée, and sprinkle with 1 teaspoon of the remaining sugar. Place the brûlées under the hot broiler for 2 to 3 minutes, or until the sugar melts and caramelizes. Place each soup plate on a serving plate covered with a doily or a folded napkin, and serve immediately.

# Alsatian Cheesecake

CHEESECAKE IS a tradition in Alsace, where it's thinner in consistency than the average American cheesecake and baked more like a pie (you won't find the unbaked type of cheesecake in Alsace). This version departs from tradition by using rum instead of kirsch—my grandmother would probably be horrified, but the result is delicious! Just so you have a legitimate excuse, this cheesecake really is best eaten immediately. Avoid refrigerating it or the light and delicate texture will be affected.

### CHEF'S NOTES

Allow about $3^{1}/_{2}$ hours to prepare. If you like, serve the cheesecake with the Raspberry Coulis (page 193).

Recommended Wine: A late harvest Alsatian Pinot Gris "Selection de Grain Nobles."

SERVES: 8

**SWEET PASTRY DOUGH**
$1^{3}/_{4}$ cups flour
$^{1}/_{4}$ teaspoon salt
2 tablespoons sugar
$^{1}/_{2}$ cup butter, cut into small pieces and chilled
$^{1}/_{2}$ cup ice water

**FILLING**
$^{1}/_{2}$ cup golden raisins
3 tablespoons dark (or light) rum
1 pound cream cheese
1 pound ricotta cheese
4 eggs, separated
$^{1}/_{2}$ cup sugar
1 tablespoon flour
2 tablespoons cornstarch
1 teaspoon pure vanilla extract
Zest of 1 lemon, grated

2 teaspoons confectioners' sugar, for dusting

To prepare the pastry dough, combine the flour, salt, sugar, and butter in a food processor, and process for 10 seconds, or until the mixture resembles coarse meal. Add the ice water and pulse 3 or 4 times; the dough should form numerous small lumps at this point. (If the dough gathers into a ball, it has been overmixed.) Immediately transfer the dough to a work surface, and using your hands, press the dough together to form a thick, flattened circle (this helps even chilling and makes rolling out easier). Cover the dough in plastic wrap and chill for at least $1^{1}/_{2}$ to 2 hours.

Unwrap the chilled dough and roll out in a circle about $^{1}/_{16}$ inch thick. Place in a 9-inch pie pan, bringing the dough up the sides and trimming off. Prick the bottom of the pastry dough at $^{1}/_{2}$-inch intervals with a fork. Refrigerate until ready to use.

To prepare the filling, warm the raisins and rum in a small saucepan over low heat until hot. Remove the pan from the heat and let sit for 15 to 20 minutes, or until the raisins have soaked up the rum and are plump.

Preheat the oven to 375°.

Combine the cream cheese and ricotta in the bowl of an electric mixer fitted with the flat beater. Beat on low speed for 5 to 6 minutes, or until smooth and fluffy. Do not overbeat or the cheesecake will be dry and crumbly.

In a separate mixing bowl, whisk together the egg yolks and sugar. Gradually add the flour, cornstarch, vanilla extract, and lemon zest, whisking until smooth. Gently add the egg mixture to the cheese mixture, scraping the bottom and sides of the mixing bowl to break up any lumps, and mix until smooth.

Beat the egg whites in a clean mixing bowl until soft peaks form. Fold one-third of the beaten egg whites into the cheese mixture until incorporated, and then gently fold in the remaining egg whites, raisins, and any rum the raisins didn't absorb. Pour the mixture into the chilled pastry shell. Bake on the middle oven rack for 15 to 20 minutes. Carefully make an incision in the cheesecake by inserting a sharp paring knife at a 45-degree angle where the custard meets the dough and running it around the edge of the pie. This will release some of the air pressure and help the cheesecake rise properly. Bake for 40 minutes longer, or until the surface has lightly browned. Remove from the oven and place on a wire rack to cool. Unmold the cake and transfer to a serving platter. Dust with the confectioners' sugar, and serve slightly warm or at room temperature.

# Chocolate Crème Brûlée with Caramelized Bananas

*I* CREATED THIS recipe for my wife, Chantal, who adores chocolate. Naturally, she tested the recipe for me, and when she gave it her seal of approval, I knew we had a "keeper." Because the chocolate creates a richness and creaminess, you need less cream and fewer eggs than traditional brûlées, although it hardly qualifies as a health food! (Pictured on opposite page with Orange-Flavored Brûlée with Roasted Apples.)

## CHEF'S NOTES

Allow about 1 hour 45 minutes to prepare. I find using a propane torch to caramelize the sugar topping is faster and easier than the broiler and gives you greater control over the brownness. Handheld propane torches can be purchased at specialty kitchen and gourmet stores. If you like, serve the brûlée with Almond Tuiles (page 200) or a dish of Dried Michigan Cherry Ice Cream (page 214).

Recommended Wine: A young Sauternes.

SERVES: 6

$^2/_3$ cup milk

$1^1/_2$ cups cream

$3^1/_2$ ounces bittersweet chocolate, chopped into $^1/_4$-inch chunks

5 egg yolks

$^1/_4$ cup plus 2 tablespoons sugar

2 small ripe bananas, peeled and each cut into 15 slices about $^1/_8$ inch thick

Preheat the oven to 250°.

Pour the milk and cream into a saucepan and bring just to a boil. Remove from the heat, add the chocolate chunks, cover, and keep warm for 5 to 7 minutes or until the chocolate is melted.

Meanwhile, whisk together the egg yolks and $^1/_3$ cup of the sugar in a mixing bowl, until slightly thickened and lemon colored. Whisking continuously, slowly add the warm chocolate mixture to the egg mixture. Strain through a fine sieve into a clean mixing bowl and set aside for 2 minutes. Skim off any foam that may rise to the surface of the custard.

Place 6 ovenproof $^1/_2$-cup ramekins or custard cups in a large baking pan, and evenly pour the custard mixture into the ramekins. Pour enough hot water into the pan to come halfway up the outside of the ramekins and carefully place the water bath on the middle rack of the oven.

Bake for about 1 hour 20 minutes, or until the custards are set but still trembling in the center. Remove the water bath from the oven, take out the ramekins, and let cool. Refrigerate if not serving immediately, but for no longer than 8 hours.

Preheat the broiler.

Fan out 10 banana slices on top of the crème brûlées and sprinkle each with 1 teaspoon of the remaining sugar. Place the brûlées under the hot broiler for 2 to 3 minutes, or until the sugar melts and caramelizes.

Place each ramekin on a serving plate covered with a doily or folded napkin, and serve immediately.

# Caramelized Apple and Pecan Gratin with Citrus and Honey Consommé

REGRETS? I'VE had a few, but not when it comes to this dessert, which I created for a special meal held in conjunction with a Frank Sinatra festival in Brazil. Tickets for each of the three shows that followed the gala meal cost thousands of dollars—by far the most elaborate and expensive event of its kind the country had ever seen. It was certainly the biggest production I've ever been involved in, and I'm glad to say the meals worked perfectly. Contrary to what you might expect, this is not a difficult recipe to put together, and the hot, crisp apple "cakes" contrast refreshingly with the cold or room-temperature broth. So "start spreading the news"—for your next big production, do it "my way."

## CHEF'S NOTES

Allow about 1 hour 45 minutes to prepare. The consommé can be prepared up to 24 hours ahead of time and kept covered and refrigerated.

Recommended Wine: A grand Sauternes.

SERVES: 4

### CONSOMMÉ

- ³/₄ cup freshly squeezed orange juice
- ¹/₂ cup freshly squeezed grapefruit juice
- 1 tablespoon freshly squeezed lemon juice
- ¹/₂ teaspoon finely grated ginger
- 1 tablespoon honey
- 1 tablespoon dark (or light) rum
- 1 banana, peeled and cut into ¹/₄-inch-thick slices
- 9 fresh blueberries
- 12 green grapes
- 12 red grapes
- 3 large strawberries, sliced
- 1 nectarine, cut into quarters and fanned
- 3 kumquats, sliced
- 8 slices star fruit
- 8 to 10 orange sections
- 12 raspberries

### APPLE GRATIN

- 1¹/₂ tablespoons butter, at room temperature
- 1¹/₂ tablespoons sugar
- 1¹/₂ tablespoons ground pecans
- 1 small egg, separated
- 2 Granny Smith apples, peeled, cored, and cut in half
- 1 teaspoon freshly squeezed lemon juice
- 2 tablespoons whipping cream
- ¹/₄ teaspoon ground cinnamon

- 4 fresh raspberries, for garnish
- 8 fresh mint leaves, for garnish

To prepare the consommé, combine the citrus juices in a stainless steel or nonreactive sauté pan. Stir in the ginger, honey, and rum, and bring to a boil. Add the banana, blueberries, and grapes, and remove from the heat. Cover, and when cool, transfer to the refrigerator and chill for 1 hour.

To prepare the gratin, whisk the butter in a mixing bowl until pale and smooth. Whisk in the sugar and pecans until thoroughly combined, and then whisk in the egg white. Refrigerate for 10 minutes.

Finely grate the apples, and using your hands. squeeze out about half of their moisture. With a spatula, gently fold the apples and lemon juice into the chilled butter mixture. Using a round, nonfluted 2¹/₄-inch cookie cutter as a mold, fill to the rim with the apple mixture, pressing down firmly. Carefully remove the mold, to leave a uniformly shaped "cake." Repeat for 3 more cakes, place on a baking sheet, and set aside.

Preheat the oven to 375°.

Whisk the cream in a small mixing bowl until stiff. Fold in the egg yolk and cinnamon. Top each cake with ½ tablespoon of this cream mixture, and garnish with 1 raspberry, placed in the center.

Bake in the oven for about 10 minutes, or until the top of each gratin turns golden brown. Remove from the oven and set aside.

Strain the chilled fruit from the consommé (this makes it easier to evenly distribute the fruit between the serving plates). Divide the fruit and consommé between 4 rimmed shallow soup plates. Using a spatula, place the hot apple "cakes" in the center of each plate. Garnish with the mint leaves and serve immediately.

# Cinnamon, Apple, and Raisin Crisp with Blond Caramel Sauce

*I* ABSOLUTELY LOVE this delicious crisp, which merges the classic apple strudel, made with phyllo dough, and the plain streusel topping that traditionally covers brioche filled with pastry cream. This popular Fleur de Lys dessert can be served warm or at room temperature; add a little whipped cream or vanilla ice cream and you'll feel like you're halfway to heaven.

## CHEF'S NOTES

Allow about 1 hour to prepare. The caramel sauce can also be served warm or at room temperature, and it's easily reheated. It's great to make up a batch and keep on hand as it's very versatile; you can pour it over ice cream, serve it over poached fruits, baked apples, or coffee cakes. Covered, it will keep refrigerated for several weeks.

Recommended Wine: A grand Sauternes.

SERVES: 6

### FILLING

3 pounds Granny Smith or Golden Delicious apples, peeled, quartered, cored, and cut into $1/8$-inch-thick slices (about 16 slices per apple)

2 tablespoons raisins

1 tablespoon freshly squeezed lemon juice

1 tablespoon butter

5 tablespoons sugar

1 tablespoon dark (or light) rum

### TOPPING

$1/2$ cup flour

$1/4$ cup sugar

$1/2$ teaspoon ground cinnamon

5 tablespoons chilled butter, diced

8 sheets phyllo dough, about 15 by 10 inches

$1 1/2$ tablespoons melted butter

### BLOND CARAMEL SAUCE

1 cup cream

2 cups sugar

$1/2$ cup water

To prepare the filling, combine the apples, raisins, and lemon juice in a mixing bowl, and toss. Heat the butter in a large sauté pan and sauté the apple mixture over high heat for about 5 minutes, stirring frequently. Sprinkle the apples with the sugar and rum, and continue cooking for another 5 minutes, stirring frequently, until tender. Remove from the heat and let cool.

To prepare the topping, combine the flour, sugar, cinnamon, and butter in a food processor and pulse until thoroughly incorporated. Refrigerate for 10 to 15 minutes.

Preheat the oven to 375°.

Brush each phyllo sheet generously with the melted butter and lay them in a buttered 9-inch pie pan; some of the dough should hang over the edge of the pan by 2 inches or so. Spread the sautéed apples in a single layer over the phyllo dough. Fold the excess dough over the filling (it will only cover the edges of the filling), and sprinkle the topping mixture all over the top of the filling and dough.

Bake in the oven for 20 to 25 minutes, or until the topping is lightly browned and the phyllo dough is golden.

To prepare the sauce, heat the cream in a saucepan over medium-high heat until just barely simmering. Keep hot until needed. Combine the sugar and water in a heavy-bottomed saucepan and cook over medium-high heat, stirring continuously, until the sugar dissolves. Bring to a simmer and cook until the mixture turns golden. Immediately remove from the heat and, while stirring continuously, slowly add the hot cream. (The caramel will bubble up as you add the cream; be careful.) Continue stirring until very thoroughly combined. Return the pan to the heat, bring to a boil, and remove from the heat. Spoon the sauce onto serving plates, cut the crisp into 6 portions, and set on top of the sauce. Serve hot or at room temperature.

# Grandma's Omelette Soufflé with Strawberries

T HIS IS one of my favorite desserts. It reminds me of home because my grandmother loved to make this recipe for us when our parents went out to eat. My brother and I looked forward to it for days, and it was a surefire way of keeping us quiet—we dared not misbehave or we knew we might miss out on it. This dessert is also special to me because it's the first thing I ever made for Chantal; who knows, perhaps it so impressed her that she made a mental note to marry me!

## CHEF'S NOTES

Allow 15 to 20 minutes to prepare. This simple and delicate dish can also be served for breakfast or brunch, as well as dessert.

Recommended Wine: A late harvest California Sauvignon Blanc.

### SERVES: 4

- 2 pints fresh strawberries (about 16 to 20), hulled and quartered
- 6 tablespoons granulated sugar
- 2 tablespoons kirsch, Grand Marnier, or Curaçao
- 6 eggs, separated
- 1 teaspoon grated orange zest
- 1 tablespoon butter
- 1 teaspoon confectioners' sugar, for dusting
- 8 fresh mint leaves, for garnish

Preheat the oven to 375°.

In a mixing bowl, combine the strawberries, 1 tablespoon of the sugar, and 1 tablespoon of the kirsch. Cover the bowl and set aside at room temperature.

In the bowl of an electric mixer, beat the egg yolks with the remaining 5 tablespoons of sugar, the remaining 1 tablespoon of kirsch, and the orange zest until thick and pale yellow. In another mixing bowl, beat the egg whites just until they form peaks (but not stiff peaks, or they will not fold in properly). Gently fold half of the beaten egg whites into the egg yolk mixture until incorporated, and then fold in the remaining egg whites.

Heat the butter in a 13-inch nonstick sauté pan (or two 10-inch pans) over medium heat and quickly pour the egg mixture into the pan, spreading it out as you pour. The mixture around the edges of the pan will brown quickly, the bulk of the soufflé will puff up after 3 or 4 minutes. Remove the pan from the heat and place in the oven for 3 to 4 minutes. (Alternatively, cover with a lid for 3 to 4 minutes to set.) Once the soufflé has begun to set, spoon half of the strawberries in the center, and return to low heat for another 1 or 2 minutes.

Taking the pan in one hand and a warm serving dish in the other, slide the soufflé out onto the dish, folding it over in half as you do so. Spoon the remaining strawberries around the soufflé, and dust with the confectioners' sugar. Divide the soufflé into 4 portions with a dessert spatula and place on warm serving plates. Garnish with the mint leaves, and serve immediately.

# Terrine of Fresh Fruit Flavored with Mint and Vanilla on a Raspberry Coulis

THIS COLORFUL, do-ahead dessert is perfect for entertaining. It looks impressive and tastes refreshing, and the coulis can be used with a number of other desserts. It almost goes without saying that this dessert is best prepared in the summer when the fruit is abundant and in season.

### CHEF'S NOTES

Allow about 35 minutes to prepare, and at least 6 to 8 hours to chill. The coulis also freezes well. The terrine is easy to serve, although you need to take care when unmolding and slicing it. For best results, use a long, sharp knife with a thin blade. A sprinkling of finely chopped pistachios can be substituted for the seasonal fresh fruit, if you prefer.

Recommended Wines: A Sauternes or Quarts de Chaume from the Loire Valley.

SERVES: 8 TO 10

1 cup chilled whipping cream

1½ tablespoons unflavored gelatin

3 tablespoons cold water

2 egg yolks

⅓ cup sugar

1 vanilla bean, split in half lengthwise

1 cup milk

8 to 12 fresh mint leaves, finely sliced

1 cup seedless red grapes

1 cup seedless green grapes

¾ cup halved fresh strawberries

1 kiwifruit, peeled and cut into 8 pieces

¾ cup fresh blueberries

RASPBERRY COULIS

1 pint fresh raspberries

Juice of 1 lemon

¼ cup sugar

1 tablespoon kirsch

2 tablespoons water

16 to 20 mint leaves, for garnish

2½ cups sliced seasonal fresh fruit (such as bananas, mangoes, peaches, figs, or orange segments)

Line a rectangular mold or 8 by 4-inch loaf pan with plastic wrap and set aside.

Place the cream in a chilled mixing bowl and beat with an electric mixture until soft peaks form. Refrigerate.

Stir the gelatin and water together in a saucepan, and let sit for 5 minutes. Place the saucepan over low heat, and stir until dissolved. Keep warm.

Beat the egg yolks and sugar together in a mixing bowl until creamy. Set aside.

Scrape the seeds out of the vanilla bean into a separate saucepan, add the vanilla pod and milk, and bring to a boil. Remove from the heat and gently stir in the dissolved gelatin. Stir into the egg yolk mixture, transfer to a clean saucepan, and return to low heat. Cook for 4 to 5 minutes, stirring continuously, or until the mixture thickens slightly; do not let it boil.

Remove the pan from the heat and immediately strain the mixture through a fine sieve into a mixing bowl; discard the bean pod. Cool the mixture over a bowl of ice water, stirring continuously with a spatula until it begins to set. Do not let it chill too quickly or it will set prematurely and have to be reheated and rechilled. As soon as the mixture begins to set, remove from the ice water and quickly fold in the whipped cream, sliced mint leaves, grapes, strawberries, kiwifruit, and blueberries. Pour immediately into the prepared mold or loaf pan. Evenly spread and smooth out the mixture. Refrigerate for 6 to 8 hours or overnight.

To prepare the coulis, place all the ingredients in a blender and purée until completely smooth. Refrigerate.

To unmold the terrine, invert it onto a cutting board. Pull gently on one end of the plastic wrap; the terrine should slide out of the mold. Cut into ½-inch slices. Pour a little coulis on the chilled plates, and top with a slice of the terrine. Garnish with the mint leaves. Divide the seasonal fruit among the plates and serve.

# Chocolate and Quinoa Pudding

*I* HAVE NEVER seen quinoa used in a dessert, which was reason enough to create this one. I am intrigued by quinoa's healthful characteristics—it is extremely high in protein, iron, phosphorous, thiamin, and vitamin B-6, among other nutrients—and I thought this adaptation of a chocolate rice pudding would be an interesting way to introduce the "mother grain" to our guests. The quinoa absorbs the intense, rich flavor of the cocoa powder wonderfully well, and its crisp texture gives this dessert body and sparkle.

## CHEF'S NOTES

Allow 35 to 40 minutes to prepare and 3 to 4 hours to chill. You can store this dessert in the refrigerator for up to 2 or 3 days, but keep it in its mold, covered, so it absorbs fewer of the other odors in the refrigerator.

I recommend serving this pudding with espresso instead of wine.

### SERVES: 6 TO 8

2 quarts plus $1/4$ cup water

5 tablespoons quinoa

2 cups milk

$1/2$ cup sugar

1 cup chilled whipping cream

1 tablespoon unflavored gelatin

6 tablespoons unsweetened cocoa powder

Brush or spray a 5- or 6-cup fluted mold (or an 8-inch cake pan) lightly with vegetable oil, and line the bottom of the mold with oiled waxed paper to facilitate unmolding.

Bring the 2 quarts of water to a boil in a saucepan, add the quinoa, and blanch for 10 minutes. Strain, and return the quinoa to a clean heavy-bottomed saucepan. Add the milk and sugar, and bring to a simmer over medium heat. Decrease the heat to low, cover the pan, and cook very gently for 20 minutes, stirring occasionally.

Meanwhile, whisk the cream in a chilled mixing bowl, until soft peaks form. Refrigerate until needed.

Stir the gelatin and the remaining $1/4$ cup of water together in a saucepan and let sit for 5 minutes. Then place the saucepan over low heat and stir until dissolved. Set aside.

Transfer the quinoa mixture to a mixing bowl and gently stir in the gelatin mixture and the cocoa. Place over a bowl of ice water to cool, stirring occasionally with a rubber spatula, until the mixture is just cool to the touch. Be careful not to let the mixture chill too quickly, or it will set prematurely. Remove from the ice water and quickly fold in the whipped cream with a rubber spatula; the mixture should then be just firm enough to keep the quinoa suspended.

Immediately pour the mixture into the prepared mold. Cover with plastic wrap and refrigerate for 3 to 4 hours.

To unmold, dip the bottom of the mold into hot water for 5 seconds, remove the plastic wrap, and invert onto a serving platter. Gently remove the mold and waxed paper.

# Clafoutis with Black Cherries and Champagne Sabayon

Clafoutis IS a type of black cherry tart that originated in the Limousin region of central France (in the local dialect, **clafir** means "to fill"). It's a popular dessert in Alsace, where cherries are an abundant and much-loved crop. If cherries are not in season, substitute pears, mangoes, peaches, apricots, or a mixture of apples and fresh prunes. Traditionally, it's important to make the sabayon (also known as zabaglione in Italian cuisine) at the last minute, and in many restaurants, it's made at the table in front of the diner. It was one of the first dessert sauces I ever made as an apprentice as L'Auberge de L'Ill; it accompanied the trademark dessert **La Pêche Haeberlin** (poached white peaches with pistachio ice cream). It really impressed me, and it's easy to prepare.

## CHEF'S NOTES

Allow about 1 1/2 hours to prepare. You can also serve the clafoutis with fresh berries, poached pears or peaches, and ice cream.

Recommended Wine: An Alsatian Riesling, such as Vendange Tardive.

SERVES: 6 TO 8

### BATTER

3 tablespoons almonds, blanched and toasted

1 vanilla bean, cut in half lengthwise, or 2 teaspoons pure vanilla extract

3/4 cup sugar

6 tablespoons flour, sifted

4 eggs

1 cup milk

1/2 cup cream

1 tablespoon kirsch

1 pound (about 2 1/2 cups) fresh black cherries, pitted

### CHAMPAGNE SABAYON

4 egg yolks

6 tablespoons sugar

1 cup Champagne or sparkling wine

1/2 cup whipping cream

2 teaspoons confectioners' sugar, for dusting

Preheat the oven to 400°. Grease a 9- or 10-inch round baking dish or pie pan with butter.

To prepare the batter, place the almonds in a food processor and grind to a fine powder. Scrape the seeds from the vanilla bean into the ground almonds (reserve the pod for another purpose). Add the sugar, flour, eggs, milk, cream, and kirsch, and process with several pulses, just until blended. Transfer to a mixing bowl and let the batter rest for 10 minutes.

Arrange the cherries evenly on the bottom of the prepared baking dish and carefully pour the batter over them. Bake in the center of the oven for 40 to 45 minutes, or until puffed up and golden brown.

Meanwhile, prepare the sabayon. Combine the egg yolks and sugar in a mixing bowl. Stir in the Champagne and place in a double boiler over high heat. Vigorously whisk the mixture for 6 to 8 minutes, or until soft peaks form and the mixture turns light and airy, and is double in volume. Remove from the heat and place over a bowl of ice water. Continue whisking until the mixture is completely chilled.

Whisk the whipping cream in the bowl of an electric mixer on high speed until soft peaks form. Gently fold the whipped cream into the egg mixture until smooth and completely incorporated. Refrigerate until ready to serve.

Remove the clafoutis from the oven and place on a wire rack to cool. Dust with the confectioners' sugar and serve warm or at room temperature with the Champagne Sabayon.

# Fleur de Lys's Chocolate Truffles

*T*HE DINING experience at Fleur de Lys would not be complete without these little delicacies at the end of the meal. They're one of our trademarks and perennially popular, so I'm sure the reaction will be just as favorable when you serve them. Always serve the truffles at room temperature so they melt instantly in the mouth; the texture will be smooth, and the fragrance of the chocolate, rum, and honey will be much more intense. These truffles may be refrigerated for up to a week before serving. Simply store them in an airtight container. If the cocoa coating becomes absorbed during this time, just roll the truffles in some fresh cocoa powder before serving.

## CHEF'S NOTES

Allow about $2^1/_2$ hours to prepare. You can roll the truffles in a variety of coatings. For example, chopped pistachios, toasted hazelnuts, toasted almonds, macadamia nuts, shredded coconut, or melted and tempered bittersweet chocolate. (Use a good-quality chocolate, such as Valrhona or Callebaut.) Feel free to substitute Grand Marnier, cognac, eau de vie, or your favorite liqueur for the rum in the recipe.

I recommend serving coffee or espresso instead of wine with these truffles.

YIELD: ABOUT 3 DOZEN

$1^3/_4$ cups cream

$^1/_4$ cup honey

1 pound bittersweet chocolate, cut into $^1/_4$-inch pieces

7 tablespoons butter, at room temperature

2 tablespoons dark (or light) rum

$^1/_2$ cup unsweetened cocoa powder

Place the cream and honey in a saucepan and bring to a boil, stirring occasionally. Remove from the heat and stir in the chocolate. Cover, and let the mixture stand for 5 minutes.

Whisk in the butter, 1 tablespoon at a time, until smooth. Transfer the mixture to a small mixing bowl and stir in the rum. Let cool for 30 minutes, then refrigerate for $1^1/_2$ hours.

Using a small ice cream scoop or a large melon baller, scoop out 1-inch balls and place on a baking sheet lined with parchment paper or aluminum foil. Refrigerate for 15 minutes.

Place the cocoa in a shallow dish and roll the chocolate balls, one at a time, in the cocoa, until completely covered. Don't worry if the truffles are irregular in shape and size—they will only look more authentic. Serve the truffles in fluted paper candy cups, allowing 3 or 4 per person.

# Rhubarb Tart with Meringue Topping

RHUBARB GROWS prolifically in Alsace, and it is a popular dessert ingredient throughout France. Although rhubarb is generally eaten as a fruit, it is actually classified botanically as a vegetable. A trick I learned from my father that reduces the natural juiciness of rhubarb, blueberry, or prune pies and prevents them from becoming too soggy is to sprinkle some bread crumbs (preferably made from brioche, old sponge cake, or sandwich bread) on the bottom of the baked tart shell. The bread crumbs, rather than the pastry crust, absorb most of the juice.

### CHEF'S NOTES

Allow about $1^1/_2$ hours to prepare. If using older, thicker rhubarb stems, you will need to peel the skin, but young rhubarb can be used unpeeled, and its skin will tint the pie filling an attractive
reddish color.

Recommended Wine: A Tokay Aszu from Hungary.

SERVES: 8

1 recipe Sweet Pastry Dough (page 198), flattened, wrapped, and chilled

FILLING

$1^1/_2$ pounds young rhubarb stalks, trimmed and diced

$^1/_2$ cup plus $^1/_3$ cup granulated sugar

3 eggs

$^1/_2$ cup cream or half-and-half

3 tablespoons bread crumbs (optional)

MERINGUE

3 egg whites

$^3/_4$ cup granulated sugar

2 teaspoons confectioners' sugar, for dusting

Prepare the pastry dough and chill for at least $1^1/_2$ to 2 hours.

Preheat the oven to 375°.

Unwrap the chilled dough on a work surface and roll out in a circle about $^1/_{16}$ inch thick. Place in a 9-inch tart or pie pan, bringing the dough up the sides and trimming off. Prick the bottom of the pastry dough at $^1/_2$-inch intervals with a fork.

Lightly butter the shiny side of a 12 by 12-inch piece of aluminum foil and line the pastry dough with it, batter side down. Cover the foil with about $1^1/_2$ cups of dry beans or pastry weights.

Bake the tart shell in the oven for 20 to 25 minutes. Remove from the oven and discard the beans (or remove the weights) and the aluminum foil. Bake for a few minutes longer, or until the tart shell turns a light golden color. Remove from the oven and place on a wire rack to cool. Keep the oven heated to 375°.

While the tart shell is baking, prepare the filling. Combine the rhubarb and $^1/_2$ cup of the sugar in a nonreactive saucepan and let stand for 30 minutes so that some of the juice drains off—this prevents the tart from becoming too soggy (use the juice for a tasty cold drink). Cook the rhubarb gently over medium heat, stirring frequently, for 6 to 7 minutes, or until it is tender but not falling apart. Remove from the heat, drain off the excess liquid again, and set aside.

Whisk together the eggs and the remaining $^1/_3$ cup of sugar in a small mixing bowl for about 2 minutes, or until well blended. Add the cream, whisk again until well blended, and set aside.

Cover the bottom of the pastry shell with the bread crumbs and spoon the rhubarb over them. Carefully pour the egg mixture over the rhubarb (if you have some custard mixture left over, bake the tart for 5 minutes, then add the extra custard).

Bake the tart in the center of the oven for 30 to 35 minutes. Remove from the oven and place on a wire rack to cool. Increase the oven temperature to 425°.

To prepare the meringue, beat the egg whites in a mixing bowl with an electric mixer until foamy. Gradually add the sugar, and beat until stiff peaks form. Transfer the meringue to a pastry bag and pipe it on top of the rhubarb in a rosette pattern. Bake tart on the top rack of the oven for 8 to 10 minutes, or until the meringue turns golden brown. Remove from the oven, dust with the confectioners' sugar, and serve while still warm.

# Honey Madeleines with Rhubarb and Orange Jam

THIS RECIPE is for all lovers of Marcel Proust, who evocatively immortalized this classic cookie in his novel, **Remembrance of Things Past**. I had to include this recipe because **madeleines** are so French, so elegant and delicate, and besides, I grew up on them. **Madeleines** are believed to have originated in the town of Commercy in nearby Lorraine, over two hundred years ago. Fittingly, the jam is based on a two hundred-year-old recipe that I made for an elaborate French breakfast hosted by Jacques Pépin in San Francisco to launch the Food Channel. The recipe makes about 4 cups. It can be halved, but you may as well make a full batch because the jam makes an ideal housewarmning or holiday gift.

### CHEF'S NOTES

Allow 2 to $2^{1}/_{2}$ hours to prepare. You can buy madeleine molds at many gourmet or kitchen supply stores. For a cooking demonstration, Chantal once made a basket of madeleines, tied each one with string, and tucked in a sprig of lavender for a stunning presentation.

I recommend serving the madeleines and jam with coffee.

YIELD: ABOUT 2 DOZEN

### MADELEINE BATTER

6 tablespoons butter

$^{3}/_{4}$ cup flour

1 teaspoon baking powder

3 eggs

$^{1}/_{2}$ cup sugar

1 tablespoon honey

Zest of 2 lemons, grated

1 teaspoon pure vanilla extract

### RHUBARB AND ORANGE JAM

$1^{1}/_{2}$ to 2 pounds young (unpeeled) rhubarb stalks (or peeled mature rhubarb), trimmed and diced

3 cups sugar

Zest of 3 Valencia or navel oranges

6 Valencia or navel oranges, seeded and sectioned

1 stick cinnamon

Lightly brush 24 madeleine tin molds evenly with melted butter and dust lightly with flour. Invert the molds and shake out any excess flour by tapping them lightly on a work surface. Set aside.

To prepare the batter, melt the butter in a small saucepan over medium-high heat for 3 to 4 minutes, or until it begins to brown and gives off a nutty aroma. Transfer to a small metal mixing bowl to stop the cooking process and let cool. Set aside.

Sift the flour and baking powder together into a small mixing bowl. Beat the eggs in a separate mixing bowl with an electric mixer on high speed for 1 to 2 minutes. Add the sugar and honey to the eggs, and continue beating for 5 minutes, or until the mixture turns frothy and thick. Reduce the speed to low, and gradually add the flour mixture. Then add the lemon zest, vanilla extract, and browned butter, and beat until thoroughly incorporated. Cover the bowl with plastic wrap and set aside for 1 hour.

Meanwhile, make the jam. Place the rhubarb, sugar, orange zest, orange sections, and cinnamon stick in a nonreactive saucepan. Gently cook the mixture over medium heat, stirring continuously, until the sugar has completely dissolved. Increase the heat to medium-high, and quickly bring to a boil, stirring occasionally. Skim off the foam, and continue cooking for about 15 minutes, until the jam thickens (the faster it thickens the brighter the color and the fresher the flavors). Remove the jam from the heat and pour into hot sterilized jars. Let cool. Keep airtight in the refrigerator. (If not using within 2 weeks, seal the jars with melted paraffin wax and store in a cool, dry place.)

Preheat the oven to 375°. Whisk the chilled madeleine batter briefly to remix it, and fill each prepared mold three-quarters full. Place the molds on a baking sheet. Bake in the oven for 10 to 12 minutes, or until golden brown. Remove from the oven and immediately unmold by tapping the tins on a work surface. (If using 12 molds, repeat the cooking process for the second batch.)

Serve the madeleines warm or place on a wire rack to cool. Serve 3 or 4 per person with the jam. They can be stored for several days in an airtight container.

# Almond Tuiles

THIS CLASSIC French cookie is almost as popular as our chocolate truffles at Fleur de Lys. **Tuile** means "roof tile" and the U-shaped cookies take their name from the curved roof tiles common in the South of France. These thin, crisp almond cookies can be enjoyed on their own or with ice cream. For a change of pace and flavor, you can substitute $^3/_4$ cup toasted and chopped hazelnuts or $^1/_2$ cup chopped pistachios, $^1/_2$ teaspoon cinnamon, or $^1/_2$ cup coconut for the almonds. Another of my favorite ways to serve them is with Champagne Sabayon (page 195).

## CHEF'S NOTES

Allow about $1^1/_2$ hours to prepare. The **tuiles** are best served fresh from the oven, but they can also be stored in your cookie jar for a few days. The raw batter will keep for up to a week in a tightly sealed container in the refrigerator, which will allow you to bake fresh batches as needed.

I recommend serving the **tuiles** with coffee.

### YIELD: 35 TO 40

$^1/_4$ cup butter

1 cup plus 3 tablespoons sifted confectioners' sugar

5 tablespoons flour

3 egg whites, at room temperature

$^3/_4$ cup sliced blanched almonds

In the bowl of an electric mixer fitted with a paddle attachment, cream the butter for 2 or 3 minutes. Mix 1 cup of the confectioners' sugar with the flour in a mixing bowl, and with the mixer on low speed, slowly add to the butter.

Slowly add the egg whites and continue beating for about 2 minutes, until the mixture is completely smooth. Cover the bowl with plastic wrap and refrigerate for at least 1 hour to allow the mixture to firm up.

Preheat the oven to 400°. Lightly butter a baking sheet (if necessary, use 2 sheets).

Using a coffee cup or glass about 3 inches in diameter as a mold, invert it onto the cookie sheet and trace a circle in the butter. Cover the sheet with as many circles as possible, spacing them about $1^1/_2$ inches apart. Spoon 1 tablespoon of the batter into the center of each circle, spreading the batter out with the back of a spoon to form a very thin layer that covers the circle. Top each circle with a few almonds and lightly sprinkle with the remaining 3 tablespoons of confectioners' sugar.

Bake in the oven for about 3 to 4 minutes, or until a $^1/_2$-inch border around the edge of the cookies turns brown. Remove the cookies from the oven, and while they are still hot, lift them with a spatula, and transfer to rest over a rolling pin or wine bottle, smooth side down, to form U shapes. If the cookies have hardened and cooled too much to shape, return them to the oven for 30 seconds, or until they are warm enough to be flexible.

After shaping, let the tuiles cool completely and carefully remove from the molds. Repeat for the second sheet of cookies, if using. Serve 3 to 4 tuiles per person.

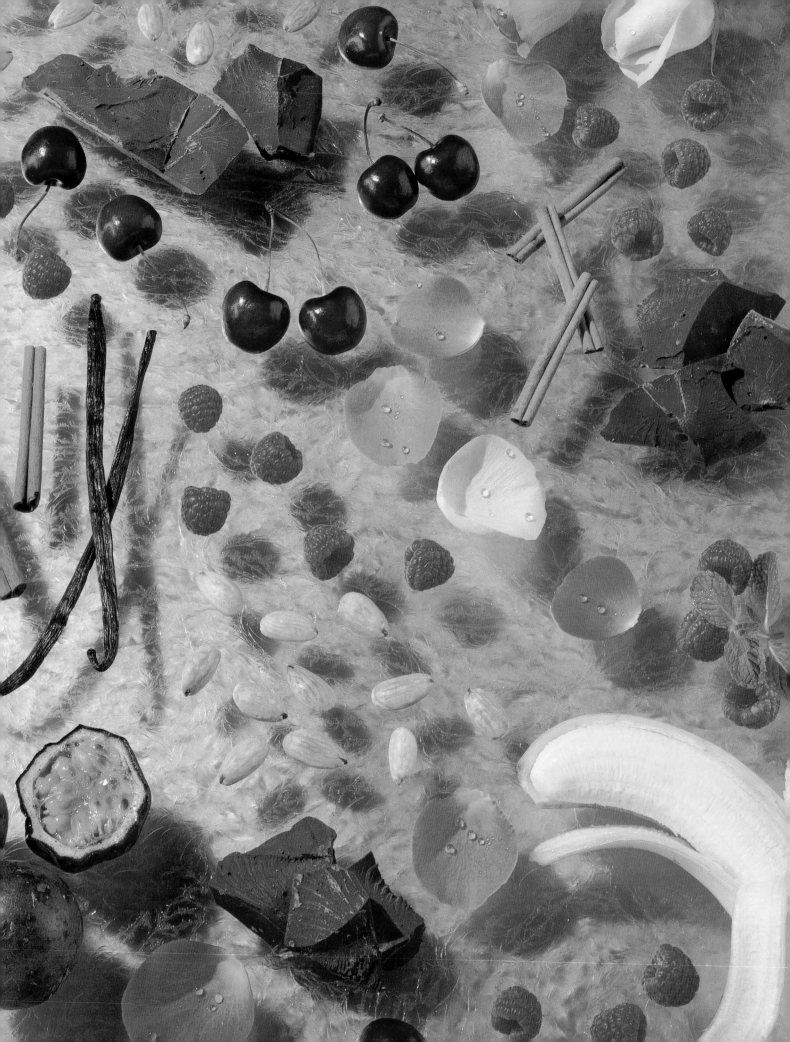

# Sorbets and Ice Creams

WHEN I was growing up in Alsace, I thought I could live on sorbets and ice creams (balanced by the occasional pastry or dessert!). It seems I've found a hospitable environment for my tendencies here in the United States. Although sorbets and frozen yogurts have surged in popularity in these more health-conscious times, Americans still love their ice cream—it's a weakness shared by most people I know.

Sorbets are a form of softly textured water-ice that never contains milk or eggs and is thus (usually) fat free. Instead, they are based on fruit juice or fruit purée, or flavored with wine or liquor, and are sweetened with sugar syrup. The correct degree of sweetness is the key to a perfect sorbet.

Culinary historians believe that the Chinese introduced **sharbets,** syrups sweetened with honey and chilled with snow, to the Persians and Arabs, who in turn introduced them to Italy, where they were called **sorbettos.** It was Marco Polo who returned from China having learned the technique of chilling with saltpeter and water, instead of ice, to cool the container. For centuries, sorbets have been served as a palate cleanser, and although this practice has become less fashionable in recent years, I like to serve them this way at Fleur de Lys.

Ice cream, based on dairy products and a **crême anglaise** base, first became popular during the mid-1600s in England, probably due to the favor it found with the monarchy. By the late 1700s, ice cream was highly fashionable in many European countries. Its popularity never waned, and ice cream has probably found its most appreciative audience here in the United States.

It seems strange now, thinking back to my youth in France some thirty years ago, that ice cream was still strictly seasonal—it was sold exclusively in late spring, summer, and early fall. Then sometime in October, my father would turn off the ice cream machine in his shop and we'd never think of eating ice cream during the winter. Slowly but surely, over time, this tradition changed; Christmas ice cream logs and other frozen desserts began to appear, and ice cream became an accepted year-round treat. Maybe "the good old days" left something to be desired, after all!

# Red Burgundy and Cinnamon Sorbet

*T*HIS DESSERT always reminds me of Mr. and Mrs. Blackburn, two of our best customers. The Blackburns live in Dallas but visit us often at Fleur de Lys, and on one occasion they flew us to Texas to cook for an important dinner party. One of the conditions was that I prepare this sorbet, Mrs. Blackburn's favorite. It makes an ideal winter dessert with its intense, warming flavors and beautiful hue.

### CHEF'S NOTES

Allow about 45 minutes to prepare. This sorbet accompanies poached fruits, such as pears, figs, or blackberries, particularly well. Although it will keep in the freezer, the longer it is frozen, the heavier it will become. Look for candied orange zest at Asian markets.

### SERVES: 6 TO 8

2$\frac{1}{2}$ cups red Burgundy wine

1$\frac{1}{4}$ cups water

$\frac{3}{4}$ cup sugar

6 to 7 cinnamon sticks

1 tablespoon candied orange zest, for garnish (optional)

Combine the wine, water, sugar, and cinnamon in a saucepan and stir once. Bring to a boil and immediately remove from the heat. Cover and let cool completely.

Strain the mixture into a mixing bowl and discard the cinnamon sticks. Pour into the container of an ice cream maker and freeze according to the manufacturer's directions.

Serve in chilled wine glasses, and garnish with the candied orange zest, if desired.

# Bittersweet Chocolate Sorbet

*T*HIS IS my wife Chantal's favorite sorbet. It is rich and creamy like ice cream but contains no eggs and has only a fraction of the fat. In fact, just think of it as a healthful chocolate ice cream!

### CHEF'S NOTES

Allow about 30 minutes to prepare. This sorbet has the virtue of being quick and easy to make. Serve it with Almond Tuiles (page 220) or sliced bananas with whipped cream.

Serves: 6

1 1/2 cups water

1/2 cup plus 1 tablespoon sugar

9 ounces bittersweet chocolate, chopped into very small pieces

Combine the water and sugar in a saucepan and stir once. Bring to a boil and immediately remove from the heat. Add the chocolate pieces to the sugar syrup without stirring. Cover and let cool for 10 minutes. Gently stir the mixture until smooth. Refrigerate for about 1 hour, until thoroughly chilled.

Pour the mixture into the container of an ice cream maker and freeze according to the manufacturer's directions.

Serve in chilled wine glasses.

# Passion Fruit and Rum Sorbet

THIS SORBET reminds me of Brazilian cocktails made with fruit and rum. My favorite was made with passion fruit, a tropical ingredient native to Brazil with which I only became familiar during my stay in Sao Paulo—in France, passion fruit are considered highly exotic. Their acidity and citrusy flavor need to be balanced with plenty of sugar, which creates an extra-smooth texture in a sorbet. The rum, which does not freeze, has the same effect, resulting in a delicious, creamy sorbet.

## CHEF'S NOTES

Allow about 45 minutes to prepare. Passion fruit are in season from March through September and are ripe when their purple skin becomes wrinkly and dimpled. Frozen passion fruit juice can be substituted, if necessary. Serve this sorbet with fresh strawberries, pineapple, bananas, papayas, or mangoes.

SERVES: 6

3 cups water

2$\frac{1}{2}$ cups sugar

2 pounds fresh passion fruit, cut in half, pulp scooped out and strained, and seeds discarded (to make about 1 cup of juice)

1 tablespoon dark rum

Combine 2 cups of the water and the sugar in a saucepan and stir once. Bring to a boil and immediately remove from the heat. Cover and let cool completely.

Stir in the passion fruit juice, the remaining 1 cup of water, and the rum. Pour into the container of an ice cream maker and freeze according to the manufacturer's directions.

Serve in chilled wine glasses.

# Rose Petal and Champagne Sorbet

FLEUR DE LYS has a deserved reputation for its intimate dining experience, and for several years now, we have been selected as the most romantic restaurant in San Francisco. In fact, **Food & Wine** magazine has selected us as one of the most romantic restaurants in the United States. The demand for reservations peaks on Valentine's Day, and I always prepare a special menu for the occasion. I created this recipe for our last Valentine's celebration, and I suspect it's going to become a tradition.

## CHEF'S NOTES

Allow about 1 hour to prepare. Make sure the rose petals are washed (stir gently but thoroughly in a bowl of cold water). Use only petals grown organically in your garden or from one of the sources on page 222. Store any leftover crystallized rose petals in an airtight container lined with parchment paper.

SERVES: 6

CRYSTALLIZED ROSE PETALS

1 egg white

12 organic red rose petals, washed, and white part removed

3 tablespoons sugar

SORBET

1 cup organic red rose petals, washed, and white part removed

$1^{1}/_{2}$ tablespoons freshly squeezed lemon juice

$1^{1}/_{2}$ cups water

$^{3}/_{4}$ cup sugar

$1^{1}/_{2}$ cups Champagne or sparkling wine

Preheat the oven to 325°.

To prepare the rose petals, place the egg white in a bowl and beat with a fork for 1 minute. Brush the petals lightly on both sides with the beaten egg white, and sprinkle with the sugar. Line a baking sheet with parchment paper. Place the petals on the prepared baking sheet and place in the oven for 10 minutes, or until crystallized.

To prepare the sorbet, combine the rose petals and lemon juice in a saucepan. Cook over low heat for 2 minutes, stirring continuously, until the petals have wilted. Plunge the petals into a bowl of cold water to maximize their flavor and brightness. Drain and set aside.

Combine the water and sugar in a saucepan and stir once. Bring to a boil and immediately remove from the heat. Cover, and let cool completely.

Gently fold the Champagne and rose petals into the sugar syrup. Pour into the container of an ice cream maker and freeze according to the manufacturer's directions.

Serve immediately in chilled flute (or standard wine) glasses, and garnish with 2 crystallized rose petals per serving.

# Frozen Raspberry Yogurt with Chocolate Meringue

*P*LAIN YOGURT can serve as the base for many flavored frozen yogurts, just like the **crème anglaise** base for ice creams. Because of yogurt's thick and creamy texture, it's an easy-to-make and satisfying frozen dessert without the eggs and high-fat dairy content of ice cream. This recipe, with its combination of yogurt, meringue, and whipped cream, is a play on the classic **vacherin glacée** or meringue **glacée** that my father sold every Sunday at his **pâtisserie**—desserts that are served in most bistros and cafés across France.

## CHEF'S NOTES

Allow about $2^1/2$ hours to prepare. The meringues can be made in advance. Just store them in an airtight cookie jar or plastic container; they will keep for several weeks.

SERVES: 4 TO 6

### CHOCOLATE MERINGUE

4 egg whites

9 tablespoons granulated sugar

$^1/_2$ cup confectioners' sugar, sifted

$2^1/_2$ tablespoons unsweetened cocoa powder, sifted

### RASPBERRY YOGURT

2 cups fresh raspberries

1 cup sugar

2 cups plain yogurt

### WHIPPED CREAM

$^1/_2$ cup whipping cream, chilled

$1^1/_2$ tablespoon sugar

6 raspberries, for garnish

6 mint leaves, for garnish

Preheat the oven to 225°.

To prepare the meringue, place the egg whites in the bowl of an electric mixer, and beat on medium-high speed for about 3 minutes, until foamy. Gradually add 3 tablespoons of the granulated sugar and continue beating for 1 minute. Increase the speed to high and gradually add the remaining 6 tablespoons of granulated sugar. Beat for 1 to $1^1/2$ minutes, or until stiff and glossy. Using a rubber spatula, gently fold in the confectioners' sugar and cocoa powder.

Place the meringue in a pastry bag, and pipe elongated ovals, about $1^1/2$ inches across at their widest point and $2^1/2$ inches long, onto a baking sheet. Meringues should be about $1^1/2$ inches apart.

Bake in an oven for $1^1/2$ hours to 1 hour 45 minutes, or until the meringues are dry and beige colored. Remove from the oven and let cool completely.

To prepare the yogurt, place the raspberries and sugar in a blender and purée until smooth. In a mixing bowl, whisk the yogurt until smooth. Stir the raspberry mixture into the yogurt, pour into the container of an ice cream maker, and freeze according to the manufacturer's directions.

To prepare the whipped cream, beat the cream and sugar together in the bowl of an electric mixture just until soft peaks form; do not overwhip. Refrigerate until ready to use.

To serve, place 2 scoops of the frozen yogurt in the center of each chilled dessert plate, and place 2 meringues on each side of the yogurt, sandwiching it. Place the whipped cream in a pastry bag, and pipe a zig-zag decorative pattern over the yogurt and meringue. Garnish each dessert with a raspberry and mint leaf.

# Banana and Ginger Ice Cream

OST PEOPLE enjoy banana ice cream, and the addition of ginger spices it up and gives it a whole new dimension. This sweet and spicy ice cream has an intriguing combination of flavors and textures. Serve it on its own or with any apple or pineapple dessert.

**CHEF'S NOTES**

Allow about 1 hour to prepare. At Fleur de Lys, we serve this ice cream with the Cinnamon, Apple, and Raisin Crisp (page 191).

SERVES: 4 TO 6

3 cups milk

1 cup cream

1 cup sugar

1 tablespoon ginger, peeled and finely sliced

6 egg yolks

2 pounds ripe bananas, peeled and cut into $^1/_4$-inch-thick slices

2 tablespoons dark rum (optional)

Place the milk, cream, $^1/_2$ cup of the sugar, and the ginger in a heavy-bottomed saucepan. Bring just to a boil, and immediately remove from the heat. Cover, and let infuse for 15 minutes.

Meanwhile, whisk together the egg yolks and the remaining $^1/_2$ cup of sugar in a mixing bowl, until slightly thickened and lemon colored. Set aside.

Bring the milk mixture to a boil over high heat, while stirring continuously. Slowly pour into the egg mixture while whisking vigorously and continuously. Return to the saucepan, decrease the heat to low, and cook while stirring gently for 4 to 5 minutes, or until the mixture is thick enough to coat the back of a spoon (the custard will read about 175° on a candy thermometer). Do not let the mixture boil.

Immediately strain through a fine sieve into a clean bowl set over an ice-water bath, and stir the custard until chilled.

While the mixture is cooling, place the bananas in a food processor, add the rum, and purée until smooth. Transfer to a large mixing bowl and stir in the chilled custard. Pour the mixture into the container of an ice cream maker and freeze according to the manufacturer's directions.

Serve in chilled bowls or frosted glasses.

# Pure Vanilla Ice Cream

*T*HIS RECIPE forms the base for other flavored ice creams. I think of vanilla ice cream as the queen of them all—it's my favorite, and it's so simple and versatile. You can serve it on its own or with all kinds of desserts, fresh fruit, chocolate, and sauces. The vanilla flavor of the ice cream will be enhanced if the custard is made the day before and refrigerated until you are ready to freeze it.

## CHEF'S NOTES

Allow about 1 hour to prepare.
The best vanilla beans come from Tahiti, Madagascar, and Réunion, a French island territory in the Indian Ocean. Fresh vanilla beans should be supple and aromatic, and they are best stored in a tightly sealed jar of sugar, which the beans will infuse. You can substitute vanilla extract, but nothing is better than fresh beans.

SERVES: 4 TO 6

3 cups milk

1 cup cream

1 cup sugar

3 plump vanilla beans, cut in half lengthwise

6 egg yolks

Place the milk, cream, and $1/2$ cup of the sugar in a heavy-bottomed saucepan. Using the back of a small knife, scrape the seeds from the vanilla beans into the milk mixture, and add the bean pods. Bring just to a boil and immediately remove from the heat. Cover, and let infuse for 15 minutes.

Meanwhile, whisk together the egg yolks and the remaining $1/2$ cup of sugar in a large mixing bowl until slightly thickened and lemon colored. Set aside.

Bring the milk mixture to a boil over high heat, while stirring continuously. Slowly pour into the egg mixture while whisking vigorously and continuously. Return to the saucepan, reduce the heat to low, and cook while stirring gently for 4 to 5 minutes, or until the mixture is thick enough to coat the back of a spoon (the custard will read about 175° on a candy thermometer). Do not let the mixture boil.

Immediately strain through a fine sieve into a clean bowl set over an ice-water bath, and discard the vanilla bean. Stir the custard until chilled. Pour into the container of an ice cream maker and freeze according to the manufacturer's directions.

Serve in chilled bowls or frosted glasses.

# Toasted Almond Ice Cream

TYPICALLY, ALMOND ice cream contains commercially ground almond powder. Here, I use toasted blanched almonds, which give a more complex and intense flavor. The tiny flecks of almond also give the ice cream an appealing textural quality. You can substitute an equal amount of any skinless toasted nut in this recipe; among my other favorites are hazelnuts, macadamia nuts, and pine nuts.

CHEF'S NOTES

Allow about 1 hour to prepare.
This ice cream goes particularly well with the Blond Caramel Sauce on page 191.

SERVES: 4 TO 6

1 cup whole blanched
   almonds, toasted

3 cups milk

1 cup cream

1 cup sugar

6 egg yolks

In a food processor, grind the almonds to a fine powder. Transfer to a heavy-bottomed saucepan and add the milk, cream, and $1/2$ cup of the sugar. Bring just to a boil and immediately remove from the heat. Cover, and let infuse for 15 minutes.

Meanwhile, whisk together the egg yolks and the remaining $1/2$ cup of sugar in a large mixing bowl until slightly thickened and lemon colored. Set aside.

Bring the milk mixture to a boil over high heat, while stirring continuously. Slowly pour into the egg mixture while whisking vigorously and constantly. Return to the saucepan, reduce the heat to low, and cook while stirring gently for 4 to 5 minutes, or until the mixture is thick enough to coat the back of a spoon (the custard will read about 175° on a candy thermometer). Do not let the mixture boil.

Immediately strain through a medium (not fine) sieve into a clean bowl set over an ice-water bath, and stir the custard until chilled. Pour into the container of an ice cream maker and freeze according to the manufacturer's directions.

Serve in chilled bowls or frosted glasses.

# Honey and Lavender Ice Cream

THE INGREDIENTS in this recipe are redolent of the South of France with its rolling, richly hued hillsides of cultivated lavender. Most people are familiar with the perfumed aroma of lavender, but are surprised by its wonderful flavor, which is delicate and not at all heavy, as you might imagine. This is an unusual but spectacular ice cream.

## CHEF'S NOTES

Allow about 1 hour to prepare. If buying dried lavender, be sure that it's organically grown plain lavender, not scented or perfumed. See page 222 for ordering information.

SERVES: 4 TO 6

### CRYSTALLIZED LAVENDER

1 egg white

6 sprigs organic fresh lavender

3 tablespoons sugar

### ICE CREAM

$^1/_2$ cup sugar

$^1/_2$ tablespoon organic fresh (or dried) lavender flowers

3 cups milk

1 cup cream

6 egg yolks

$^1/_3$ cup honey

Preheat the oven to 325°.

To prepare the crystallized lavender, place the egg white in a bowl and beat with a fork for 1 minute. Line a baking sheet with parchment paper. Brush the lavender sprigs lightly with the beaten egg white, and sprinkle with the sugar. Place the lavender sprigs on the prepared baking sheet, and place in the oven for 10 to 15 minutes, or until crystallized.

To prepare the ice cream, combine the sugar and lavender flowers in a food processor (or blender), and process for about 2 minutes, or until ground to a fine powder.

Place the milk, cream, and powdered lavender mixture in a heavy-bottomed saucepan. Bring just to a boil, and immediately remove from the heat. Cover, and let infuse for 15 minutes.

Meanwhile, whisk together the egg yolks and honey in a large mixing bowl until slightly thickened and lemon colored. Set aside.

Bring the lavender mixture to a boil over high heat. Slowly pour into the egg mixture while whisking vigorously and continuously. Return to the saucepan, reduce the heat to low, and cook while stirring gently for 4 to 5 minutes, or until the custard is thick enough to coat the back of a spoon (the custard will read about 175° on a candy thermometer). Do not let the mixture boil.

Immediately strain through a fine sieve into a clean bowl set over an ice-water bath, and stir the custard until chilled. Pour into the container of an ice cream maker and freeze according to the manufacturer's directions.

Serve in chilled bowls or frosted glasses, and garnish with the crystallized lavender sprigs.

# Dried Michigan Cherry Ice Cream

HERRIES AND kirsch are two familiar and favorite flavors back home in Alsace. My father used to make **brie au kirsch**—a cake layered with a frozen kirsch-infused crème anglaise—in his **pâtisserie**. I've reinvoked that combination, adding dried cherries soaked in kirsch to ice cream to create an appealing chunky texture as well as a heady flavor.

## CHEF'S NOTES

Allow about 6 hours to macerate the fruit and 1 hour to prepare. Try serving this ice cream together with the Bittersweet Chocolate Sorbet (page 205). Alternatively, you can serve it with the Chocolate Meringue (page 208) and whipped cream.

SERVES: 4 TO 6

1 cup dried Michigan cherries (or other dried cherries)

1/2 cup kirsch

3 cups milk

1 cup cream

1 cup sugar

6 egg yolks

8 mint leaves, for garnish

Place the dried cherries and kirsch in a nonreactive container and cover with a tight-fitting lid. Let the fruit macerate at room temperature for at least 6 hours or overnight.

Place the milk, cream, and 1/2 cup of the sugar in a heavy-bottomed saucepan. Bring just to a boil and immediately remove from the heat.

Meanwhile, whisk together the egg yolks and the remaining 1/2 cup of sugar in a large mixing bowl until slightly thickened and lemon colored.

Slowly pour the milk mixture into the egg mixture while whisking vigorously and continuously. Return to the saucepan, reduce the heat to low, and cook while stirring gently for 4 to 5 minutes, until the mixture is thick enough to coat the back of a spoon (the custard will read about 175° on a candy thermometer). Do not let the mixture boil.

Immediately strain through a fine sieve into a clean bowl set over an ice-water bath, and stir the custard until chilled. Stir in the macerated cherries and kirsch, and pour into the container of an ice cream maker. Freeze according to the manufacturer's directions.

Serve in chilled bowls or frosted glasses, and garnish with the mint leaves.

# Glossary of Ingredients

**Black Beans (or Turtle Beans)**
Native to Central and South America, and the Caribbean. These beans are widely used in Southwestern cooking, no doubt because of their robust, assertive flavor. As with other types of dried beans, it is important that black beans are under a year old, or they will be dry, hard, and tough. It is best, therefore, to purchase them from a source with a high turnover.

**Bouquet Garni**
A mixture of herbs used to flavor soups, stocks, sauces, and other dishes. See recipe on page 22.

**Caraway**
The aromatic seed of an herb in the parsley family used as a flavoring, especially for rye bread, marinades, cakes, desserts, and cheese. Caraway has a nutty flavor with tones of anise and fennel.

**Caul Fat**
The thin, lacy weblike internal membrane (usually from sheep or pigs) used to wrap meats and pâtés for cooking. The caul fat melts away during the cooking process. You may need to ask your butcher to order it for you.

**Celeriac (or celery root)**
The roundish, brown-skinned vegetable root of a type of celery grown specifically for the root (the stalk and leaves are inedible). It has a crunchy, white flesh and strong celerylike flavor with tones of parsley. It can be eaten raw or cooked. Celeriac is in season from the fall through the spring.

**Celery Leaves**
See page 138.

**Cheese**
French President Charles de Gaulle once asked, "How can you govern a country that has 246 varieties of cheese?" Some experts claim there are over 700 types of French cheese. We serve many types for the cheese course at Fleur de Lys, but the main varieties I use in the recipes in this book are as follows:

> **Comté:** A member of the Gruyère family (see below). A flavorful cow's milk cheese originating in the Franche-Comté region of France.
> **Emmentaler:** A cow's milk cheese originating in the Swiss Alps with a mellow, nutty, and fruity flavor. The cheese contains large holes. It is exported in the form of huge wheels.
> **Gruyère:** A cow's milk cheese originating in Switzerland with a sweet, nutty flavor. It is usually aged, and the cheese contains small holes.
> **Parmesan:** A hard, dry cow cheese originating in Italy that is perfect for grating. Its flavor is rich and sharp.
> **Swiss:** Any Swiss-style mellow, nutty-flavored cheese with large holes, such as Emmentaler or Gruyère (see above).

## Chervil

An aromatic herb related to parsley. Chervil is widely used in France and is an important ingredient in **bouquet garni** and **fines herbes.** It has a delicate flavor with anise and fennel tones. To preserve its flavor, add it at the end of the cooking process.

## Chestnuts

Called **marrons** in France, where they are very popular raw or roasted, used in stuffings, puréed and used as a side dish, and candied **(marrons glacés)**. Chestnuts have a sweet flavor and meaty texture. They should be peeled and the bitter inner skin removed before eating or cooking. Fresh chestnuts are in season during the fall and early winter, but dried chestnuts are available year-round.

## Chives

An aromatic herb related to onions and leeks, with a mild onion flavor and a hint of garlic. They should be snipped with sharp kitchen scissors so they do not turn brown where cut. To preserve their color and delicate flavor, add chives at the end of the cooking process.

## Cilantro

Also known as fresh coriander or Chinese parsley, cilantro is a member of the parsley family. Cilantro is probably the most widely used herb in the world. Rarely used in French cuisine even twenty years ago, it has become popular because of its pungent, sweet flavor and bright green color. Cilantro is best stored with its roots in water. Cilantro is not interchangeable with coriander seed.

## Cocoa Powder

Commercially processed and highly concentrated finely ground unsweetened chocolate. Because most of the cocoa butter has been removed, it has the advantage of being relatively low in fat compared with chocolate.

## Coral

The roe of crustaceans, such as lobster. So called because it turns an attractive coral red color when cooked.

## Crayfish (crawfish)

Freshwater crustaceans that look like miniature lobsters. They usually measure 3 to 6 inches long and weigh anywhere from 2 to 8 ounces. Very popular in France, where they are known as **ecrévisses**.

## Croutons

Small cubes or slices of bread that are toasted (or fried) and served as a garnish for soups, salads, or sauces.

## Cumin

An aromatic spice with a nutty, earthy flavor that combines well with other spices and herbs. Cumin is related to the carrot and parsley families. It is available in seed and ground forms, but I recommend buying it in seed form and grinding it yourself. This makes it fresher as well as easier to toast, if necessary (see page 20).

## Dijon-Style Mustard

A creamy, pale style of yellow mustard with a distinctive, sharp flavor. One of the best known brands in the United States is Grey Poupon. As the name suggests, this style of mustard originated in Dijon, France, which has been the center of the mustard trade since medieval times.

## Dill
A feathery-leafed herb in the parsley family with a delicate, refreshing flavor. It goes particularly well with most types of fish. To preserve its flavor, add it at the end of the cooking process.

## Endive
The slightly bitter-tasting Belgian or French endive is a member of the chicory family. It is cigar-shaped, measuring about 6 inches long, with tightly overlapping, elongated leaves. The crisp leaves are white or cream colored due to the growing process (blanching) which deprives the plant of light so that it will not turn green. Peak season is November through April.

## Fava Beans
Also known as broad beans or horse beans, and resembling baby limas. The flat-shaped fava bean is popular in France, especially the south. They are quite labor intensive as they need to be removed from the pod, blanched, and peeled. Fava beans have a pleasant, slightly bitter aftertaste and a grassy flavor.

## Fennel
The fennel plant has a bulblike base, which is cooked as a vegetable, and feathery leaves that can be used like dill or as a garnish. The bulb or root has delicate, sweet tones of anise and licorice, with a texture when cooked rather like celery. Peak season is fall through spring.

## Foie Gras
Considered one of the greatest delicacies, foie gras is the very rich, smoothly textured liver of fattened geese or ducks. It is a specialty of Alsace (as well as the Périgord region in southwestern France). In the United States, foie gras is made from fattened duck livers. Foie gras is also made into pâtés, terrines, and potted products. Foie gras should be creamy beige or white, with a rosy tinge, and very firm in texture.

## Ginger
Best when young and pliable, when it has more flavor. I recommend using a little less than the amount called for in recipes as it can be strong, and you can always add more to taste. The flavor of minced ginger will diffuse more readily than if you use whole crushed ginger.

## Haricots Verts
The French term (commonly used in the United States) for fresh green beans, also known as French beans.

## Jicama
A large, light brown-skinned root vegetable that resembles a turnip and is sometimes called "the Mexican potato." The crisp, juicy texture is like radishes or water chestnuts, even when cooked, and it is delicious raw in salads. Jicama has a delicate, nutty flavor. Peak season is November through May.

## Juniper Berries
The dark blue-black berries have an aromatic, pungent, and astringent flavor and are commonly used in marinades and sauces, especially for red meats. They should be crushed before using to release their flavor.

## Kirsch
A colorless cherry brandy (or eau de vie) that originated in Alsace. It should not be confused with the sweetened cherry brandies made by some liqueur companies; I particularly recommend the Trimbach brand.

## Lemongrass

The fragrant stalk of an herb that is a key ingredient in Thai cuisine. As the name suggests, the aroma and flavor are lemonlike, but unique; there is no good substitute. Use the lower part of the stalk, peel off the tough outer layers, and crush to release the full flavor.

## Lentils

A pulse that is popular in France as well as many other parts of Europe. I prefer the green, or French, lentils, which turn brown when cooked, or brown lentils. Orange lentils tend to fall apart when cooked. Some soak lentils before cooking them to soften them and puff them up, but this can cause them to ferment and begin the sprouting process, making them indigestible.

## Mushrooms

In addition to regular white (or button) mushrooms, I use a number of other different mushrooms in the recipes in this book.

**Chanterelle:** An apricot-, gold-, or orange-colored wild mushroom shaped like a trumpet flower. Meaty in texture and delicately nutty in flavor, chanterelles are in peak season during the summer, fall, and early winter. Black chanterelles are a rarer delicacy with similar qualities.

**Morels:** A wild mushroom closely related to the truffle. Morels vary in color from white, to yellow, and black. The spongy caps are aromatically nutty and earthy in flavor; the stems of true morels are hollow. Peak season is spring and early summer.

Porcini (or **cêpe):** Pale brown wild mushrooms with a meaty texture and a pungent, woodsy flavor. If using in dried form, rehydrate in warm water for 20 minutes or so.

**Shiitake:** Brown-capped, meaty Japanese mushrooms. They are now being grown in the United States, where they are also known as golden oak mushrooms.

## Oils

Most of my recipes call for **virgin olive oil,** which comes from the second pressing (the first olive pressing creates the rich and flavorful extra virgin olive oil). Virgin olive oil has the advantage of a milder, more subtle flavor and higher acidity than extra virgin oil, although a pleasant and distinctive nuttiness remains that does not overwhelm most ingredients. It is important to choose a fresh, good-quality brand. Sometimes, other oils are appropriate. **Canola oil** has a completely neutral flavor and is good for frying as it has a high smoking point. It is also considered a "healthy oil" in that it is low in saturated fat and has the lowest (cholesterol balancing) mono-unsaturated fat of any oil. I use nut oils—**almond oil, hazelnut oil,** and **walnut oil**—for the particular rich and distinctive flavors they impart, especially in vinaigrettes and sauces. Nut oils should be stored in the refrigerator as they spoil easily.

## Olives

To me, olives epitomize the intense flavors of the Mediterranean, where they have been cultivated for thousands of years. I generally prefer the small, flavorful dark brown niçoise olives from the South of France, or the large, black kalamata olives from Greece. All black olives are ripe fruit; green olives are immature. All olives must be cured to eliminate any bitterness and preserved in brine or oil.

## Paprika

Dried and powdered sweet red pepper used to season or garnish a variety of dishes. Although it ranges in heat from mild to pungent, I use only the mild type, usually for its intensely red color.

## Peppercorns

I like to use different colored peppercorns for certain culinary purposes, either because of their different flavor qualities or for their specific color. Black, white, and green peppercorns are the berrylike fruit of a climbing vine native to Southeast Asia. **Black peppercorns** are those picked before maturity and dried, resulting in a strong flavor and piquant heat. **White peppercorns** are harvested at the same point as black, but their skin is removed before drying. **Green peppercorns** are the unripe fruit that are preserved in brine, giving them a fresh flavor and milder quality. **Pink** and **red peppercorns** are the dried berries of an unrelated plant grown in Madagascar. They have a sweet and pungent flavor. They are available freeze-dried or preserved in brine.

## Phyllo (Filo)

Derived from the Greek word for "leaf," phyllo refers to very thinly layered sheets of feathery-light pastry or strudel dough made with wheat flour. Brushed or basted with oil or butter, phyllo becomes crisp and flaky, making a perfect wrapping or covering for ingredients. Phyllo is sold fresh (mostly in Middle Eastern markets) or frozen in most supermarkets.

## Quinoa

Quinoa was such an important staple to the Incan civilization of South America that it was referred to as the "Mother Grain." It is still used extensively, but until recently it was rarely found outside its native Andes. Now, for example, it is being cultivated in the northwestern United States. Quinoa, like amaranth, is a "complete protein" that is low in carbohydrates and a source of important nutrients. When cooked properly, quinoa has a springy, crunchy texture, rather like caviar.

## Saffron

The dried stamens of a type of crocus used for its vivid yellow-orange coloring. Because of the highly labor-intensive harvesting process, saffron is the most expensive spice of all.

## Salt

I recommend using sea salt, which is extracted by evaporation from sea water, because it's the purest form of salt. It's available in most supermarkets or specialty stores. If you can only get it in coarse granules, grind it to the same fineness as table salt. I find table salt and kosher salt less satisfactory because their flavors are too assertive and sometimes a little chemicaly.

## Scallops

I like to use both sea scallops and the sweeter, tiny bay scallops. You can substitute sea scallops for the less available bay scallops by quartering them. Buy scallops fresh and in loose form, whenever possible; they should be sticky and stick to each other. Avoid buying scallops sold in plastic-wrapped trays or sitting in a milky liquid, which is added to extend their shelf life and make them weigh more. Scallops will release this milky liquid when they cook, making searing and sautéing less effective.

## Sorrel

Perennially popular in France, but comparatively underused in the United States. Sorrel is related to buckwheat and rhubarb; the arrow-shaped leaves are a little sour. It is most commonly used in salads or puréed and added to sauces and soups. Peak season is the spring.

## Split Peas (or Field Peas)

Type of pea specifically grown for drying.

## Tarragon

An herb used widely in France. Its tart, assertive, yet subtly aromatic flavor means that it is best used sparingly; a little goes a long way. It is used as a component in **fines herbes** and **bouquet garni.**

## Tomalley

The soft green liver of crustaceans such as lobsters, considered a delicacy to many. It is often added to sauces.

## Truffles

"The black diamond of the kitchen" is how nineteenth-century French gourmet and writer Brillat-Savarin described this subterranean fungus and highly prized delicacy. Truffles are scarce and expensive; however, only a little of their intense and delicate, yet earthy, flavor and aroma is needed to transform a dish delightfully. They vary in color from black to off-white and look rather unappealing. Truffles are located and rooted out by specially trained pigs and sometimes dogs. The best truffles of all come from the Périgord and Lot regions of France. Fresh truffles are usually in season from mid-December to mid-March, but you can substitute frozen truffles, which are more aromatic and flavorful than canned truffles (use these only as a last resort).

## Vanilla

A flavoring native to the Americas, known to have been cultivated by the Aztecs. Vanilla is extracted from beans that grow on a plant in the orchid family. The best vanilla in the world comes from Tahiti, although it is also grown in Mexico, Madagascar, and Indonesia. When buying vanilla, choose beans that are plump, flexible, and moist, or alternatively, use pure vanilla extract.

## Vinegars

"Vinegar" means distilled white vinegar to many people, but the wide variety of flavored vinegars that are available can add wonderfully subtle or assertive flavor elements and acidity to dishes, depending on the results you are seeking. Among the vinegars I use are the following:

**Balsamic:** A full-flavored, high-acid yet sweet vinegar that ranges from mild to pungent. Made from Trebbiano red grapes and aged in wooden casks for 3 to 50 years. Balsamic vinegar has a particular affinity for tomatoes and strawberries.

**Cider:** Made from fermented apple cider, the hint of sweetness from the apples balances the acidity of the vinegar. Good-quality cider vinegars with a pleasantly fruity aroma are available from most health food stores.

**Red Wine:** A full-bodied, pungently flavored vinegar that is particularly suited to vinaigrettes or sauces with red meat or other ingredients with strong flavors. Red (and white) wine vinegars are the preferred varieties in French cuisine.

**Rice Wine:** Unseasoned rice vinegars, usually from Japan or China, are made from fermented rice. They have a lower acidity than most other vinegars and a natural sweetness, making them more mellow and delicate in flavor. Rice wine vinegars are available in Asian markets and in the Asian section of many supermarkets.

**Sherry:** Made from sherry and aged in wooden casks. I recommend buying Spanish sherry vinegar because the finest authentic sherry is made in Spain. Sherry vinegar has a natural, subtle sweetness and a rich flavor.

**Tarragon:** Of all herb vinegars, this is my favorite, perhaps because of the French affinity for tarragon. It is made simply by steeping tarragon in vinegar, and it adds a wonderfully aromatic herbal touch to dishes.

## Watercress

The peppery flavor of the small, dime-sized leaves and substantial stems adds spice to salads, soups, and garnishes. Good-quality, fresh watercress is crisp and dark green in color, with no yellowing. To preserve its freshness, keep watercress cold and moist. Available year-round.

# Sources for Equipment and Ingredients

## Baking and General Equipment

Draeger's Supermarkets, Inc.
1010 University Dr.
Menlo Park, CA 94025
(415) 688-0688
(415) 322-7958 (fax)

Sur La Table
84 Pine St.
Pike Place Farmers' Market
Seattle, WA 98101
(800) 243-0852

King Arthur Flour
P.O. Box 876
Norwich, VT 05055-0876
(800) 827-6836

Williams-Sonoma
P.O. Box 7456
San Francisco, CA 94120-7456
(800) 541-2233
(415) 421-5133 (fax)

## Wines (including Alsatian) and Spirits

Kermit Lynch Wine Merchant
1605 San Pablo Ave.
Berkeley, CA 94702-1317
(510) 524-1524
(510) 528-7026 (fax)

## Foie Gras

D'Artagnan
399 St. Paul Ave.
Jersey City, NJ 07306
(800) DARTAGN

Michael Ginor
AGY Corp.
Rte. 1, Box 69
Ferndale, NY 12734
(516) 773-4400

Polarica / Game Exchange
107 Quint St.
San Francisco, CA 94124
(415) 282-7878
(415) 647-6826 (fax)

## Edible Flowers

Maxi Flowers a la Carte
1015 Martin Ln.
Sebastopol, CA 95472
(707) 829-0592

## Information about Cooking Classes and Events

Fleur de Lys
777 Sutter St.
San Francisco, CA 94109
(415) 673-7779
(415) 673-4619 (fax)

# Index